MY CURIOUS LIFE

*If My Grandkids Ask About Me,
Tell Them This*

ROBERT DANNA

Visit the Official Website at: MyCuriousLife.net

Printed in the United States of America

First Printing: April 2024

Published by Ibis Books, 2349 Hyde Park Street, Sarasota FL, 34239

IBIS BOOKS

Paperback ISBN: 978-1-956672-28-2
eBook ISBN: 978-1-956672-27-5

This book may be purchased for educational, business or sales promotional use. Special discounts are available on quantity purchases. For more information, please contact me:

Website: www.mycuriouslife.net
Email: bobdanna@mycuriouslife.net

DISCLAIMER

While the author and publisher have strived to be as accurate and complete as possible in the creation of this book, readers are cautioned to rely on their own judgment about their individual circumstances to act accordingly.

The author and publisher are providing this information on an educational basis and will not be liable for damages arising out of, or in connection with, the use of the content in this book. This is a comprehensive limitation of liability that applies to all damages of any kind, including (without limitation) compensatory; direct, indirect or direct, indirect or consequential damages; loss of data, income or profit; loss of or damage to property and claims of third parties.

While all attempts have been made to verify information provided in this publication, the author and publisher assume no responsibility for errors, omissions, or contrary interpretation of the subject matter herein. Any perceived slights of specific persons, peoples, or organizations are unintentional. This book details the author's own personal experiences and opinions.

You understand that this book is not intended as a substitute for consultation with a licensed professional. In the event you use any of the information in this book for yourself, which is your constitutional right, the author and publisher assume no responsibility for your actions or outcomes.

For
Sean and Kyle
and
All the Curious Children in
This Crazy World

ABOUT THE COVER

The cover illustration is very special to me. The core of the cover pays homage to the thousands of incredible people I had the privilege of working with for more than 15 years at General Physics Corporation (1980–1996). I pulled several of the graphic figures from a brochure that I used to support the marketing and promotion of the group that I led, the Engineering and Applied Sciences Group, containing all the company's engineering and scientific staff (with multiple company officers, directors, managers, project managers, and engineering and laboratory staff).

The solar eclipse illustration is a nod to my life-long interest in science, having seen five solar eclipses over the past 50 years. The slide rule provides acknowledgement of where I started in the 1960s—with literally no technology as a physics student—the advancement of science and math are my life's passion.

The flipchart contains a cutaway of the Three Mile Island Nuclear Plant. Much of the first 15 years of my career were focused on nuclear propulsion in the navy and commercial nuclear power plants throughout the U.S.

Finally, the picture of me was taken around 2010 (at around 60 years old) in New Delhi, India, where I participated on an expert panel, sponsored by India's business publication, *Business Today*, which was focused on my experience in creating a business learning culture for continuous life-long learning. My curiosity as a lifelong learner is the bedrock and driving force for my entire career.

CONTENTS

PART 3

Curiosity and Knowing Oneself
What Does it All Mean?

PART 4

Continually Curious

PROLOGUE

I WOULD NOT have written this memoir ten years ago. This collection of stories, reflections, calls to action, and hard-earned insights is a direct response to a very particular stimulus: my grandkids, Sean and Kyle.

They are still young, but one of my favorite things in this world is to watch them grow from tiny creatures that barely filled my hands to self-propelled little humans who have actual agency and insatiable curiosity.

Their physical presence the last few years has *changed* me. The curiosity that comes so naturally to them—and to all children, really—brings me immeasurable joy. At the same time, I fear their curiosity will wane, or be squashed out of them by the pressures of this accelerating world.

Of course—and I'm sure many of you fellow grandparents reading this now will knowingly nod along with me—their youth also serves to remind me that I'm getting older. I refuse to say I'm old, but as a scientist and engineer, I understand I'm aging.

I have so much to tell Sean and Kyle, so much to teach them. But what if I'm gone before they are old enough to understand, much less know to ask? That's why I'm writing all this down. So, my grandkids have a record of Grandpa, even if (when…) I'm not around.

That's why I'll be addressing the rest of this book to them. I invite you to step into their shoes and remember what it was like to listen to your own grandfather. Read my book as though you and I are two generations apart but entirely matched in curiosity.

I think I know who I am. You and my grandkids may reach very different conclusions once I tell you my stories, but this is the way I would describe myself to someone who does not know me, or even more importantly, to someone who thinks they do know me.

I am:

- Progressive, secular humanist, rabid gun-control advocate, open-minded, anti-fascist, pro-democracy, extrovert, travel and experience junkie, lover of science and reason, art collector, rock music lover, non-believer in anything supernatural—yes, all of these. You are forewarned.
- A grandfather, father, partner, and friend and colleague to many good people that I have met during my journey—you bet.
- Financially secure and happy with my day-to-day life—absolutely.
- Healthy and vital man for my age. Genes, chance and luck only get you so far. I still put in the work every day.
- Continuing to contribute my wisdom, expertise, and energy to my business ventures, personal interests, and community—as much as I can.
- A hard worker and driven to succeed and please—for sure, and often to excess.

The ***Values and Guiding Principles*** that I try to live by have been developed, tested, challenged, and reinforced throughout my life. I believe I have been true to these, but I will leave it to you to judge whether I have achieved this goal.

- Live the Golden Rule—treat others as you would like others to treat you.

- Be curious and always skeptical.
- Work hard and never stop learning.
- Do not compromise your integrity.
- Value honesty and openness.
- Be responsible and accountable.
- Live Aloha.

One additional thought: On January 20th, 2022, I learned that Michael Lee Aday—professionally known as Meat Loaf—had died. It struck me like a ton of bricks. He was born around four years before me and was my absolute favorite music artist. I was a fan since the mid-1970s. I must have listened to his songs thousands of times, seen him perform live a number of times and actually have a signed, stage-played guitar, from Meat Loaf's *Bat Out of Hell III* tour hanging in my living room. Life is here and then it is gone. Done. Forgotten? Not for Meat Loaf, but probably for me.

A year later, almost to the day, on January 18th, 2023, David Crosby, from the rock bands Byrds and then Crosby, Stills, Nash and Young, died. He, too, was one of my favorite musicians. One of his songs, *Almost Cut My Hair*, kept running around my head that day.

Almost cut my hair
It happened just the other day
It's gettin' kinda long
I coulda said it wasn't in my way

But I didn't and I wonder why

I feel like letting my freak flag fly Yes, I feel like I owe it to someone

"I feel like letting my freak flag fly. Yes, I feel like I owe it to someone." I was a long-haired, bearded, hippy freak in the late 1960s and early 1970s, and that person is actually still inside of me. I did cut my hair in the mid-1970s and joined the other baby boomers that would change the world. But no one is ever just one person in their lifetime, are they?

This is why I feel I owe it to my grandkids to get it down so they may learn something from the life I lived and the insights I developed over the years. How many different people are inside those two beautiful boys? What adventures and challenges and decisions await them? I want them to know that Grandpa was once their age, and once had long hair, and more than once rocked out to Meat Loaf.

Above all, I want them to always and forever remain *curious*. My name is Robert Danna. This is my story.

PART 1

If My Life Were A Play

What is Past is Prologue

"(And by that destiny) to perform an act Whereof
what's past is prologue; what to come, in yours and my
discharge."

—*Antonio tells Sebastian*
The Tempest by William Shakespeare

Coming of Age

MY HERITAGE IS 100% Southern Italian. My ethnicity is 67 percent Southern Italy, 21 percent Aegean Islands, 7 percent Northern Italy, 3 percent Balkans, 1 percent Northern Africa, and 1 percent Basque. I can now trace some of the branches of my tree to the mid to late 1600s—back more than ten generations. Many of my relatives came from Calabria, chiefly from Cosenza—which is the story that was told around the Sunday dinner table by my grandfather (your great, great grandfather), mother (your great grandmother) and her four sisters, and now validated with a DNA test and extensive genealogical research.

My grandparents came to the U.S. in the late 1800s and early 1900s

My maternal grandparents— Pasquale Damiano (Papa) (1892-1965) and Elvira Chicchitelli (Mama) (1891-1957) in front of their shoe repair shop in Brooklyn—this is how I remember them—they were warm and loving people

through Ellis Island and settled in Manhattan, then Brooklyn and finally Queens in New York City. They worked hard, bought homes and raised families in the New York Area. Census records indicate they had a fifth-grade education and none ever spoke English, only Italian. All their grandchildren were born in New York City, including me. One of my granddads owned a shoe repair shop; the other was a factory worker.

Immigrants have never been accepted by the people already living in the U.S. They are portrayed as poor, uneducated, lazy, dirty, criminals, and diseased. Italians in the early 1900s were portrayed as such, and my grandparents faced all the challenges and barriers you would expect. Today, it is much the same: different groups of immigrants, same reaction of those individuals in this country that feel they have a "birth right" because they were born here, even though not so many generations ago, their ancestors were immigrants, too. So, in August 1921, Pasquale, living in San Marco, Italy, with his wife, Elvira, emigrated to the U.S. They traveled to Naples and boarded the SS Taormina, crossed the Atlantic Ocean, arrived in New York City, passing the Statue of Liberty in NY harbor, were processed through Ellis Island, and entered New York, living in a tenement apartment just like millions of other immigrants to the U.S. Your great, great grandparents were heroes although they never considered themselves as such. They came here with nothing, and their grit powered them to build a life for their children and descendants. They petitioned for Naturalization and were made citizens of the U.S. on December 10, 1936. Pasquale was 44 years old. You would not be you without Pasquale and your other ancestors who took the enormous risks to come here and build a life and our country.

Neither my dad (born in 1919) nor mother (born in 1927) graduated high school. My dad was a teenager during the Great Depression. He enlisted in the Civilian Conservation Corps (CCC) and worked to build infrastructure in the national parks in the Western U.S., chiefly in Washington State. I believe this was his first exposure to being outside of New York City and left a lasting mark on him. He loved to travel and see new things and exposed my brother and me continually to new experiences.

My dad was a mechanic on the Long Island Railroad, and my mother was a housewife and worked part time in the public-school kitchens. My younger brother (by 11 months) and I grew up as part of the lower middle class in a 2-bedroom, 900 square foot home, first in Levittown and then in Farmingdale on Long Island. My dad took us to the railroad repair shop where he worked in Queens. It was a pretty horrible work environment. He wanted to make sure that we were motivated to work hard in school to have a better work life than he had. It definitely worked. I greatly appreciate those who work hard with their hands for a living and are part of strong unions. I try to earn my place in society every day with the work I do.

My father changed his name from Mastantuono to Danna in 1950—the year before I was born—because he wanted his children to grow up as "Americans" and not feel the discrimination that he experienced as an Italian-American in the 1930s and 1940s. It worked; I never did. Although my dad told us several stories about why he chose Danna as his new surname, none really seemed to make sense. It appeared to be quite random to me as a child. I never really questioned it. It was just my name. I was Bobby Danna.

I was born in Bedford-Stuyvesant, Brooklyn in 1951 and almost immediately moved to Levittown for five years and then to Farmingdale where I went to elementary, middle, and high school graduating in 1969. I was given every opportunity to get a great public education and took them all.

Between my mom and dad, I had 20 aunts and uncles and over two dozen first cousins all living in Queens and on Long Island. It was a typical Italian family, lots of love, some typical sibling in-fighting and an incredible opportunity to spend time at family get-togethers. I was one of the older first cousins and loved interacting with everyone. We also spent time with my mom's aunts, uncles, and cousins (my second cousins), mostly in Camden, New Jersey. Unfortunately, as happens in most families, we scattered across the country as we grew up and had our own lives to live. I lost personal touch with most of them.

I was raised as a Catholic, baptized, received my first communion, and then I completed confirmation. Although my brother and I attended public school, we were also enrolled in the Church's Confraternity of Christian Doctrine (CCD) classes, commonly known as Catechism. I started to question the doctrine around the time of my Confirmation at age 13 and ultimately rejected belief in religion by 17. My mother remained a believer for her entire life and was never happy with my choice to become an atheist. I have never questioned my rejection of organized religion. It is antithetical to my guiding principles.

My dad was an archconservative, a John Bircher, supporter of George Wallace and Barry Goldwater, and a Kennedy-hater. He tried his best to indoctrinate me in the early 60s by giving me books to read by Phyllis Schlafly and others in the conservative movement, but it did not go well. He and I never agreed on anything political, and I started to build my social awareness as a young teenager and as a liberal Democrat. He hated that. It is funny that he would be so bigoted and openly discriminated against others being the son of immigrants and with his experience living through the Great Depression and with experiencing discrimination himself. We lived in a segregated community on Long Island made up of families of mostly European decent. Our schools were almost all White.

The 1960s taught me how to work hard with a great learning opportunity as a paperboy delivering Newsday six days a week to a route containing more than 70 homes for more than three years as a young teenager. The paper sold for five cents per day (30 cents per week). I received eight cents per home per week, and Newsday received 22 cents per home per week. It was my responsibility to collect weekly from my customers at each home (which I did on Saturday morning) and to sell new subscriptions to new homes on my route (which I did whenever I saw new folks in the neighborhood while I was delivering papers). By the way, I delivered papers in the hot summer, snowy winters, and rainy spring and fall days. There was no excuse for not completing your route.

I also learned the importance of tipping. My customers would typically give me a tip of five or ten cents per week. I still remember the guy who would give me a 20-cent tip—the best that I would generally get. He would give me two quarters and say keep the change. I try to be that guy and always tip generously. Everything that I now know about selling and delivering service was learned in those three years.

During elementary school, I started to play the alto saxophone. I was in the band and really enjoyed practicing with the group and being part of the "concerts" we performed. In middle school, my brother joined me playing the tenor saxophone as well, and we played together in the band and in a sax quartet. We went into competition with me playing the baritone sax and won as part of a quartet playing "Beguine for Saxophone." The lead alto sax player was a kid named Jay Beckenstein. Jay was a fabulous sax player and went on to found the jazz group Spyro Gyra—one of the few times that I was actually in presence of greatness and knew it—even at 13 years old. I have seen Spyro Gyra in concert multiple times over my lifetime—same Jay, same incredible talent. I continue to listen to his albums often on my iPhone when I just want to relax. I continued playing in the band through high school. I could not make the cut as a saxophonist, so I changed to bass clarinet, which I played until I graduated from high school. I definitely qualified as a band "geek" and was proud of it.

I fell in love with science and math in middle school and initially decided that I wanted to be a scientist. Next, in high school, I was exposed to chemistry and physics and was convinced that what I really wanted to be was a physicist. My mom and dad had no idea what that even was. With that said, I believe they felt it was their responsibility to give my brother and me every opportunity to be exposed to as many experiences as they could afford. We drove cross-country to California and then several years later up to

Canada and down to Florida. My brother and I were responsible for navigation using AAA-prepared customized *TripTik* books. We learned U.S. geography by being there. We visited Washington, D.C. multiple times including the Capitol, White House, every museum, and the Cherry Blossom Festival. We frequently visited Manhattan (including every year to see the Radio City Christmas Show), and went to two World's Fairs. They did a good job exposing us to history, geography, culture, and our country. Your great grandmother would save a dollar here and a dollar there in envelopes in her closet and used that money to fund all this travel. We drove or took trains to all these places. I did not get on a plane until I was in college and able to pay for it myself.

The New York World's Fair in 1964 and 1965 changed my life. I saw things that were unimaginable as a young teenager in the 1960s.

A few more thoughts on the two World's Fairs: The first was in NYC Flushing Meadow in 1964 and 1965; the second was in Montreal in 1968. I went 17 times to the New York World's Fair including on school trips, with my family, and with just my brother. Yes, do the math; I was around 13 and my brother was 12, and my mother let us get on the train on Long Island and travel almost two hours to the Fair including changing trains on our own. Whoa—that is not likely today. The technology, science, engineering, global cultures, and excitement about the future was everywhere, and I wanted to be part of it all. I visited a number of the pavilions multiple times including IBM (computers), Bell Telephone (communications), Ford (transportation), Sinclair (energy), General Electric (consumer products, future technologies and nuclear power), and countries from all over the world.

Tools in the late 1960s to support the sciences and math were few. I became extremely adept in using the slide rule, could program using the FORTRAN computer language, and truly understood math as well as I could speak English. FORTRAN stands for Formula Translation (created in 1957) and was the first high-level programming language developed by IBM. It was used by scientists and engineers to develop very detailed computer models and simulations for NASA's space missions, nuclear power and weapons, structural analysis, aircraft design and a million other applications. Each equation or logical instruction was distilled into a line of computer code, often punched onto hundreds or thousands of computer punch cards, combined into a deck of cards (the deck), fed into a card reader, assembled and run by a computer (the size of a small house), and then the results were printed out on sheets of paper - lots and lots of sheets of paper. I needed to truly understand what I was programming, what was a realistic result, and whether the output actually made logical sense.

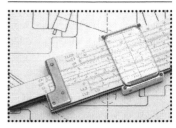

We were doing sophisticated scientific and mathematical calculations on a piece of bamboo. There were no calculators or other tools for us to use.

I also fell in love with folk and rock and roll music buying albums with money that I earned from several retail jobs and going to my first live concert—Jefferson Airplane. In 1969, I also bought my first car using the money that I saved from my paper route. It was a maroon 1964 Ford Galaxie 500 XL with beige leatherette interior, front bucket seats, and almost 200 HP. I could not believe how happy I was driving that car. It was also the place where I had my first car accident, went to the drive-in with my girlfriend, got my first speeding tickets, and experienced what it felt like to do 120 MPH on the highway. Actually, this is an example of one of the many stupid things I have done in my lifetime. I do not recommend it. But, if you do, please try to do it "responsibly."

ACT II

Finding My Way

IN THE LATE 1960s, New York City offered free public college education to its children. Having no money to pay for college, I applied to Hunter College of the City University of New York, was accepted and declared as a physics major and a math minor. That never changed during the three and a half years it took me to be awarded my bachelor's degree. The education that I received was outstanding with most of my professors having Ivy League degrees and being amazing teachers. One additional note: My grandfather passed away a few years before I entered college and left my brother and me $3,000 each to help with our future education. That was a big help during my freshman and sophomore years to keep me going when I had no income to support my day-to-day life.

By the way, Hunter had no dorms and was considered a commuter school, which I initially did from Long Island and then from Astoria in Queens. The ride started before 6 AM from Long Island. It required driving to the Massapequa Railroad Station and taking the LIRR (with a free pass my dad got for me) to Penn Station in Manhattan, changing to a subway train to Times Square, then changing to a subway train to Lexington Avenue, and again changing to a subway train to the Hunter College Station at 68th Street and Lexington Avenue. I repeated this in the afternoon. Fourteen-hour days were the norm for me. I did much of my homework and studying at Hunter during my class breaks and on the LIRR.

During my sophomore year, the College selected me to be a tutor for the freshman physics course which came in three variations: a one semester course for non-science majors, a two-semester course without calculus, and a two-semester course with calculus. I did this for three years, was paid $5.25 an hour (a lot of money in 1971 when the minimum wage was under $2 per hour) for as much time as I could apply to this activity. I learned an incredible amount of foundational physics, completed and could explain every problem in all three textbooks, and discovered that I was a pretty good communicator and teacher. I also got my first piece of technology to support my physics courses, a Hewlett-Packard scientific calculator—the HP35—and learned to calculate using Reverse Polish Notation (RPN) used by scientists to more efficiently stack and perform complex calculations. I still use an HP calculator with RPN to this day, although not the original one I had in the early 1970s.

I experienced my first Total Solar Eclipse. This is the eclipse in 1972 on Prince Edward Island in Canada. It was spectacular. I have repeated that experience multiple times during my lifetime.

Going to college in NYC in the early 1970s was unbelievable—anti-war protests (yes, I marched and was an active anti-Vietnam War protestor and hippy freak), dozens and dozens of live folk and rock concerts (including the Concert for Bangladesh), supporting our Amazing Mets (winning the World Series in 1969), and developing deep relationships with an incredibly diverse group of friends—guys, girls, Blacks, Puerto Ricans, Muslims, Jews, refugees from the Soviet Union, homosexuals. We socialized together and enjoyed one another's company. We all came from working-class backgrounds and embraced the "lovechild" generation culture of the late 1960s and early 1970s. I lived in Astoria and Glendale in Queens and was a New Yorker in every way possible. To this day, I am a New Yorker no matter where I live or what I am doing with my life.

The early 1970s were the start of several other adventures that are now some of my favorite things to do. I learned to snow ski in Vermont and turned out to be pretty good. I traveled to view the first of many total solar eclipses that I would see over my lifetime. The first was in 1972 in Prince Edward Island in Canada. Carly Simon mentioned this eclipse in her song "You're So Vain," always one of my favorites. We drove there from NYC in a Volkswagen Bug, although I would have preferred the Learjet she wrote about in the lyrics to her song. We also had no money for hotels. So, we camped all the way there and back.

I jumped from a small single-engine plane. A few of us read an article in the New York Times about the Rhinebeck Aerodrome and the fact that you could do static line parachute jumping from a small plane using army surplus parachutes. We decided to do it. I solo parachute jumped, actually hit the target, limped away, and never did that again.

I worked in the evenings and weekends on research and writing computer programs to analyze electric signals from weakly electric fish.

Back to Hunter: Three of my professors asked me to assist them with their research as an undergraduate—one supporting NASA and the manned moon missions, one doing chemical physics in the early years of nuclear magnetic resonance (NMR), and one in the psychology department working at the American Museum of Natural History's research department on the interaction of weakly electric fish. Talk about drinking from a firehose as a 20-year-old. I began writing FORTRAN scientific programs to support this research and was routinely typing computer punch cards to run these programs on an IBM 360. The power of this room-filing computer is less than today's tablet, but it changed science and engineering—and me. In 1972, I was elected a member of Sigma Pi Sigma, the National Physics Honor Society.

After graduation, I went straight on for my Master's degree in physics at Hunter which I completed in two years including research and a thesis in chemical and nuclear physics. The College also asked me to join the faculty as an adjunct lecturer, ultimately teaching the two-semester "physics without calculus" course to undergraduate students. It was a good thing that I did all of that tutoring as an undergraduate. I was rated as one of their best lecturers and loved teaching. They paid me $23 per contact hour. I was delivering around eight contact hours per week. That's around $6,500 per year. In the early 1970s that was a lot of money since I was only paying around $150 a month to rent an apartment in Queens. I was also working on a research grant, tutoring nursing students at the Hunter-Bellevue School of Nursing and at the Fashion Institute of Technology (in their organic chemistry lab as a lab assistant). Every dollar I could earn made a difference.

I was married for the first time in the summer of 1974. Janice was a year younger than me, a math major at Hunter (where we met), extremely smart, and one of the most challenging physics students that I tutored. She wanted to solve every problem in the "physics with calculus" textbook—which we did. I was in the middle of my master's degree, and she had just completed her bachelor's degree. We were both making a little money and had saved for this wedding. So, we splurged on a honeymoon in Canada, visiting Niagara Falls, Montreal and Quebec City. In Quebec City we stayed at the Chateau Frontenac and ordered breakfast in bed. That was way better than the camping that we were doing as undergraduates. This definitely reset my expectations for what future vacations should look like.

A Ph.D. in physics was the obvious next step for me and continuing on for a master's degree was part of her plans. In 1975,

I applied and was accepted to complete my Ph.D. in physics at Brown University. This year was very pivotal for us driving considerations of our future and what we wanted to do with the rest of our lives.

During the summer of 1975, I was invited to apply to join the team at the U.S. Navy's Office of Naval Reactors. I applied and was invited to Naval Reactors in Crystal City, Virginia for interviews with the leadership team and with Admiral Hyman Rickover. The interviews went well, and they offered me a direct commission as a naval officer to serve as an instructor at the U.S. Navy's Nuclear Power School. That was a bit of a major turn of events; I was ready for a change of direction so I accepted, raised my hand, took the oath and became a Navy Ensign in September 1975 reporting for active duty in January 1976 to Newport, RI for five weeks of Officer Indoctrination School and then on to Orlando to serve at the Navy's brand new Naval Nuclear Power School. It was one of the best decisions I ever made. The Ph.D. would need to wait. My mentor was not very happy with my decision, but I just felt that I needed to get on with my life. I never completed the Ph.D. but additional degrees and credentials in engineering were definitely in my future.

By the way, I was anti-war, not anti-military. There is a difference. Deterrence and defense are good, politically driven offensive actions and unjustified wars are very bad. I then served in a time of "peace" for 13 years between the end of the Vietnam War and the beginning of the first Iraq War.

I spent four years on active duty in Orlando as an instructor and division director. They were intense. The Navy asked a lot, and I delivered, teaching a three-month long atomic and nuclear physics course and a three-month long reactor principles course to enlisted personnel, and a three-month long reactor dynamics and core characteristics course to naval officers all of whom were destined to operate the Navy's nuclear reactors aboard submarines and aircraft carriers. Additionally, my last year at the Nuclear Power School was as the head of the physics division, where I led around

20 naval officers, all of whom held master's or Ph.D.s in physics. My division trained thousands of naval personnel per year. I completed active duty as a Lieutenant (O-3) and then continued service as a reserve officer.

During these four years in Orlando, I completed another Master's degree (paid for by the Navy). This one was in environmental engineering which was just becoming an area of concern for the U.S. and the world. I also obtained my private pilot's license. In 1979, I was able to take my mom and dad on a plane ride

I learned to fly in a Piper Warrior single engine aircraft and got my pilots license in July 1978.

over Walt Disney World. They were incredibly excited to do that with me and could not believe that I was actually piloting the plane.

On a very dark note, Janice's younger brother, and only sibling, committed suicide. He was enrolled in college in Boston, and on a trip home to Brooklyn, took his own life. To today, I cannot fathom how someone can get to a place where that is their only option. It is probably a shortcoming in my personality and attitude, but I cannot imagine why an individual decides that the people who love them, their friends, everyone around them can't help. I have now been confronted with people who I know committing suicide—my reaction is always the same. I break down in disbelief and say "why would you do that to yourself—what could drive you to do that?" Like I said, I just need to keep trying to learn more about what that must feel like so I can be more aware and sensitive to the indications of this possible situation. Heartbreaking.

In 1979, during the writing of my master's thesis on the environmental impact of commercial nuclear power plants, the Three Mile Island accident occurred. I was able to incorporate my analysis of the accident into my thesis which had a major positive impact on my job hunting for the civilian job that would follow active duty. Amazingly, everyone wanted me to join their teams—the U.S. Nuclear Regulatory Commission, General Physics Corporation (the largest training and consulting firm in the commercial nuclear power industry), two nuclear reactor manufacturers, and several other engineering consulting firms. Janice completed her master's degree in operations research, applied for jobs in Maryland, and landed a great position as an analyst at the Johns Hopkins Applied Physics Lab.

We were putting in 13 to 14-hour days seven days a week for the duration of the four years in Orlando. At the end of the four years, we were 28 years old. We did party a bit as well. Our Navy friends and colleagues came from all over the country. They were quite an interesting bunch of folks.

I joined General Physics Corporation (GP) at the beginning of 1980 as a senior engineer in their Columbia, MD headquarters. Columbia was a new, completely planned, community—beautiful, lots of open space, socially conscious, completely diverse and integrated, with health and athletic community centers and programs. The center of town had a lake, mall and Symphony Woods. It was heaven. We bought our first home there for $95,000. Mortgage interest rates exceeded 12 percent per year. Life continued at the intense pace that we had become accustomed to in Orlando. Housing prices are much higher, and mortgage rates are lower, today. Ultimately, just live life within your means, and it will all work out.

The early 1980s continued to be very life changing. I decided to focus on getting all the credentials that I needed to be recognized as a consulting design engineer. This required me to again put in long days of study to allow me to take and pass the Engineer-in-Training Exam and then sit for the grueling Professional Engineer Exam. I did both in Maryland passing both exams the first time and was certified as a Professional Engineer (P.E.) in March 1982. I proudly carried the P.E. designation for almost 30 years after that retiring my registration in 2009.

My mom and dad, your great grandparents, were now living in Orlando. On August 1, 1982, my dad died suddenly and instantaneously of a massive stroke. I had no chance to say goodbye. I still feel bad that his life ended this way, with no chance to say goodbye—he or me. He was 63 years old and generally not well, probably because of his smoking, work in the "pits" under the Long Island Railroad's passenger cars fixing the train's brakes (his specialty), exposure to asbestos and many other environmental issues that he probably worked with. Based on his wishes, he was cremated, and his ashes were spread from an airplane over Walt Disney World. He loved going there.

I now split my time at GP developing and delivering engineer training programs at commercial nuclear power plants throughout the U.S. in response to the findings from the Three Mile Island nuclear accident. I began to develop and apply my engineering skills assessing the integrity of pressure vessels and systems at nuclear power plants and NASA research facilities including the Jet Propulsion Lab (JPL). I also started to be published with peer-reviewed papers and articles accepted by the American Society of Mechanical Engineers (ASME) and the American Nuclear Society (ANS). The P.E. license, publications, professional society presentations, and engineering projects that I led all contributed to me being recognized as one of the leading engineers at GP and in the engineering community. I was promoted to manager, then director, and finally chief engineer and vice president during the 1980s. I was also listed in *Who's Who in Engineering* by the American Association of Engineering Societies and became a member of ASME's new High Pressure Vessel Code Committee.

The Beginning of You, My Grandkids

ON A PERSONAL note, I was divorced from Janice in early 1984 and married your grandmother, Janis, later in December of that same year. Pretty crazy that they had the same name. Your grandmother and I met at the Jet Propulsion Laboratory (JPL) during a multi-year project that I directed for GP. That was both a tough and very happy year for me. In 1985, we took a two-week honeymoon in Asia with stops in Tokyo. We also visited my final World's Fair—Tsukuba Expo'85 which was taking place just outside of Tokyo. We also visited Mt. Fuji, Kyoto, Osaka, Taipei, Hong Kong, Macau, and Guangzhou. This was my first exposure to Asia. Luckily, I have been back dozens of times since then. Your grandmother and I bought a new home in Columbia, MD and settled into life there.

I was then asked to relocate to San Diego in 1985 to help lead GP's geographic expansion in the Western U.S., which I happily did, continuing to carry my responsibility as head of engineering in addition to the leader of GP's Western operations. We sold our home in Columbia and bought a new home in Carlsbad/La Costa north of San Diego. San Diego is still one of my favorite places on earth. Your mom was born in March 1986, and we settled down for a life in Southern California. I was 34 years old and was now ready for the next chapter of my life as a father of a beautiful baby girl (your mom).

I was on the road almost continually—first, all over the country and then all over the world for both business (mostly) and pleasure (whenever we could). I developed a five-day nuclear codes and standards course for GP for engineers at commercial nuclear power plants. It turned out that I was one of the only ones who could deliver it. Everyone wanted it presented at their power plant. In addition, our NASA and Air Force rocket launch and research facility system integrity programs were incredibly successful. I led business development, proposal writing, and directed most of these multi-year, multi-million dollar programs country-wide. During this time, I also became a registered professional engineer in Florida and Tennessee and a registered mechanical engineer in California. I now sat on an ASME code committee on high-pressure vessels, was delivering expert witness testimony to government safety committees, and presenting engineering workshops internationally.

I was also an early adopter of technology. GP allowed me to be one of the first to use the new technologies that were being introduced into the business environment. I carried and used the first Compaq Portable Computer. It was one of the first IBM PC compatible systems and was a beast, barely portable. I also used the Toshiba T1000, the world's first mass-marketed laptop computer. I could create presentations, write proposals and reports, and be independent. I was no longer tied to an office or an admin to get my work done. It was liberating. This was 1988. We also got our first home computer which your mom started to use when she was three years old—one of the original pre-internet platforms. It was the Prodigy online content portal. I also carried and continuously used a pager to keep in contact with my office and colleagues, airport pay phones (you can't find those anymore), one of the first car phones and a portable "bag" phone.

During this time, I continued my military service in the Navy Reserves, first as a member of the Theater Nuclear Warfare Project Office in Crystal City, VA and then as a member of the Office of Naval Research in Pasadena, CA. I held a Top Secret security clearance with compartmented access to Critical Nuclear Weapons Design Information. I received an honorable discharge from the Navy as a Lieutenant Commander (LCDR) in April 1989 after 13 years of service.

These are my LCDR shoulder boards.

Your mom was still a young child at this time. Whenever she, your grandmother, and I would travel together, we would be going on vacation. Your mom got very mad at me whenever I would go away on business and leave them at home, which was pretty often. We finally asked her why she was so mad. She said she wanted to know why dad was going on vacation and not taking them with me. Whoa, I would have never guessed that. So, on my next business trip, which was to work with my NASA client and our team in Cleveland, I took your mom and grandma to Cleveland. I usually stayed at a hotel next to GP's Cleveland office. When we got up the next morning, I had her watch me walk to the office from the window in our hotel room so she could see that I was not on vacation but actually just going to work in a different city. They came to lunch with me at the office and met the GP team there. I still had a wild travel schedule, but at least she knew I was not going on vacation without them.

I would also routinely take your mom to my office in San Diego, Columbia, and Sacramento on Saturday mornings to catch up on business if I traveled during the week. She loved to be there and would have the run of the office, often playing on the whiteboards, "delivering" presentations in the conference room, and on one occasion in San Diego watched the circus come to town. Our office was in Old Town, San Diego, and all of the circus animals came right past my office window on their trip from the train station to the circus location.

We really geared up our personal travel during the late 1980s and early 1990s with our first Caribbean Cruise, our first extended vacation in Hawai'i (O'ahu, Kauai and the Big Island) with your mom (she was 18-months-old), and our first weeklong trip to Paris. We also became season seat holders for the San Diego Chargers and had annual passes to Disneyland, the San Diego Zoo, and SeaWorld. All were special to us and quite different from one another. As you know, your mom remains a big fan of these and has now introduced you to them. My favorite remains Disney, both California and Florida.

In 1991, we took part in a weeklong cruise to see a total solar eclipse. The centerline of the eclipse, with maximum duration of totality of around seven minutes, was to occur between Cabo San Lucas and Mazatlán in the Sea of Cortez. It was a total "geek-out" cruise filled with scientists, astronomy lectures and incredible conversations. It also became a thing for me looking for the next time that I could stand in the shadow of the moon. That came in San Diego soon after when we witnessed an annular eclipse at sunset. It was spectacular but paled in comparison with a total eclipse. Finally of note, as a senior exec at GP, we were invited to attend the four-day 1993 Super Bowl event as a guest of Avis Car Rental at the Rose Bowl in Pasadena.

Your mom and I also developed an "imagine" game that we played for years. We called it the "travel game." From all of my travels, I would bring back my plane tickets (they were paper back then!), car rental agreements (paper too), hotel stationery (paper and envelopes), hotel pens and pencils, hotel brochures, drink coasters, and whatever else I could get for her to represent my travels. She had a couple of baskets at home filled with this stuff. She had been on multiple trips with your grandma and me so she knew the whole travel routine, making reservations, checking in at the airport, getting the rental car, checking into the hotels, going to places and restaurants. Yes, she knew all of it. So, the game at home was a "make-believe" game that had us doing all of this. We had an old computer keyboard that she used to "make" the reservations, gave me the tickets (from her basket), moved to the next room in our house with her keyboard to get the rental car (she had the car rental folder ready to go), and then moved to the next room to check into our hotel. It was so cute. We played this game for hours every time we could.

GP was sold, restructured, and reorganized in the late 1980s and early 1990s. Luckily, I was continually recognized as one of the company's key leaders and was given more responsibility within the company during each change. In the early 1990s, I was asked to relocate back to Columbia, MD to assume an Executive Vice President and Chief Operating Officer position. We sold our home in California and bought a new home in Columbia, MD. I was now routinely traveling back and forth to Asia-Pac and Europe helping GP build their international operations. I was now in my early 40s and started to consider what I wanted to do with the rest of my life. I had been working incredibly long days for around 25 years now with extensive domestic and international travel, sometimes involving multiple cities in a week. It was getting old, or I was getting old, or both.

My team in San Diego had a caricature created when I moved to Columbia in the early 1990s. It was very funny and very true. It was a crazy time, indeed. I was given the Ayatollah name in 1979 by my team in the Physics Division at the Nuclear Power School. It stuck for over 30 years until the early 2010s.

During the early 1990s, I was asked to sit on the business advisory board for the Dean of Sciences at Hunter College. It was great to return to Hunter and provide my support to the college's success in biology, chemistry, and physics—both in research and academics. In 1993, the Alumni Association of Hunter College named me to the Hunter College Hall of Fame in recognition of my outstanding achievement—an honor that was offered to only around 10 alumni per year.

My business travel continued to be intense at this point as GP was developing its Asia-Pac and European operations. I did some fun things during all these trips including walking on the Great Wall of China and visiting the Forbidden City, being in Beijing and Shanghai before they were fully open to western travelers (we were required to stay at the Diaoyutai State Guest House with a minder since there were no western hotels at that point), and spending extended stays in Singapore and Malaysia, including having a Singapore Sling at the Long Bar at the Raffles Hotel in Singapore. I also got to have a meeting in the Kremlin while working in Moscow. The best part was having time to spend with the people. Most of GP's teams were locals, and that gave me the opportunity to get out with them to see how locals really lived.

The mid 1990s at GP were incredibly intense. I led the largest proposal effort ever to be undertaken by GP. It was a half a billion-dollar effort to take over operations of the Air Force's Arnold Engineering Development Center in Tullahoma, TN. It required us to take part in the creation of a joint venture with Computer Sciences Corporation and DynCorp. I worked for around six months on this effort along with all my other duties. We won, and I was named to the Board of Directors of the joint venture. I was now one of the two top operating executives in GP—me as the "COO" and my colleague as the "CFO"—although we co-shared operational leadership for the company. We now had almost 2,000 professionals located worldwide. I was on the Board of Directors (GP was listed on the NY Stock Exchange) with a retired congressional representative and a Nobel Prize-winning physicist, and was a group president of engineering and technical services. In 1995, they decided to select one of us for the CEO position. The CFO was selected, and I went to work for him. I did not enjoy working for an accountant. That may sound harsh, but it was just how I felt.

During my work in Singapore, Malaysia, the Philippines, and Thailand I developed a relationship with the founder and CEO of Resource Management International (RMI), headquartered in Sacramento, CA. He initially wanted to buy GP's Asia-Pac operations to add to their foothold in Manila. We were not able to come to terms on a deal, and he offered me a prominent position to join him as part of his leadership team in Sacramento. I accepted, resigned from GP after nearly 16 years of service, and moved your mom and grandmother to Sacramento. As it turned out, he and I did not see eye-to-eye, and I decided to leave RMI after just one year. I am sure that I had missed many cues that I should have picked up during my many conversations before accepting the offer and probably did not adjust quickly enough to the new business environment to be successful in the new company.

On a high note, we went to the Summer Olympics in Atlanta in 1996 for five days. It was incredible. We got to see the women's gymnastics competition and the U.S. "dream team" performance.

Luckily, I had built a large network of folks who knew and respected me and my work ethic. I immediately got hired by RWD Technologies (some of the team from the original GP organization who left after GP's acquisition in the late 1980s), got set up in a one-person temporary office in Sacramento (where we lived), given a laptop, internet connection, a mobile phone, fax machine and a printer, and asked to build their West Coast operations. I did so in a matter of three years on the basis of supporting the deployment of newly developed enterprise resource planning (ERP) software and the Y2K (Year 2000) scare that was overtaking the business world in the late 1990s. We opened two offices, hired dozens of professionals, and supported some of the largest ERP implementations in the country. I also developed deep relationships with PricewaterhouseCoopers International Limited, SAP, PeopleSoft and Business Objects, putting in place partnerships and joint ventures (JV) with these firms including establishing a JV with SAP

Asia operations (headquartered in Singapore) to deliver ERP training support throughout Asia-Pac. We had offices throughout the region, including Tokyo, Singapore, and Sydney. I led the operations hiring almost all locals to staff the offices and traveling to and from Asia and Australia at least every other month. It was a wonderful time again. We started a routine of going to Hawaii, cruising, and traveling for pleasure as much as we could. Thank goodness for all those Hilton Hotel frequent stay and United frequent flyer points.

The highlight of 1999 was we spent two weeks in Europe, first a week in London, including a tour of Buckingham Palace, then on to Paris for a few days, and then on to Vienna. As part of the plan, we coordinated the trip to coincide with a total solar eclipse with its centerline just south of Vienna. We were there. Once again, I was in the shadow of the moon, and it was thrilling. Then, we partied like it was 1999. Actually, it was 1999, and we were in Las Vegas at a New Year's Eve party hosted by Pat Benatar and Neil Giraldo. Like I said, this was a pretty cool year.

As a side note, during the 1990s, GP and RWD conducted a number of personality assessments to assist senior managers in understanding their own personality types and traits and use this to better understand how to manage and interact with others—supervisors, peers and subordinates. It turns out that on a Myers-Briggs Type Indicator (MBTI) assessment, I am an ENTJ—Extroversion (you prefer to focus on the outer world of people and things), Intuition (you tend to focus on the future with a view toward patterns and possibilities), Thinking (you tend to base your decisions primarily on logic and on objective analysis of cause and effect), and Judging (you like a planned and organized approach to life and prefer to have things settled). Yes, that's me. This assessment result was corroborated using the Predictive Index System, Harrison Assessment, one-on-one executive development assessments, and other related coaching assessments. There is definitely something to be said for knowing oneself. I am convinced the earlier you understand what your core personality is, the better life decisions you will make.

In fact, there are several personality tests for kids that might be useful to consider. The bottom line is that personality appears very early in life. I can already see it in you, my grandkids. So, which are you?: the dominant child, the expressive child, the analytical child, the loyal child? Some combination? I will hold my opinion for now. It will be wonderful to see where you each land. My personality definitely guided my journey through life, probably appearing about the time I took my first steps. That goes for you, too. Just ask your mom.

In the early 2000s, I turned 50 years old and joined a ".com" learning technology startup as a senior vice president, funded by the Charles Schwab family. This ".com" ultimately failed, and was shut down. I started my own consulting firm that was very successful but not what I wanted to do with the rest of my career. I co-founded and co-funded a knowledge management and learning startup that I ultimately joined full time but then left after a disagreement with my co-founders. During all this time, I continued traveling a lot for business, domestically and in Asia-Pac. We also bought our first timeshare weeks in Florida, Canada, and Hawaii, spent time skiing in the Sierras and Whistler, Canada, and spent as much time as we could on the Big Island in Hawaii. We went on more cruises, got into wine tasting, attended the Winter Olympics and totally enjoyed family life in the foothills of El Dorado County in California.

On the morning of September 11, 2001, the world changed. We were living in El Dorado Hills, CA, and I was on business travel getting ready for a meeting in Maryland, just north of D.C. The feeling of horror, despair, uncertainty, anger, and every other reaction was happening at the same time. I was a New Yorker and watched the Twin Towers being built when I went to college in Manhattan. Your mom, grandmother and I had been to the top of the towers, and I had meetings there. As a naval reserves officer, I had meetings in the Pentagon. It was horrible beyond words. Everything shut down—including all the air traffic throughout the U.S. I had no way to get home. Luckily one of my best friends lived in Virginia and I could get there. The drive around the D.C. Beltway was surreal. There was no traffic going into D.C.—only traffic coming out of D.C. with rumors flying around on the radio about a massive attack on our Country. I was grateful for the ability to be with friends but had no way to get home to your mom and grandmother.

On Friday, U.S. airspace reopened. It was chaos. I was able to get to Dulles Airport, use my status as a frequent flyer to get through security and on to a flight to Denver, where there were hundreds of planes stranded on the tarmac. I used my United 1K status again to get a flight to Sacramento, being one of the first to fly cross-country after 9/11. I got home to your mom and grandmother and thought I was one of the luckiest guys in the world.

Thousands of people would never get home to their families, and hundreds of thousands of people were dislocated for weeks. Sadness was everywhere, and then the feeling of revenge percolated everywhere. That would change the U.S. and its politics for decades—even today.

I did not agree with the Country's response to 9/11—not in Afghanistan and especially not in Iraq. The damage that we caused in the aftermath of 9/11 far exceeded the horror of 9/11 itself. The "War on Terror" was a total failure and hundreds of thousands of innocent people died unnecessarily.

In 2002, my mom—your great grandmother—contracted pancreatic can-

This is one of my favorite pictures of my mom and me—taken in 1978 in Orlando—definitely a proud mom and her grateful son.

cer. She was diagnosed in the Spring, and on September 22, 2002 she passed away at the age of 75. That was 20 years after my dad died. During those twenty years, she had built an enjoyable life for herself in the Orlando area. She started to work in the retail shops at Walt Disney World, became involved in the church and in her community, and made lots and lots of friends. Everyone loved Anna. I guess I have not mentioned it before—my mom's name was Anna Danna.

Before she died, your grandmother, your mom and I took her to lots of places to just have fun so all of us could have great memories of her and not dwell over the last few months of her life. It was a good time for all of us, and her passing, although tough for me, was associated with a celebration of a life well-lived. My mom loved art collectables. They were all over her house, hundreds of them.

After her passing, my brother and I took a few of the collectables to remember her by and decided to do something very different. We donated her furniture to her church for their "young adult" rec center. We then scheduled a night to celebrate her life inviting all her friends from work, her church, neighbors, the community and anyone she touched during her life. I called them all to invite them for the evening. My brother and I then set out all the collectables. When folks arrived, we encouraged all of them to share stories about her and take as many of the collectables they wanted to remember Anna. At first, no one wanted to take anything. We then individually asked that they take something, and by the end of the evening, almost everything went home with someone. I now know that every day someone looks at one of those collectables in their homes and remembers your great grandmother. This is really the only way that we "live" past our current too short lives. She asked to be cremated and have her ashes spread near a lake in Vermont. My brother and I did this later that year. Your grandmother and your mom went along with us.

Your mom now graduated high school and went off to college. We put a pre-construction contract on a condo unit in downtown

San Diego on Pacific Highway and sold our home in El Dorado Hills. We moved to San Diego in 2005 into a brand new, incredible unit at the Grand North, one of the premier condo towers in the newly revitalized downtown, directly across from the Cruise Terminal and one block from San Diego Bay. My home office looked out onto the airport and the cruise terminal. I could watch the planes land and take off and the cruise ships embark and disembark. I could also see the Navy's nuclear aircraft carriers docked at North Island—an added bonus to a guy that trained the sailors who were operating the nuclear reactors on those ships.

In December 2005, I joined another startup, a research and analyst firm that focused on corporate learning and human resources. I was a member of the senior leadership team. It was started by Josh Bersin who is respected globally as one of the leading analysts in this area. Over the next seven years, I helped him build the company to have more than 500 global clients and over $10 million in annual revenue.

We also continued to add to the timeshare portfolio, traveled yearly to Hawaii, completed transatlantic and Mediterranean cruises, wine tasted in Tuscany, traveled to Greece, Turkey, and India, and totally enjoyed living in San Diego. We also bought a second home in Las Vegas and moved our residency to Nevada.

ACT IV

Finding Robert Danna

2012 WAS THE toughest year of my life. I was serving as the Executive Vice President and Chief Operating Officer of Bersin & Associates. We had engaged an investment banker to raise $10 million in investment capital earlier in the year and then, by midyear after several organizations expressed interest to buy Bersin, a full-blown Merger & Acquisition (M&A) initiative took place. I was also in the middle of a divorce from your grandmother. Your mom and dad were getting married with a destination wedding planned on the Big Island of Hawaii. I bought a home out of foreclosure in the Traccia Community in Las Vegas during the very bottom of the Great Recession's housing crisis. I was also working 12 to 15 hours per day to drive the growth of the company in the face of all the M&A activities. I started to date Laci as well.

I was at my wit's end most days and felt like the world was pressing in from all sides. I dug deep and called on every bit of energy, grit, and capability that I had. I probably pissed off everyone that came in contact with me at one point or another that year—your mom, your grandmother, friends, colleagues, probably everyone. I can remember one evening in the Spring of 2012. I was on a business trip in New Jersey with two colleagues getting ready for a major proposal presentation to a client the next day. Over dinner, I concluded my colleagues were not prepared to deliver a presentation that could win the work. During dinner, I received a call from my attorney in Las Vegas telling me about another issue that I needed to address immediately in the divorce proceedings. I went back to the proposal-prep dinner meeting, and it got worse. I would need to rewrite the entire presentation probably requiring the entire night. Then, Laci called from her home in Phoenix on my way back to my hotel room at around 11 PM ET to tell me about an issue she had with her car. My response was quick and to the point: "MY PROBLEM BASKET IS FULL," and I hung up.

It took a number of years to repair much of the damage that was caused during 2012. But, with everything going on, I still tried to do my best. My adherence to my values and guiding principles were bent and twisted that year, but ultimately held firm. Good thing; I would need them in 2013 to be even stronger to help me navigate all of the changes that were going on in my life. I did learn a lot about asking for forgiveness, acknowledging wrong-doing, forgiving others, extending grace, accepting that failure is a chance to learn and grow, "fall down eight times get up nine." It is not pretty, nor easy, and the scars stay with you for the rest of your life. It also forces you to try to do better in all of your relationships. The Golden Rule, Living Aloha, and all of my other guiding principles become the starting point for making things better for all involved. I hope that when asked, everyone would say that Bob was definitely not perfect (for sure), but he tried (and succeeded) more often than not to be a good person.

Luckily, by the end of the year, Bersin & Associates was sold to Deloitte Consulting. I was asked to stay on as a managing director (a level equivalent to a non-owner partner) in the firm's Human Capital Practice, a billion-dollar part of the global consulting firm. The divorce was finalized. Your mom and dad got married in an incredible wedding at the Hilton Waikoloa on the Big Island in Hawaii. Many of our family and friends were able to be there.

I was able to get most of the repairs completed on the home that I bought out of foreclosure. Laci, and her daughter Ali, relocated from Arizona to Las Vegas. Like I said, this was quite a messy year. I also turned 61 that year and was feeling more like 80.

The 10 years between 2012 and today have had their challenges as well, but there have been many more good things that happened than bad. I wanted to be as good a Managing Director at Deloitte as I could be, looking to place a capstone on my professional career. Since I loved to travel, I wanted to continue to cruise, spend more time exploring interesting places around the world, and to spend extended stays in Hawaii. Also, I wanted to work on making my new relationship with Laci as deep and meaningful as I possibly could. Finally, I planned to ensure that my relationship with your mom and dad is solid and continues to mature as we move into the next stage of our lives—your mom and dad into their thirties and forties, and motherhood and fatherhood, and me into my old age and becoming your grandfather. I think I made progress to accomplish this during the past 10 years and am still working every day to try to ensure I continue to accomplish these more personal goals for the rest of my life.

After almost five years of service as a Managing Director at Deloitte, I retired in June 2017. That ended my more than 40 years of full-time employment. Those 40+ years were intense, with little "balance" between my work and my life; although, I did try to perform that "balancing act" every day, a successful career requires too many compromises often prioritizing work over life (family, friends, personal interests, and personal time). I have tried to do better during the past six years since "retiring," however, once you have established a routine over almost 50 years (if you want to count those crazy college days), it is hard to break it.

During the last 10 years, Laci and I have developed a deep and rich relationship. We are inseparable. Her older daughter, Taylor, who was living in Cleveland with her father through high school after Laci's divorce, started to look for colleges. She wanted to study Hospitality Management. Laci and I helped her decide on a school, flying around the country to look at colleges that might be a good fit. She selected UNLV and moved to Las Vegas to attend college. Her sister, Ali, did the same, and both now live in Las Vegas, have solid careers and have established lives for themselves within 20 minutes of us, with Ali having two kids, Parker and Carter. Taylor and Ali (along with the kids) have become the closest of close friends of mine and are now part of my extended family.

Laci and I have continued to travel extensively with eight cruises on Royal Caribbean including three transatlantic cruises, spending six to seven weeks per year in Hawaii (now owning timeshares in O'ahu, Maui and the Big Island), and travel throughout the U.S. and Europe. I became an investor in a startup which, unfortunately, failed because of the Covid-shutdown of the economy. I also became a limited partner in a Venture Capital firm, an advisor to a Workday integrator, executive chairman of an executive networking firm, and a member of the UCF Dean of the Business School's advisory board—all at once and all part time. Gotta watch out for that intense personality of mine, my need to always be doing something, and the issues I now have, after 50 years, in getting that work-life balance right.

The Undiscovered Country

So, THE TWO of you arrived in my life during the past seven years. After the birth of your mother, the days of your births were the most amazing thing that I have ever experienced. I still get choked up thinking about it. Watching you grow and now become little kids is so cool, and I can't wait to see you every time we get together. I also can't wait to see what you become as you grow up. The world is filled with infinite opportunities for you to take and never-ending challenges for you to face. As I think about my past 70 years, I also consider your next 100 years, or more. I have seen such wonders. What will you see? I have had amazing experiences. What will you experience? I have had incredible joys and as well as my share of heartaches and challenges. What will you have in your lives? I have met incredible people worldwide. Who will you have as your friends, colleagues, and acquaintances? I have had only three deep relationships in my life. Who will you develop relationships with that will change your lives?

The world is getting to be a very scary and confusing place, one filled with an incredible amount of misinformation and disinformation. We live in a place where facts, evidence, truth, the scientific method, reason, logic, and integrity are no longer valued nor understood by many people and especially individuals like media personalities, politicians, religious leaders, "online influencers," and the like.

Scientists, engineers, intellectuals, committed skeptics, and humanists are never included in the conversation. They are marginalized or otherwise ignored when they try to explain what is really happening based on facts and evidence.

I hope you, my grandkids, don't fall into the trap of believing in, following, or being complicit in supporting, these liars, half-truth tellers, charlatans, conspiracy promoters, and others that have big megaphones, lots to say, but little or no integrity nor truth in what they are saying. It will be very hard for you to resist the pressure from these people. Conformance to the positions espoused by the majority is easy; sticking to your principles may be much more difficult.

I also fear that you will be affected by the results of our inaction over the past 50 years and not be part of taking action—of being part of the solution—but rather continue to be part of the lack of action to address the effects of climate change, the carnage associated with gun violence, the intolerance shown to those who are different from the dominant white, heterosexual, religious, right-leaning, male-dominated conservative political, religious and business elites, and the intensifying bifurcation of the country's population—far-right and far-left.

I also fear that you may not understand that you need to work hard to truly succeed in this world. The decisions you make will actually change the course of the rest of your lives for good and/or for bad. You should expect to have a very long life, possibly well over 100 years, with multiple careers, experiences, relationships, and joys and heartaches. Embrace it, enjoy it, and live it to the max. My fear is that you won't. My hope is that you do.

I want you to be able to ask, "What would Grandpa say about this?" If I am alive, I would like to think that you would ask me. If I am gone, I would like to know that you have a reference to go to for an answer or some guidance. This memoir is my first chance to capture these perspectives, reflections, and insights in one place. Once this memoir is complete, I plan to put my thoughts into an application like *StoryFile Life* to ensure that you can continue to ask me questions through this online platform. I will be just one of those apps on your iPhone or iPad: *Let's just ask Grandpa*.

During my past 70 years, I have lived through some of the greatest changes in human history—in society, technology, globalization of the population, science, engineering, philosophy, politics, economics, medical, culture, self-identification, and efforts to erase the marginalization of select groups (gays, women, minorities, differently-abled, etc.)—and much more.

During the next 100 years, I expect many of these changes to accelerate. Some will spin out of control; some may be sidetracked; and, several could end in chaos for humanity. There are probably many things that will show up that are completely unpredictable at this point. The bottom line is that "change" will be the absolute norm in the future and being able to address and adjust to these changes will be critical to having a happy and productive long life. Is that a real danger? I would say yes, yes, absolutely yes. I can't wait to sit and chat with you as you grow. Because here's the thing about curiosity… sure, I have a lot to share with you, but I have even more to learn from you!

PART 2

Deconstructing My Curious Self

Intellectual

Naval Officer

Physicist

Engineer

Business Leader

ONE

Being an Intellectual and a Word About Curiosity

"Curiosity—in a nutshell—is the desire to challenge status quo, explore, discover, and learn."

—*Stefaan van Hooydonk*
—*Global Curiosity Institute*

MY PARENTS NEVER had money to send my brother and me to summer camp (or any other summer activity). So, my mom needed to find something for us to do during the summer break to occupy our time; otherwise, we two young boys would make her completely crazy. Although, I am sure she would say that we had already accomplished that.

In the early 1960s, she discovered that the public library, which was within walking distance from our home in South Farmingdale, had a free summer reading program. You would check out books to read and when you returned them, you would get stickers that could be collected to get prizes at different tier levels. She enrolled both of us in the summer program, and we were off to the races. My brother and I read non-stop, lots of science fiction, hard science, history, books about different cultures, and lots of other subjects. This summer was probably the start of my genuine love of science, geography, U.S. and world history, art, and learning about different cultures from around the world.

I like to think of myself as a Renaissance Man, or maybe just someone having a strong renaissance personality—an extrovert, a scientist and engineer, a lover of music and art, a world traveler, and an "experience" enthusiast. I am principled, logical, skeptical, reason-oriented, and very, very curious about everything in the world and the universe. I enjoy reading about science, history, politics, religion, sociology/cultures, and never get tired of studying the geography of the world, our solar system, the galaxy, and the universe. My brain is a very cluttered and busy place. I continually joke that my brain is a storage container for an incredible amount of useless information.

The Rolling Stones sang *(I Can't Get No Satisfaction)* about that useless information. It actually does fire my imagination, and I get an enormous amount of satisfaction from it. I believe curiosity and open-mindedness are the keys to a full and productive life. I hope that you, my grandkids, and your kids and grandkids are sponges for knowledge, learning, questioning, and to being continually curious about everything in the world. You will never know when that bit of useless information becomes the cornerstone of a thought, a key element of a reasoned argument, or the seed of something that grows into a new concept worth sharing with others. In 2021, I had a chance to spend some time with Stefaan van Hooydonk, the founder and head of the Global Curiosity Institute,

"When I'm driving in my car
When a man comes on the radio
He's telling me more and more
About some useless information
Supposed to fire my imagination"

and found his Curiosity Diagnostic very insightful. He described Curiosity in three dimensions: cognitive curiosity (our curiosity of

the world), empathic curiosity (our curiosity of others), and reflective curiosity (our curiosity of self). I scored highest in cognitive curiosity and lowest in reflective curiosity. In particular, my highest three scores within the more granular data were in *joyous exploration* (100%), *openness to ideas* (89%), and *insight through self-reflection* (87%). My lowest three scores were *recognizing the need for reflection* (62%), *engagement in self-reflection* (64%), and *openness to emotions* (74%). This is quite interesting and does a pretty good job of describing me. It is funny how those internal personality traits drove my lifetime choices and decisions, and who I am as a person. So, you might ask whether it's nature or nurture that drives most of life's decisions. I believe it is mostly nature, combined with chance and luck (being in the right place at the right time). Nature and personality set up the foundation of your life and then attitude, chance and luck present you the building blocks with which to construct your life. Oh, and you then need to put in the energy and hard work to live a fruitful and valued life. Sounds complicated? I'd say that is true.

One additional thought: I am always passionate about what I believe, in the way I behave, and how I communicate. Most of my friends and colleagues would describe it as "wearing my emotions on my sleeve." This is me, although maybe not always a good thing. No one can ever question that I am not going to state my position in a clear and unfiltered way. In this case, my brain, filled with data, facts, perspectives, experiences, and knowledge, provides me a valuable tool to drive a discussion and conversation. It is actually nice to be an intellectual and have a *renaissance personality*. I hope you got some of my curiosity genes. I highly recommend it to you.

As a quick aside, my favorite book is *Contact* by Carl Sagan published in 1985. This is a "hard science" fiction book, my favorite form of fiction. Its hero, Ellie Arroway, is an astrophysicist, a researcher in the Search for Extraterrestrial Intelligence (SETI), a passionate scientist, a leader, a skeptic, incredibly articulate, and an atheist. How many times will you find that in a book, let alone the movie that was later made with the same name?

In addition, the book (not the movie) includes an interesting twist. It proposes what may be acceptable evidence for the existence of intelligence behind the creation of the universe that would be able to be found and interpreted by any intelligent being anywhere in the vastness of the universe—the only way this evidence would make any sense.

In the last chapter of the book titled "The Artist's Signature," we find a description of what that evidence might look like. "Acting on the suggestion of Ted, Ellie works on a program to compute the digits of Pi to heretofore-unprecedented lengths. When Ellie looks at what the computer has found, she sees a circle rasterized from 0's and 1's that appear after *1020* places in the base 11 representation of Pi (π). This not only provides evidence of her journey, but suggests that intelligence is behind the universe itself." By the way, in case you have forgotten, π is a transcendental number that is the ratio of a circle's circumference to its diameter, literally *the* universal constant. Every intelligent being in the vastness of the universe would recognize this ratio and the number associated with it.

So, what do you do with being an intellectual, a curious person and with a renaissance personality? There is no badge, no certificate, and no recognition for achieving this distinction. But you now, in fact, have all the tools to *think critically*. When I say "critically," I would like to refer to the root of the word, originally from the Greek word kritikos, meaning "able to judge or discern." This is similar to the "J" in the Myers-Briggs personality assessment mentioned in the Prologue and later in these reflections. I am a "J" and very comfortable with critical thinking. In fact, it is core to how I approach everything in life—often to the discomfort of the people with whom I converse.

At this point, I will steal the thoughts of others about what makes for good critical thinking. Then, I'll mash them up into a few sentences for you to think about. A number of writers have distilled the characteristics of critical thinking into open-mindedness, respecting evidence and reasoning, being able to consider different perspectives and points of view, not being stuck in one position, skepticism, and clarity and precision. You probably realize at this point that I likely check every one of these boxes and totally agree that living your life as a critical thinker is better than any other option. How do you do this? Critical thinkers ask questions, define problems, examine evidence, analyze assumptions, steer away from emotional reasoning, avoid oversimplification, and tolerate ambiguity. They push themselves and others to think critically even if it is scary.

> "Come to the edge," he said.
> "We can't, we're afraid!" they responded.
> "Come to the edge," he said.
> "We can't, we will fall!" they responded.
> "Come to the edge," he said.
> And so they came. And he
> pushed them.
> And they flew.

My favorite poem is Come to the Edge attributed to Guillaume Apollinaire. The publish date is unknown (probably early 1900s).

I will share multiple stories and examples of how this works in the real world and in my life in the next chapters. This is easy to do, but it will not make you popular in a lot of circles. Be prepared to be shunned because of your lack of adherence to the "party line" and the dogma adopted by the group—sometimes adopted by the masses. Ultimately, it is my hope that logic, reason, evidence, and critical thinking drive you and the future of the U.S. Don't get distracted by the demagogues, liars, cheats, self-serving politicians, and religious leaders, and others who have illogical or unreasonable agendas that they want you to embrace.

Ad in the 1964/1965 New York World's Fair guidebook for the General Electric pavilion—a life changer for me as a young teenager

I would like to give you a little background about how, in my teens and as a young adult, science, reason, logical and critical thinking, and a love of knowledge, took root and began to establish themselves as the core drivers of who I am now and who I have been throughout my entire life. My visits to and experiences at three World's Fairs are a good place to start. I was able to totally immerse myself in the New York World's Fair in 1964 and 1965 when I was 12 to 14 years old visiting the Fair 17 times over a two-year period. This was followed by a family visit to Expo'67 in Montreal, Canada in 1968 when I was 17 years old and Expo'85 in Tsukuba, Japan in 1985 when I was 33 years old. Each was incredibly impactful on my thinking about the world, other global countries and cultures, business and technology, and our place in the global community.

General Electric Corporation (GE) was one of the most respected companies in the world in the 1960s. As a kid, I knew the name, recognized the logo and many of their products. The World's Fair showcased GE in a pavilion that contained a one-hour show that dramatized the changes that electricity brought to American life from the late 1800s to the present (the 1960s) with a glimpse of what the future would hold for us. The Walt Disney Company was contracted to develop the core of the pavilion, the Carousel of Progress, which contained animatronic figures that showed life at four different periods in America's history. The moving animatronic "people" were amazing, and the way it showed the history of the use of electricity in daily life stuck with me even through today. Animatronics (essentially robots) were brand new, and Disney was experimenting with them at Disneyland and in four pavilions at the World's Fair: Ford, GE, Pepsi-Cola and Illinois (where Abraham Lincoln stood up from his chair and recited lines from several speeches from his time as president during the Civil War.) In fact, "he" was capable of more than 250,000 combinations of actions, including gestures, smiles, and frowns; the facial features were actually taken from Lincoln's life mask. To me, as a young teenager, this all was amazing, and I was more convinced than ever that I wanted to be someone who could understand how this all works.

The GE pavilion was all about the excitement of progress and the potential for a better future powered by electricity. One element of GE's presentation was very interesting. As described in the NY World's Fair Guidebook: "In a spectacular demonstration of controlled nuclear fusion, a magnetic field squeezes a plasma of deuterium gas for a few millionths of a second at a temperature of 50 million degrees Fahrenheit. There is a vivid flash and a loud report as atoms fuse and free energy is created." Wow, I was totally sold. I probably went back to see the one-hour show 20 times. By the way, this is 1965. We are still trying to develop nuclear fusion into a power source for the country and the world today. Again, I walked away convinced that I wanted to be part of all of this. As you will definitely see in many of my reflections in this book, this was a seed that was planted in me and steadily grew into my love of physics and engineering. GE also turned out to be one of the companies I tried to learn from during the early part of my business career. I hope you get to see a lot of today's technology stimulate your interest in your future career decisions and spark a passion in you to do great things in your own way.

The World Fair had about 160 pavilions, venues, and locations. I believe my brother and I probably saw them all over our multiple visits. We would try to get to the Fair when it opened and leave when it closed just in time to catch the last train back from the Long Island Railroad's (LIRR) station near the Fair to our home on Long Island. My Dad, who was a LIRR employee, was able to get us free passes for the day to go to and from the Fair on the train. Without that, we probably wouldn't have been able to afford the cost of the train fare and entrance fee to the Fair.

In 1968, my mom and dad planned a trip to see Canada, including Niagara Falls, Toronto, and Montreal. As part of our time in Montreal, we planned to visit Expo '67 which was still running in 1968. The Expo, titled Terre Des Hommes (Man and His World), was completely different from the New York World's

Fair. By the way, we lived in a very male-dominated world in the 1960s, something that we have continually tried to move beyond for many decades. We have made some progress toward equality for women, along with the multitude of minority populations. I will leave it to you to continue to work on this problem and hope that future generations finally get our society to embrace equality, equity, democracy, and acceptance of all people really being equal.

$1.00

TERRE DES HOMMES

MAN AND HIS WORLD

GUIDE

Montréal   OFFICIEL/OFFICIAL

Expo'67 could not have been more different from the NY World's Fair—an eye-opener on how the U.S. saw itself, compared to the rest of the world, including Canada.

Now back to the Fair: The pavilions were much smaller, very few companies represented, and a very focused effort to showcase international cultures, countries from all continents, and a feeling of a global brotherhood of humankind. Wow, this was a real eye-opener for a 17-year-old American's first exposure to being "outside" of the U.S. and now fully exposed to people and cultures from all over the world. The guidebook was in French and English—the whole thing, every page and every word. In fact, French was first and English second. We were in Canada but actually in Quebec, "French Canada." We only had a few days there but were able to see almost all the pavilions and venues. I took it all in—the countries from Asia, Africa, Europe and North and South America along with pavilions named Humor, Mirror of Man, Man the Explorer, Polymer, Flight, the Biosphere, The Face of Winter, the Indians of Canada and Education Through Stamps. Everything was very Canadian in every way and so different from what I saw at the New York World's Fair. I came away with a new appreciation of what it meant to be a "citizen" of the world and not just a citizen of the U.S. This was just starting to be a thing in the late 1960s and the experience at Expo'67 solidified my thinking. I walked away from this experience saying, "I want to see the world" and be part of everything it has to offer, not just what New York City, the East Coast, or the U.S. has to offer. Being a "poor" kid from Long Island, it would take a little while for me to make that happen, but my mom and dad planted the seed and I am forever grateful for them exposing my brother and me to these experiences.

During the 1970s, I had the opportunity to realize several dreams, the seeds of which were planted during my experiences at the New York World's Fair including getting advanced degrees in physics and engineering, becoming an expert in nuclear power, and getting exposed to technology on a grand scale. It was not until 1985 that I had the opportunity to venture overseas to experience other cultures and countries first-hand.

Expo'85 had a very similar feel to Expo'67 in Canada but with a very strong corporate presence. One other difference: we were one of the only Americans there—most attendees were Japanese.

I was divorced from my first wife and then married your grandmother in 1984. We postponed our honeymoon until 1985 when we would do a once-in-a-lifetime trip to Asia including Japan. I will have more to say about this trip in the chapter on my world travels. One highlight of the trip was the opportunity to go to Tsukuba Expo'85, called Quest, located in Japan's "science city"—Tsukuba, a train ride outside of Tokyo. Navigating Japan at that time was quite difficult. Everything was written in Japanese and very few people spoke English although everyone we met were extraordinarily helpful to us which is core to the Japanese culture. We were able to navigate our way on our own to the train station, and after a train ride to Tsukuba, we went on to the Expo.

Walking into the Expo and seeing all the pavilions was overwhelming. We saw Hitachi, Toshiba, Mitsui, Sumitomo, NTT, Mitsubishi, IBM Japan, Fujitsu, Matsushita, Sony, Daiei, NEC, Midori-Kan. We saw robots, telecommunications, technology, power, transportation, and on and on from dozens and dozens of countries exhibiting. The U.S. had a place in the International Pavilion. The theme was *Artificial Intelligence: Amplifying the Mind.* The exhibit traced the progress made in the study of artificial intelligence and recognition from earlier mainframe computers to modern microprocessors. Remember, this was 1985. That was it for the U.S. and U.S. companies and technology. Japan demonstrated to me how resilient, hardworking, innovative, and proud they were of what they had been able to accomplish since the utter destruction of the Second World War which ended only a few decades before the Expo.

This was modern-day Japan completely coming into its own and showing itself for everything that it was about to become over the next few decades. I loved seeing the world, technology, and culture from an entirely new point of view. Expo'85 was a microcosm of Japan and all things Japanese. We went back to the rail station and took the train back to our hotel in Tokyo with a whole new appreciation of Japan and the world. Luckily, I would be back multiple times to work in Tokyo with my Japanese colleagues and friends over the next 25 years.

Like I said at the beginning of this chapter, I have no shortage of "useless" information rattling around in my brain. Well, maybe not so useless. It turns out that it is only useless if it does not fire your curiosity and critical thinking. Under most circumstances, it is actually all useful, even though you might not realize it at the time. It has definitely been that for me over my lifetime.

TWO

Being a Naval Officer

Oath of Office

I, Robert Danna, do solemnly affirm that I will
support and defend the Constitution of the United
States against all enemies, foreign and domestic;
that I will bear true faith and allegiance to the
same; that I take this obligation freely, without
any mental reservation or purpose of evasion; and
that I will well and faithfully discharge the duties
of the office on which I am about to enter.

WHEN I WAS around 10 years old, for Christmas, I received an
incredible present from my parents: a three-foot-long gleaming
white, nuclear-powered ballistic submarine with a removable
plexiglass deck so you could see all the interior compartments, an
"operational" nuclear reactor which glowed when switched on,

missile tubes with missiles, a conning tower, torpedoes that could be fired with a pushbutton, and a crew of sailors that you could place throughout the submarine. This toy was released at the same time the USS George Washington (SSBN-598) was commissioned in Groton, CT. It was the first in class of the Navy's new nuclear-powered ballistic missile submarines. It was my favorite toy for years.

1. Integrity
2. Ownership
3. Level of Knowledge
4. Questioning Attitude
5. Formality
6. Procedural Compliance
7. Forceful Backup

The Nuclear Navy's 7 Core Principles

I never intended to join the military. Everything about it sounded horrible. During both undergraduate and graduate school, I qualified for a deferment, and in 1975, when the Vietnam War ended, the draft became unnecessary. In 1975, I became aware of a program that was looking for scientists, engineers, and mathematicians to support the Navy's nuclear power program in their headquarters in Crystal City, VA or newly consolidated Nuclear Power School in Orlando, FL.

I applied and spoke to a recruiter in Newark, NJ. My qualifications looked perfect to support this program. I was invited to Crystal City for interviews with the staff at Naval Reactors (NR) and the father of the naval nuclear propulsion program himself, Admiral Hyman G. Rickover. Every officer who would be part of the Navy's nuclear propulsion program, including all the officer candidates who would staff the nuclear submarines and aircraft carriers, had to pass the interviews. The interviews were quite grueling and included written exams as well. I was also introduced to the Admiral's core principles for the program. I will never forget reading the short list of principles on which he built the most successful program in the military. I use these principles to this day as the underpinning of my own set of values and guiding principles for my life.

The scariest part of the day was the series of short prep sessions designed to get everyone ready for their one-on-one interview with the Admiral. There was a map of his office, the outer office where his secretary sat, the path that we were to follow to the chair in front of the Admiral's desk, what to say and not say to the Admiral, and how to answer his questions—single word answers or just enough to specifically answer the question that he asked—nothing more and nothing less. By the way, say nothing until you are spoken to. Well, for a hippy from NYC (I did cut my hair for the interview) this seemed a bit over the top, but I was definitely interested by now to be part of Admiral Rickover's nuclear navy.

I passed the tests; the interviews went well. I was ready for my Admiral Rickover interview. By the way, I had heard of nightmare scenarios of individuals going into his office and pissing him off. The interview could, in fact, end badly. Fortunately, my interview was relatively uneventful. I was escorted through the outer office into his office and sat in the chair across the desk from this very old and seemingly frail man—the man whose will of purpose had created the entire naval nuclear propulsion program—wow. I was in the presence of greatness, and I knew it. He looked up, asked me a few questions about why I wanted to join his program, whether I was married and how many children I had. My answers were short and to the point, and when I told him I had zero children (the shortest and most exact answer I could think of), he told me to get out. I had survived my Admiral Rickover interview completely unscathed. I would find myself participating in similar meetings involving the Admiral as part of the Nuclear Power School's leadership team (as head of the Enlisted Physics Division) for the Commanding Officer's regular call with Naval Reactors (NR). It would feel the same in structure but way more real in content.

As part of the exit interview, I was told I would be invited to join the program as an instructor at the Naval Nuclear Power School in Orlando, FL. I would be offered a direct commission as a Non-Warfare Qualified Unrestricted Line (URL) Officer in the U.S. Navy Reserves (USNR)—as an Ensign with a Navy designator of 1105. I would be part of Admiral Rickover's Nuclear Navy. It could not get better than that.

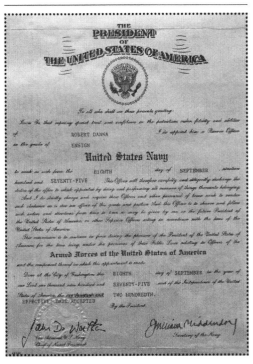

My Commission as an Ensign in the U.S. Navy

I got back to NYC. I had a conversation with my first wife, Janice. We decided that this was something that we wanted to do. I scheduled a session with my recruiter in Newark. I went to his office; I raised my hand; I recited the oath of office, and I walked out as a Navy Ensign. The direct commission was a major advantage since I would not have to go to Officer Candidate School. I was scheduled to report for active duty for a 5-week program in Newport, RI starting in January 1976— the Officer Indoctrination School (OIS). Then, I received orders to report to the Nuclear Power School in Orlando in February 1976. The Navy packed us up, and we moved to Orlando. We were assigned Navy housing—a brand new three-bedroom townhouse at the Navy's McCoy Annex on the west side of the Orlando Jetport. I reported for duty to the new Nuclear Power School located on the Naval Training Center east of downtown Orlando. Janice was able to get a job at a new laser manufacturer in Orlando and then move to Martin Marietta's missile manufacturing plant. She was a very smart and capable mathematician and was quickly recognized as a major technical contributor to very male-dominated teams at both companies. We were both now fully engaged in our careers. I was 24, and she was 23.

Nuclear Power School (NPS) was a six-month program for officers and enlisted personnel who were selected to operate the navy's nuclear power plants on submarines and aircraft carriers. It consisted of three months of "basics"—atomic and nuclear physics, mathematics and heat transfer and fluid flow, followed by three months of reactor plant systems, engineering and operations. Each class was two hours, five days per week of intense training followed by assigned problem solving, study and test preparation that usually required about 10 to 12 hours per day for the students and 10 or more hours per day for the instructional staff including scheduled after-hours tutoring, watch standing, qualification (each instructor was required to take and pass all the courses as well), additional training, and other military duties (performing inspections, conducting investigations of enlisted personnel for Captain's Mast, and the like). Every instructor was required to review and grade all assigned work daily and monitor the progress of all their students (usually more than 60 students across their two assigned classes). Following the six months of academics at NPS, the students would then report for six months of hands-on operational training and qualification on one of three Navy shore-based "prototype" reactor plant sites in Idaho, New York or Connecticut. I will have more reflections about my exposure to the Connecticut prototype later. With that as a bit more background to help you better understand NPS, I can tell you a little about my four years at the school. As you have probably guessed by now, I do not shy away from a challenge, and NPS did not hesitate to provide me as many challenging assignments as I could handle. To today, I am forever grateful for it. The Nuclear Navy and NPS changed my life in so many ways, and I continue to reflect every day on the way that it shaped my entire career and who I am as a person.

Reporting for duty in February, I was assigned to the Physics Division in the Enlisted Department and began my three-month qualification process to teach the physics course to enlisted personnel. Since I was already an experienced instructor and, frankly, knew the physics inside and out, it came down to learning the "Navy" way of presenting the content and the flow of the day-to-day activities associated with assignments, tutoring duties, and other NPS responsibilities including getting my secret security clearance completed. By the way, our tools for presenting the material were just a blackboard, chalk, a slide rule, technical manuals, books for student note taking, and a book of assignments for each day after class. That's it. Hand-held scientific calculators were introduced during my time at NPS. And by the way, everything was classified; so, the maintenance of the material was rigorous. Every word that went into the students' notes had to be written on the blackboard by the instructor. So, everyone's notes were exactly the same and could be audited by the instructors for accuracy. Since we were continually writing on the blackboard during the class, as well as answering questions and providing additional insights, the most interesting tidbit of advice that I received during my qualification process from the experienced instructors was to "erase the blackboard up-and-down rather than side-to-side", because if you erased side-to-side, your ass would wiggle while you erased the board. Okay, pretty good advice for sure. Yeah, these guys were funny, too.

My qualification process progressed well, and, in fact, maybe too well. During the three-month qualification, I was approached by the heads of the Physics Division (a lieutenant) and Enlisted Department (a lieutenant commander) with my first challenging assignment at NPS. There was an immediate need to have an instructor qualify to deliver the second half Reactor Principles Course (the one that follows the first half physics course), and they wanted to know if I would want to finish qualification to teach the physics course and then, while teaching the physics course for the first time, go through the qualification process to teach the Reactor Principles course. I would take my first cohort at NPS through the full six months of academics—first physics and then reactor principles—nonstop with the same students. Again, a little aside for context, this had never been done in NPS history. Of course, I said yes. So, by the end of the year, I had qualified to teach two courses, taken most of the rest of the NPS courses as part of my personal development plan, and now resided in the Reactor Principles division as a fully qualified instructor. Oh yeah, now that is what I am talking about! I now already had a reputation for performance more than what they had seen in the past from any other newly commissioned instructor.

The next year progressed well with me getting completely immersed in everything NPS including the culture, social life, friendships, and the life of a naval officer. It was a terrific experience. I learned a lot about physics, nuclear engineering, values and principles, teaching, coaching, interpersonal relationships, and life in general.

Instructors for the second half of NPS were mostly comprised of sea returnees since the courses

This is our class picture. I am LTJG Danna sitting in the front row immediately to the right of the Captain of NPS. Yes, I had a beard! The front row were the instructors that taught these Petty Officers for their six months of NPS.

were more about systems operations and onboard engineering details. There were a few of us who were direct input into NPS with no sea experience. We used the sea returnees (both officers and senior enlisted personnel who had operated the nuclear propulsion plant on board submarines and aircraft carriers) to better understand the details of what we were presenting in class and mine the sea stories to add color to our presentations. That was good but not enough. NPS had two solutions to help us. One, send us to one of the operating nuclear plant prototypes for an accelerated "qualification" process and two, have us spend several days on an operating ballistic missile nuclear submarine (SSBN) at sea. I did both. It was a great experience and helped with my ability to bring my classes to life for my students.

One experience is worth sharing with you. I received orders to join an SSBN for several days as part of their operations sailing from the Naval Base at Port Canaveral. The captain and crew were terrific and did everything they could to help me see most aspects of the nuclear plant operations. After an intense, in-depth immersion into the operations of the nuclear reactor propulsion plant, the captain asked me if I would like to go up to the sail of the submarine as we came back into port. It was one of the most amazing things I have ever done. I was standing on the top of the sail of one of the most powerful warships in the world (capable of utterly destroying dozens of cities anywhere in the world within a moment's notice) sailing into Port Canaveral at sunset with a pod of dolphins playing in the bow wave of the submarine. It was thrilling, humbling, and totally surreal.

The Navy does performance appraisals on a routine basis called fitness reports in which they rate all the officers in a particular rank against each other (top 1%, top 5%, top 10%, etc. of the Navy—you have the idea). There were around 80 Ensigns at the command, and I was rated in the top 1% of the Navy. For the top 1%, they then rank them from 1 to the number of Ensigns whose performance was rated in the top 1%. I was recognized as #1 in the top 1%—the best Ensign in the entire command. Wow! I could not be prouder for the recognition—no more money, no medal, no nothing. I was just given the next challenge.

Lieutenant (junior grade)
Danna—LTJG (O-2) in 1977

At the end of this year, I was again asked to take on another challenging assignment: to move to the Officer Department and qualify to teach their second half course in Reactor Dynamics and Core Characteristics, probably the most challenging course in the whole Navy. Again, of course, I said yes, and I qualified and began teaching the course early in 1978. I also started my master's degree in engineering (which the Navy paid for), began taking ground school and flying lessons for my private pilot's license, and was taking on additional assignments at NPS that involved interactions with NR, General Electric, Westinghouse reactor designers, and the leadership team at NPS. I totally loved what I was doing. I was easily putting in 12 hours a day and most weekends at this point but was continually energized by what I was learning and doing. I do highly recommend it at 26.

We also had some fun although it was pretty much limited to Saturday evenings. Orlando was a tiny town in the late 1970s. There was a group of around 10 of us who went out together regularly. There was one live music venue, Rosie O'Grady's, and Apple Annie's (at Church Street Station) that we frequented. The live music, dancing on the bar at Rosie's, and folk music at Apple Annie's definitely was a nice escape from the intensity at NPS. We also frequented a great dessert place in Winter Park, FL, the East India Ice Cream Company. That was typically our 11 PM stop before heading home after a night out. There was also Disney's Magic Kingdom. It was only open a few years at that point and the only amusement park in town. The Navy Exchange had deeply discounted tickets (they came in a paper ticket book) for military personnel. All the tickets in the book were E-tickets getting us on all the best rides at the park. We went to Disney dozens and dozens of times during our four years in Orlando and loved it.

Finally, I was asked to take on one more assignment before completing my four years of active duty. For the last year, I moved back to the Enlisted Department and took charge of the entire Physics Division, consisting of around 20 officers, most of whom held Master's or Ph.D's in physics. We were training thousands of enlisted personnel a year at this point, restructuring the entire curriculum to an objective-based training program, and now training women as part of the Nuclear Navy. I was part of the senior staff of around 20 at NPS, had my photo at the quarterdeck at the entrance to the school, and was known by, and knew, everyone. Wow, not bad for four years. I turned 28 in 1979, got promoted to Lieutenant (O-3), and successfully finished active duty. I would not trade the experience for anything. In the prologue, I indicated that I could have taken another path to a Ph.D. in physics at Brown. Hindsight is always 20-20, and I can't believe I would have had a better life doing that. I would recommend military service especially in a highly technical field and as a non-warfare qualified officer to anyone looking to kickstart a great career. My active duty ended in February 1980, and I transitioned into drilling in a navy reserve unit.

These are my Gold Oak Leaves. They are indicative of an officer at the O-4 rank.

During the early 1980s, the Chief of Naval Operations determined that the Navy was not well prepared to address "tactical" nuclear warfare at sea. He directed the setup of a new office to address this and a new program manager, PM-23, (the Theater Nuclear Warfare Program Office), was responsible for nuclear warfare considerations. One of my best friends from NPS joined the reserve unit associated with PM-23 and asked if I would be interested in joining the unit. I said yes, interviewed with the commanding officer (CO) of the unit, and was invited to join, which I did. This now required me to obtain a Top Secret (TS) security clearance and access to Critical Nuclear Weapons Design Information (CNWDI). I received the clearance and started to drill (two weekend days per month and two weeks per year) with the reserve unit in Crystal City, VA. One of the two weeks of active duty is worth sharing. For two weeks we traveled to Los Alamos National Laboratory, Sandia National Laboratories, Lawrence Livermore National Laboratory, the Nevada Test Site, and several other nuclear weapons sites. The trip involved TS CNWDI briefings, discussions, tours, and nuclear weapons "museum" access at multiple sites—all designed to support our work at PM-23.

During my time with PM-23, I was selected for promotion, and on January 1, 1985, was appointed to the rank of Lieutenant Commander (O-4) after just over 9 years of military service.

Because I was relocated to San Diego by my company, General Physics Corporation, later that year I needed to affiliate with another reserve unit in California to continue to serve in the Navy Reserves. I was recommended to join a reserve unit associated with the Office of Naval Research which drilled in Pasadena, CA. I joined the unit and continued my service until it became too hard to juggle the

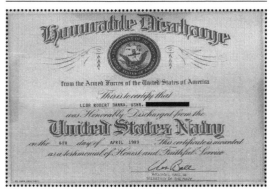

This is my Military I.D. Card. My Social Security Number was redacted.

responsibilities of my civilian job with expanding duties associated with the Reserves. I received an Honorable Discharge in April 1989 after 13 years of service.

It was an honor to serve in the U.S. Navy especially on active duty as part of the Nuclear Navy, Admiral Rickover's Navy. The adherence to a core list of principles was evident every day in everything we did. The experiences I had and the internalizing of those core principles have driven my decision-making and choices for the rest of my life.

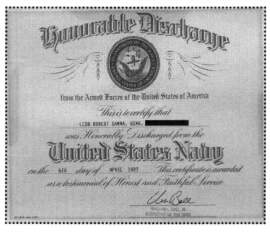

This is my Honorable Discharge. My Social Security Number was redacted.

In recognition of everything that the Navy gave to me, I have decided, when I die, to be cremated and interned at the Fort Rosecrans National Cemetery in San Diego, CA, if still open, and if not at Miramar. I hope that you, your children, and your children's children will visit me there and think about this story.

THREE

Being a Physicist

> "It's that the entire point of physics is to create a model of the Universe in maths—a set of equations that remain true when we plug in numbers from observations of physical phenomena."
>
> —*Dr. Katie Mack, Hawking Chair in Cosmology and Science Communication at the Perimeter Institute for Theoretical Physics*

THE FIRST TIME I thought science was really cool was in fifth grade. Mr. Cantor was my science teacher, and I could not wait to get to his class each day. The science homework and projects were always the first ones I would do when I got home. I also became aware of the connection between science and a lot of things that I was seeing around me including watching Walter Cronkite on the CBS Evening News. He did an incredible job of showing the excitement of science and the space program. I also enjoyed school trips to all the New York City museums as well as family day-trips to Washington, D.C.

Let There Be Light

$$\nabla \times \mathbf{E}\,(\mathbf{r}, t) = -\frac{\partial \mathbf{B}\,(\mathbf{r}, t)}{\partial t}$$

$$\nabla \times \mathbf{H}\,(\mathbf{r}, t) = \frac{\partial \mathbf{D}\,(\mathbf{r}, t)}{\partial t} + \mathbf{j}\,(\mathbf{r}, t)$$

$$\nabla \cdot \mathbf{D}\,(\mathbf{r}, t) = \rho\,(\mathbf{r}, t)$$

$$\nabla \cdot \mathbf{B}\,(\mathbf{r}, t) = 0$$

I wore a tee shirt in college that had the Maxwell equations and statement on it—blasphemous and geeky: "In the beginning God said, 'The four-dimensional divergence of an antisymmetric second rank tensor equals zero, and there was light, and it was good. And on the seventh day, He rested."

I was first exposed to physics as a junior in high school—the models, equations, experiments, data collection, history of questioning the status quo, and understanding our ability to build on others' knowledge to create new thinking about the world we live in. Physics is different from every other science. It is actually different from everything. By the end of my junior year, I was convinced I wanted to be a physicist. I was 16 years old. I was accepted to Hunter College in Manhattan and declared as a physics major and a math minor. I successfully completed freshman physics and calculus and found out that I had no idea what physics really was but was surely about to find out—not just formulas and experiments but the ability to model and predict the behavior of everything physical from the smallest subatomic particles to the end of the observable universe. Try to wrap your head around that!

Luckily, I was pretty good at physics and math and fully dove into my course of study. You will find that you are pretty good at one or more things based on your personality and "nature" (in an earlier Nature vs. Nurture comment). I encourage you to pursue your inherent talents and take advantage of what you are born with, including your personality. Use me as an example of what your journey might look like, not what it should be. There will be lots of times when chance and luck will take over (just like mathematical probabilities). The result will be your journey through this very curious life.

My first true exposure to "real" physics was when I learned about the Maxwell equations of electromagnetism (published by James Clerk Maxwell in 1865 by the Royal Society in London). These four equations describe the behavior of electric and magnetic fields and how they relate to each other. They prove that electric and magnetic fields are manifestations of the same phenomena. These equations also result in our ability to model light as a propagating wave of electric and magnetic fields—an electromagnetic wave. This is the basis of our understanding of electromagnetic radiation. You might say... so what? Well, next time you punch that button on your microwave, get an x-ray or MRI, see a photo from one of our space or radio telescopes, get into your self-driving car, use your smart phone or any of a million other things you do every day, you can thank Maxwell and the thousands of physicists that came before and after him. Talk about modeling the Universe in maths—I got it and now was on my way to being a physicist.

I took every physics course available at Hunter, attended physics lectures and seminars around New York City, and started to work with some of my physics professors on their research projects. I completed my bachelor's degree in physics, with a math minor, in three and a half years. It was hard to consider yourself a physicist with only a bachelor's degree, but I did wake up every morning thinking, breathing, talking about and loving physics. This was January 1973 and a great time to be a scientist. I applied for the master's program in the Physics Department at Hunter, got accepted, was awarded a tuition waiver, a position as an adjunct lecturer and a research assistantship with one of my professors, Bob Marino. Dr. Marino had a Brown University Ph.D. in physics. I was going to be involved in a new cutting-edge line of research in nuclear quadrupole resonance (NQR) spectroscopy. I did kind of feel a bit like a physicist on most days.

I worked with Bob to formulate a course of study for my master's thesis based on experimental research with models using the newly emerging field of NQR and its set of equations, and a computer simulation using the FORTRAN computer language and the college's IBM 360 computer. We were still using punch cards. Each line of code was a separate punch card.

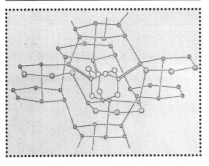

I studied the Hexamethylenetetramine Hexahydrate molecule using the quadrupole Nitrogen nucleus as a "quantum" probe. This was completely modeled using my computer simulation.

As a quick aside, I was living in Astoria in Queens and would take the elevated train into Manhattan on most days. This one day I decided to drive into the city rather than take the train. I came out of my apartment, placed a 10-inch stack of computer cards (carefully rubber banded together into a solid stack) on the roof of my car while I got the rest of my books and papers into the car. You can probably guess what happened. I drove away with the stack of computer cards—months of work in developing, debugging, refining, and running the program—still on the roof. I probably drove a few blocks, and then I heard a big bang as the deck slid off the roof, hit the trunk, and exploded into a cloud of hundreds and hundreds of computer cards now fluttering down onto a busy street in Astoria. I immediately stopped, jumped out, and started running around like a headless chicken. I am sure no one around me, including all the drivers who were now stopping, had any idea what just happened. I retrieved most of the cards and over the next few days reassembled them into the original deck re-punching what was missing, debugging

A portion of a page from my 60-page thesis. I was modeling my experimental data and merging NQR theory and other electrodynamic physics models.

again, and moving forward with the research. Luckily, I probably knew that deck better than I knew my home address at that point. Two years of course work and my research would result in a master's in physics and a well-received thesis entitled *Hexamethylenetetramine Hexahydrate: A Study of the Broadening of NQR Lines Due to an Internally Induced Stark Effect.* This was original research which is another key element of being a physicist—working on something that has never been done by anyone before. Building on the shoulders of many other scientists but adding a new piece of thinking, insight, and knowledge is foundational to continue to move the science forward.

Physics is never "done." Models continue to evolve; new data emerges from observation or experiments that challenge the current theories or models; the ability to question the status quo is core to the scientific method and, especially in physics, is seen every day. Remember, we are modeling the Universe in "maths" and not just solving a problem to get an "answer." We learn from

This is my Hunter I.D. as a member of the instruction Staff. It is hard to believe that they would let anyone that young teach physics at the University level. I was 21 when I started to teach. My Social Security Number was redacted.

the outcome from the research (from both theoretical and experimental physics) and then determine what can be leveraged in the real world and applied to our daily life. During the three years from January 1973 to January 1976, I served as an adjunct lecturer in the Physics Department. I got to teach at least two classes per semester and really honed my skills in presenting, explaining, and bringing physics to life to many undergraduate students. It was gratifying to do this, and I learned more about how to deliver very complex material to an audience of both science and non-science majors.

I was accepted into Brown University's Ph.D. physics program to continue my research in NQR spectroscopy and would have probably received a Ph.D. within two or three years. I also became more and more immersed and interested in nuclear physics. NQR was more chemical physics than nuclear physics, although there were multiple elements that were shared by both disciplines. An opportunity arose from the Nuclear Navy that gave me an alternative to the Ph.D. that would allow me to continue to grow as a physicist and go a lot deeper into the application of nuclear physics than I could ever expect from my other options. I opted to join the Naval Reactors program and hone my skills in that area.

Being a physicist is more than doing research. Many physicists, including myself, applied their education and experience to the design and manufacturing of lasers, anything using electromagnetic radiation (including medical devices and equipment), computers and quantum computing, nuclear power, nuclear weapons, and a variety of other applications. This is called applied science or applied physics.

From 1976 through almost 1990, I leveraged my experience as a nuclear physicist to support the Navy's nuclear propulsion and nuclear weapons programs, commercial nuclear power plant operations, and related work in nuclear waste management. Also, without my expertise in nuclear physics, I would not have been able to teach at the Naval Nuclear Power School or develop and deliver courses for the commercial nuclear power industry.

This is a picture of a total solar eclipse. I have seen one of these multiple times since my first experience on July 10, 1972. It is always thrilling, never gets old and I would recommend it to everyone. (Composite photo created by Fred Espenak, AKA Mr. Eclipse)

Even today, I enjoy reading books about physics and keep up with advances in the fields of atomic and nuclear physics, and astrophysics—from the very small to the very, very large. My commitment to the areas I love is part of who I am, and lifelong learning should be part of everyone's core principles.

Getting together in the Physics Major's lounge (Room 1313 in the main building) at Hunter College definitely stimulated conversation and thinking about so many interesting things. In early 1972, we started to talk about an upcoming total solar eclipse that was going to occur in Canada on July 10 of that year. Several of us said that we needed to see it in person. How many opportunities would we ever get to actually see this incredibly rare phenomenon where you can stand in the shadow of the moon?

The shadow is in fact only a few tens of miles wide and moves incredibly fast with the duration of totality being only a few minutes. As you probably have learned by now, an eclipse occurs when the moon periodically moves in front of the sun during its orbit of the Earth. Coincidentally, even though the moon and the sun are incredibly different sizes, the moon being much closer to us, appears to be exactly the same size as the sun on those occasions when the earth, moon, and sun align. By covering up the disk of the sun (which is impossible to look at without eye protection), you can see the atmosphere of the sun, which is called the corona, along with enormous pillars of fire called solar flares. There is absolutely no need for eye protection during totality. Get those binoculars, telescopes, and telephoto cameras out, and enjoy, enjoy, enjoy.

So, let's go back to the discussion in the Physics Major's lounge. We looked at the maps of the path of the eclipse and determined that Nova Scotia or Prince Edward Island (P.E.I.) in Canada would be the best viewing spots. Checking the historical weather reporting for July, we decided on Prince Edward Island. You definitely did not want it to be cloudy for the three or four minutes of totality. P.E.I. was almost exactly 800 miles from New York City. We were poor college students. So, this was going to be a drive. We did petition Hunter College for a small grant to help pay for the trip. I believe they gave us around $500 which would cover some of our expenses.

Ultimately, we decided on three cars to carry the group to Canada: an old Volkswagen Bug, an older Volkswagen Microbus, and an ancient Fiat Spider. We planned to camp up and back between NYC and P.E.I. We also planned to bring a large telescope that would be mounted on the Bug (with its four wheels jacked off the ground for stability), solar filters to view the sun before and after totality, binoculars, still cameras, and a super-8 movie camera that could take single shots to make into a stop-action movie of the entire two hours of the eclipse event.

So, around the 7th of July, we loaded up cars with tents, camping gear, all of our eclipse "viewing" equipment, and us, including my brother (your grand-uncle Al), and headed for Canada. In Maine, we hit a little snag. The Fiat died. I guess we could have tried to get it repaired to allow us to travel on as a group, but we planned to get to P.E.I. by the 9th and there was no time to repair the Spider. We decided to consolidate everyone into two cars, pushed the Fiat to the side of the road and left it there until we drove back after the eclipse. Hopefully, it would still be there on our ride back. It was. One additional highlight on our drive up to P.E.I. was an overnight in the Bay of Fundy National Park in Canada. We pulled in very late and found the park infested with porcupines. They were everywhere. There were really big ones—2 or 3 feet in length. So, we set up our tents on one of the side roads in the park and spent the night with these critters all around us. This was definitely different for a bunch of us from New York City.

We arrived at P.E.I. on the 9th and took the ferry across to the island and found a campground to set up our tents, sleeping bags, camp stoves, and our equipment to view the eclipse. We jacked up the Bug and mounted the telescope on its roof rack. We were ready for the next day. We chatted with several folks that were camping around us. Some knew about the eclipse, and like us, they were excited about being able to witness this once-in-a-life-time event. Some were there for vacation and did not even know that a total solar eclipse was occurring there. Then, wait for this, some said that they heard the moon was going to focus the sun's rays and blind you if you looked at the sun during totality. They planned to keep themselves and their families inside of their tents during the entire eclipse event. We explained what was going to happen and what they should do to safely observe the entire event. We, of course, were physicists, and they could believe us. Well, no. They still planned to keep the children safe—and dumb—because someone who was totally ignorant told them that it was too dangerous to view the Total Solar Eclipse! It is amazing how ignorant the general population is especially when it comes to science. They are not stupid; they are just lacking in curiosity, education, and a willingness to understand something that might not be part of their day-to-day experiences. The 10th arrived, and we were ready. The telescope was mounted on the Bug and now had a solar filter covering the lens so we could take pictures of the sun as the moon started to cover the disk of the sun. Tripods were set up for the additional cameras and the movie camera. I would be doing the stop action filming using the movie camera. The weather looked good, although they were predicting scattered clouds around the time of the eclipse. Everything worked. The eclipse began with first contact. I started to shoot the stop-action movie. The team started to take pictures through the Bug-mounted telescope and others were taking pictures and observing the transition from full sun to totality. During the transition, the sun begins to dim, slowly at first and then more rapidly as it approaches totality. It gets cooler. The birds and other wildlife think it is dusk and get ready for nightfall.

Then, as we get closer and closer to totality, the excitement peaks. Here it comes. Totality! We remove the solar filters from the telescope, from the movie camera, and from the other cameras, and look up. Unbelievable. The corona is bursting out from behind the moon. We can see solar flares. We can see the stars and the planets. They are lining up. We are in the solar system. It is like looking into a hole in the sky at night, but it is midday.

Look, look, look. Grab the binoculars. Keep pressing the stop-action button on the movie camera; keep taking pictures through the telescope. We only have a few minutes. The team was incredible. The experience was incredible. Then, the sun bursts out from behind the moon—the diamond ring. It is done. It's still dim, but even a small sliver of the sun is quite bright. It is too bright to look at directly. The corona is gone; the flares are gone; the planets are gone; the stars are gone, but the memory of what I had just witnessed is burned in my brain forever. We hooted. We hollered. We shouted. Wow, wow, wow—where can we go next to experience this again?

We got back to Hunter that summer and started to work on the stop-action "movie" of the eclipse, develop and catalog all the photographs and create a presentation documenting our experience. Two of us delivered a briefing in the physics department and started to research where we should go next to field a real scientific expedition to view a total solar eclipse.

When I say real scientific expedition, I mean one that does science in addition to just viewing or taking photographs. One of the classic scientific experiments involving a total solar eclipse was to confirm Einstein's theory that predicted the bending of light as it passes a large mass, like our Sun. One should be able to see a star located behind the Sun during an eclipse because the light from that star would bend around the Sun and become visible during an eclipse because of the intense glare of light from the Sun under normal conditions. Although this has been confirmed before, it was never attempted or completed by physics students from Hunter. Now, that would be pretty cool. The next eclipse that would be suitable to

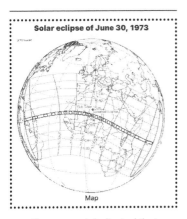

Solar eclipse of June 30, 1973

Map

Our research indicated that we could field a true scientific expedition to Mauritania in Western Africa to see 7+ minutes of totality, one of the longest duration solar eclipses.

do this was going to occur on June 30, 1973. Totality was going to be over seven minutes in duration, one of the longest durations for totality. Perfect—well, not completely perfect! The best place for us to view it would be in Mauritania in Western Africa.

Well okay, we should see if we could make it happen. We did get a small grant to support our P.E.I. adventure. So, two of us started to estimate the cost of the expedition for a small group of us to develop a grant proposal and socialize it with a few of the professors in the physics department. The cost was going to be way more than going to P.E.I., like at least 10 times more. The physics department, nor the Dean of Sciences, said they could not fund the expedition. So, it looked like our only option was to go to Hunter College and see if we could get the College to fund this. The College had a grant funding process for major college initiatives that we could use.

There was a formal grant proposal process and a structured evaluation process for selection, and there would be one big grant per year. We went all in. We were convinced we could win this grant. After multiple tiers of competitive evaluations, it came down to two finalists. Yes, we were one of the two finalists. A big meeting was held to have a final presentation and a vote from the selection committee on the winner of the grant. Oh, I forgot to mention who our competition was. The other finalist was seeking funding to set up a

The formula for the Drake Equation is as follows:

$$N = R^* \times f_p \times n_e \times f_l \times f_i \times f_c \times L$$

Whereas N is the number of civilizations in our galaxy that we might able to communicate with, R^* is the average rate of star formation in our galaxy, f_p is the fraction of those stars which have planets, n_e is the number of planets that can actually support life, f_l is the number of planets that will develop life, f_i is the number of planets that develop intelligent life, fc is the number civilizations that would develop transmission technologies, and L is the length of time that these civilizations would have to transmit their signals into space.

Frank Drake—the father of SETI and the Drake Equation

daycare center for student moms attending Hunter. Remember that this was a college-wide grant-sourcing program.

Although I was quite liberal and thought the daycare center was a good idea, I obviously thought that we had a slam-dunk academic proposal that should align totally with the academic goals of the College. Wrong. The daycare center was awarded the grant. The school newspaper published some pointed comments from me, but that was it. The expedition was not to happen. It would be nearly 20 years before I would see another eclipse. In 1990, your mom, grandmother, and I were living in Carlsbad, CA. One evening when we were together with some of our friends, we started talking about an upcoming total eclipse in 1991 and the opportunity to take a seven-day cruise chartered just to see the eclipse. On July 11, 1991, the path of the total eclipse would cross the Sea of Cortez in Mexico, and midway between Cabo San Lucas and Mazatlán was the point of maximum duration—more than seven minutes.

Wow, this was the same series of eclipses as the one I missed in Mauritania nearly 20 years before. Before the night was over, we decided we would do it. Your mom, only five-years old at the time, would stay home with your great-grandparents.

The cruise would be dedicated to science for the seven days with space science lectures by eminent scientists, lectures by astronomers to prepare us for the eclipse, and general interest science lectures, events, and activities. It was a total science "geek week." The lead scientist and lecturer on board was Frank Drake, the father of the Search for Extraterrestrial Intelligence (SETI) and the Drake Equation.

The day of departure for the cruise was an amazing scene. There were hundreds of people showing up to board with huge telescopes, boxes of scientific equipment, and astronomical binoculars, not to mention their usual luggage for the seven-day Mexican Riviera Cruise to Cabo San Lucas, Mazatlán, and Puerto Vallarta. We did not bring a telescope but planned to enjoy the eclipse by taking in all the sights and sounds of the event combined with using our large binoculars to see every detail of the eclipsed Sun, the stars, the planets and enjoy our place in the solar system and the galaxy, while in the shadow of the moon. Seven minutes is actually a long time, and we also planned to take in the view of the horizon as well. In fact, the shadow of the moon is very narrow. You can see light on the horizon in all directions where the shadow ends—very surreal.

The eclipse was to take place at midday with the Sun directly above us. So, we had plenty of time to get ready for the event. Our cruise ship made its way to the maximum duration centerline point between Cabo San Lucas and Mazatlán, stopped its engines, and dropped anchor. We noticed two other cruise ships pull up next to us, stopping their engines and dropping their anchors. There we sat. We were surrounded by three large cruise ships stopped in the middle of the ocean filled to the brim with science geeks waiting for the event of the century. It does not get better than that.

We set no tasks for ourselves—no pictures, stop-action video, no notes, no nothing—just taking in the energy and excitement of a spectacular total solar eclipse. It was that, and more and more. Again, all these science geeks are hooting and hollering, cheering and acting crazy, even though most had seen an eclipse before. It never, ever gets old. The whole cruise is burned into my memory. We enjoyed the rest of the cruise, but those seven minutes were the total highlight of the seven days. We got home, and I started to plan the next opportunity to stand in the shadow of the moon hopefully sooner than 20 years from then.

Well, we did not have to wait long for another spectacular event. This time it took place in our back yard. The moon, in its orbit around the earth, is not always at the same distance from the earth. The

An annular eclipse (Ring of Fire) at sunset

last two eclipses were at that perfect distance where the disk of the moon exactly covers the disk of the Sun allowing the corona to be seen in all its glory. If the moon is a little closer to the earth, the disk of the moon does not cover the entire Sun, and a ring of the Sun is still visible. This is called an annular solar eclipse or the "Ring of Fire" solar eclipse. It was to occur on January 4, 1992 at sunset over the Pacific Ocean. We could drive 10 minutes to Sunset Beach in North County San Diego and watch it. Your mom (who was still five years old), your grandmother, and me would watch it. The crowd applauded as the moon moved in front of the Sun at 4:50 PM. I can't remember any hooting or hollering. It was amazing but paled in comparison to a total solar eclipse. We needed to plan for another one of those again as soon as we could.

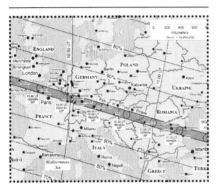

Path of the August 11, 1999 total solar eclipse in Europe

I purchased a book of total eclipse paths and dates and started to see when the three of us could see a total solar eclipse. There were a few options, but none seemed appropriate for a family with a small kid (your mom). Then I found one that occurred at around noon with a maximum duration of a bit over two minutes in Austria (south of Vienna) on August 11, 1999. Your mom would be 13 years old; we could combine it with stops in England and France, and make it a two-week vacation in Europe topped off with the last total solar eclipse of the millennium. Perfect, I started to plan for it. We were now living in El Dorado Hills in California. The fact that it occurred in August meant that I could try to get tickets to tour Buckingham Palace while the Queen was away on holiday, see a Shakespearian play at the Globe Theater in London (performed as it was 400 years ago), catch a couple of shows in London's West End, plan to walk down the Eiffel Tower, take a night boat ride on the Seine, visit the Rodin Museum, and a dozen other things that we could combine into a great vacation.

It all came off flawlessly. So, on August 11 we were staying at a Hilton on the Vienna Ring Road. The eclipse centerline and location of the maximum duration were to occur around 50 KM south of our location. We had a rental car, so the trip was a no-brainer. When we arrived at the small Austrian town where we planned to see the eclipse, the party had already started—street fair, music, lots of crowds, and a ton of excitement everywhere. The two-hour eclipse event proceeded as it had before with

"first contact" occurring when the disk of the moon makes contact with the disk of the sun. That was followed by the continuous process of the dimming of the sunlight—first slowly and then more and more rapidly. The air temperature began to drop rapidly, and then the two minutes that this whole trip was planned around—totality. The corona burst out from behind the moon, and everyone starts to cheer, hoot, holler—this time in more languages than I could count. Ah, it is good to be standing in the shadow of the moon again even if it was for only two minutes. Your mom, grandmother, and I wrapped up the day and headed back to Vienna. We spent another day in Austria and then headed back to California. I am not sure I could have planned a better vacation. Your mom probably has lots of her own memories about the trip. I hope she can tell you about it from her point of view as a young teenager on her first trip to Europe and her first experience with a total solar eclipse.

I am sure you understand by now that the unique feeling that I get from standing in the shadow of the moon is unimaginable. It is almost another 20 years before I would have the opportunity to do it again. We were now all living in Las Vegas. Your mom grew up, graduated college, got married, and had the first of the two of you. I got a divorce from your grandmother and now had a long-term relationship with my partner, Laci—your play-day and hide-and-seek buddy. In 2016, I started to plan a trip to see the next total solar eclipse for me and the first for Laci. It would be on August 21, 2017. The centerline would come through Idaho Falls and have a duration of totality of about three minutes. We would drive to Idaho Falls and experience the eclipse from there. About a month before the trip, I came down with a medical condition that should have caused us to cancel the trip. That was not going to happen. Laci was a trooper and drove most of the way there and back and doctored me along the way.

These are solar filter glasses used to look at the sun during the period before and after totality. There is no need to use the glasses for the 3 minutes of totality—just use the binoculars and take it all in.

Even though I was feeling quite ill, I still totally loved the experience. Being there with someone who had never seen a total eclipse before was very exciting. The dimming of the light, the cooling of the air temperature, and then the burst of the corona from behind the moon was just as before. But seeing Laci's reaction to it made the day. What was particularly funny was the "goody" bag that the Hilton gave to all of their guests. It contained these eclipse viewing glasses but also a box of the "famous" Idaho potatoes along with a few other items. It felt very local. We drove home with another great memory for the brain to process. Next up is a total solar eclipse in Texas for 2024. We will be there with the Planetary Society. It's obviously a thing, and actually, it's obviously my thing—time to geek out again.

In addition, being a physicist taught me to be skeptical, ask questions, and always challenge dogma. Evidence, facts, and truth-telling should always be the starting point for determining what is real and what is a lie. There are plenty of people who do not have this as part of their core principles. Always be on your guard and aware.

One additional thing is worth sharing. Science, especially physics, is understood by very few people in the world. It is not celebrated in art, music, awards, in the media, or literally anywhere else. You will find a few references to physics in museums and might know a couple of names of legendary physicists like Newton (F=ma) or Einstein (E=mc²). You can probably name dozens of movie stars, musicians, sports stars, media personalities, leaders in the religious community, and current and historical political figures.

This is Laci in her eclipse glasses and small binoculars. I had the astronomical binoculars at the ready.

This is very unfortunate since, if not for physicists, we would not have the modern world or all of the technologies you take for granted every day. In all of my travels, I found one piece of art that captures my love of physics. It was made by Lladro, a Spanish creator of porcelain sculptures.

Lladro describes the sculpture as follows: "The mind and reason guide man in his search for knowledge." The mind and reason, allied to man throughout history, help him to find wisdom. Scientia's base is engraved on its four faces with essential formulas of physics and mathematics: Einstein's Theory of Relativity, Newton's Law of Gravity, Heisenberg's Principle of Indetermination, etc., These formulas remind us of humanity's effort to unlock the secrets of science.

I have this in my office and look at it multiple times a day. It is my favorite piece of art I own. One additional item about this piece—the man on top of the base is outlining a circle with his hand. Yes, you remember the significance of the circle. It represents the universal knowledge that would be shared by every intelligent being in the universe. They would all know about the circle, the significance of the ratio of its circumference to its diameter (π), and they would know physics.

Scientia Man

FOUR

Being an Engineer

"Engineering is an important and learned profession. As members of this profession, engineers are expected to exhibit the highest standards of honesty and integrity. Engineering has a direct and vital impact on the quality of life for all people. Accordingly, the services provided by engineers require honesty, impartiality, fairness, and equity, and must be dedicated to the protection of the public health, safety, and welfare. Engineers must perform under a standard of professional behavior that requires adherence to the highest principles of ethical conduct."

—National Society of Professional Engineers
—Code of Ethics for Engineers

WHEN I WAS around 10 years old, my dad built a wooden box for me that had dozens of screws in lines on the top of the box with a combination of questions on the left and answers on the right. It also contained a light at the top of the box and two wires to touch the question and answers next to the screws. The best part of the box was underneath. The back contained wires that connected the correct answers to the questions and then to a battery and the light. When you touched the screw on the question with the correct answer, the light lit up. This was my first exposure to engineering. Soon after, I was taking it apart and putting it back together myself.

Having decided to be a physicist, I never thought of being an engineer. Physicists and engineers have different goals and approach problem-solving in different ways. Physicists seek to describe and understand the natural universe and use mathematical models, experimentation, and observation to evolve their knowledge and thinking about what is reality. Engineers consider data, codes, standards, historical experience, laws, regulations, and other criteria and constraints to design products, solutions to problems, or other systems or processes.

My arrival at the Nuclear Power School in 1976 changed my thinking about what an engineer does and whether or not I should consider evolving my focus to include developing an expertise in engineering as part of my future career direction. By 1977, I had decided to pursue another master's degree, this time in engineering. I first thought nuclear engineering might make sense but then changed to focus on environmental engineering, a discipline that was just starting to emerge. A very small university, the Florida Technological University (FTU), located on the far east side of Orlando, had a good engineering program. I applied and was accepted into their engineering program and started study that year. You would know FTU as the University of Central Florida (UCF) today, one of the largest public universities in the U.S. FTU changed its name in 1978 to UCF while I was in the middle of my master's degree. The Navy supported my seeking the additional education and paid for most of my tuition for the degree.

The University also required that I research and write a detailed research report as part of the requirements for the degree. Since I was deep into nuclear power as part of my work at NPS, and also had developed interest in the impact of industry on the environment, I chose to focus on the environmental impact of commercial nuclear power plants. The 70-page research report was entitled "Critical Exposure Pathways: An Analysis of the Environmental Impact of Gaseous Effluents from Light-Water-Cooled Reactors."

The report was scheduled to be completed and defended at the beginning of May 1979 to complete my requirements for my master's degree. Now, for the interesting part of the story. At 4 AM ET on March 28, 1979, six weeks before I was to deliver my research report, the main feedwater system of Three Mile Island, Unit 2 (TMI-2) malfunctioned. TMI-2 was a light-water-cooled commercial nuclear power station designed by Babcock & Wilcox and operated by General Public Utilities in Pennsylvania.

Mechanical failures and human errors contributed to the accident. Following the main feedwater failure, the auxiliary feedwater system then failed to start automatically. The steam generators dried out resulting in a rise in primary system temperature and pressure. The turbine generator tripped, and an over pressurization signal "scrammed" (shut down) the reactor plant. A relief valve located on the top of the pressurizer lifted due to the excessive pressure in the primary system. The primary coolant was piped to a tank located in the containment building. The relief valve failed to reset and remained in the open position. The primary coolant continued to discharge to the quench tank in the containment building. The emergency core cooling system (ECCS) started automatically.

Now, the real problem begins. To this point, everything was operating as planned for such an emergency situation. The starting of the ECCS was overridden by an operator erroneously reading a meter. The water is suspected to have flashed to steam within the reactor vessel. The quench tank continued to fill, and after approximately 15 minutes, it began to overflow onto the floor of the containment building. The coolant began collecting in the building sumps and was pumped to a storage tank in the auxiliary building. This tank also began to overflow; however, it overflowed onto the floor of the auxiliary building. Volatile gases were released into the atmosphere of the building and ultimately the environment. The core of the reactor no longer had water covering it, and the incident was now the worst nuclear power plant accident in U.S. history.

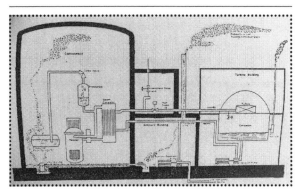

This is a drawing of the TMI-2 nuclear accident with radioactive gas pathways. This figure is taken from my master's research report.

I understood every bit about this. The combination of my NPS experience as an instructor of the Navy's Reactor Dynamics and Core Characteristics course, my physics background, and my master's research work over more than a year on gaseous releases from commercial nuclear power plants, made me uniquely positioned to understand what was going on. I completed and submitted my research paper, including a section on TMI-2, and was told by the director of my research report, Waldron McLellon, Ph.D., P.E., this was one of the best research reports and presentations he had ever seen. Thank you, UCF. I received my second master's degree, and in June 1979, started to apply for a position as an engineer in the civilian world once my commitment to active duty ended in February 1980. I sent tailored cover letters and resumes to engineering consulting firms (especially those focused on the nuclear power industry), designers and manufacturers of nuclear power plants, Federal regulators of the nuclear industry, and others in the burgeoning environmental consulting area.

I was invited to speak with more than a dozen organizations and invited for interviews with most of them. Three of note were Babcock & Wilcox (B&W) (the designer and builder of TMI-2), the Nuclear Regulatory Commission (NRC) (responsible for regulation of nuclear plants in the U.S.), and General Physics Corporation (GP) (an engineering consulting and training company specializing in the U.S. commercial power industry). B&W offered me a role on the very team tasked to analyze the results of the TMI-2 accident; the NRC offered me two positions, one as an environmental project officer and one on their regulatory standards team; and finally, GP offered me a position as a senior engineer working as part of their team tasked to address the corrective actions dictated for all the other nuclear plants in the country. One thing I really wanted to do as I entered the civilian world again was to gain all the experience, credentials, and recognition that I would need to be seen as a bona fide expert in the engineering field. GP would give that opportunity to me, and I accepted their offer and started work for them in February 1980 in Columbia, MD.

Experience required work on, and then leadership of, engineering projects. The specific *credential* that I would need was registration as a Professional Engineer (P.E). *Recognition* would come from the authoring, or co-authoring, of peer-reviewed articles accepted and published in industry journals and presented at technical society meetings. I set off to get all of this accomplished in the

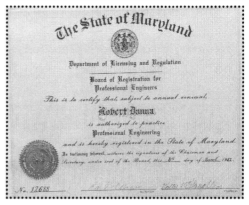

My first P.E. Registration was in March 1982 and issued by the State of Maryland's Board of Registration for Professional Engineers.

first three years at GP, probably the quickest possible timeline to accomplish these three items.

GP had no shortage of engineering consulting projects and engineer training programs to work on. Within six months, I was taking the lead on some of them. I took on more and more responsibility and within two years was promoted to Manager in the Engineering Services Department. The P.E. would be a lot more challenging. I would need to study for, and take, two eight-hour exams and provide evidence of engineering project work before I could achieve registration as a P.E. Each state is responsible for doing this, and I started the process in Maryland, the state in which I resided. Again, the study material was hundreds of pages and required the completion of thousands of study/practice problems and hundreds of possible design questions. I sat for both proctored exams, passed them on the first attempt, and was awarded my P.E. after just two years of joining GP.

As a quick aside, the proctored P.E. examination was held in a large hall where all the candidates would sit for the two, four-hour exam sessions. It was an open-book exam. The Board of Registration would allow you to bring in your reference material to support your work on the eight exam questions—four in the morning and four in the afternoon. All the candidates, including me, carted boxes of reference books into the hall and were assigned a large round table to work at during the exam, one person to a table. You will find that open-book exams are the hardest exams you can take. It really tests your understanding of the materials and requires you to present the answers in a form that is more like a small design report than an answer to a math or science problem that you may be used to in your classes. The answers to the questions were more than 10 hand-written pages each and were graded individually by experienced P.E.'s.

I was now Robert Danna, P.E. I would proudly use that title until 2009 when I retired my P.E. license since I was no longer practicing engineering. The final item that I described was getting my first publication and presentation as an engineer. This occurred in 1983 at the age of 31. I served as a lead author of a paper entitled *"Failure Prevention Program Development: An Application of Pressure Vessel and System Recertification and Inspection Planning,"* contained in *Failure Prevention and Reliability—1983* by the American Society of Mechanical Engineers, pp. 109–117 (1983). I also presented the paper at the 1983 ASME Design and Production Engineering Technical Conferences in Dearborn, MI. A sampling of publications and presentations that I led or co-authored/co-presented from 1983 to 1998 is contained in Appendix B to this book. In the early 1980s, GP's commercial nuclear utility clients requested that we help them address a need that was becoming very troublesome during construction and operations of their nuclear plants. Their plant engineers and managers needed to better understand how U.S. law, Federal regulations, and industry codes and standards all combined to ensure the safe operation and continued updating of the nuclear plant. A colleague, another P.E., and I took on the challenge. We developed the first Nuclear Codes and Standards course in three and five-day versions. Everyone wanted it, and I was one of the few individuals in the country who could deliver it. So, in addition to my core engineering work, I returned to the road as a teacher again going to many of the country's nuclear plants to deliver this course. You may or may not know that utilities generally do not locate nuclear plants near populated areas. This meant that I found myself going to many small towns and staying in one- and two-star motels.

One, in particular, has stayed with me for all of these years. We were contracted to deliver the course at the River Bend Station, a General Electric Boiling Water Reactor plant located in St. Francisville, LA. GP made reservations for me at the Ramada Inn in St. Francisville. I arrived late the night before the course was to be delivered and was told that the hotel was full, but they had made arrangements for me to be at their overflow location—The Myrtles, advertised as "One of America's Most Haunted Homes." Really?

Well, pulling into the Myrtles property at around 11 PM, with no lights, moss hanging off the trees and an owl hooting in the background, meeting the caretaker on the porch, and being escorted to my room was certainly an experience not to be forgotten. It's a good thing that I do not believe in ghosts because in the early 1980s, The Myrtles was one spooky place. By the way, we were asked to come back and deliver the course again. You can probably guess what happened. I got to the Ramada late in the evening; the front desk said they were full but they had made arrangements for me at their overflow location; and, wait for it… welcome to The Myrtles. It was no less spooky the second time.

I am particularly proud of my registration as a Mechanical Engineer in California. I received this through something called comity—where California agreed to accept my credentials from Maryland but with additional substantiated evidence.

Starting in 1984, I was a recognized expert in an emerging area of engineering called Process Safety Management doing work at commercial nuclear power plants, NASA and the U.S. Air Force rocket launch and aerospace research facilities, and petrochemical and oil and gas process facilities. I subsequently got registered as a professional engineer in Florida, Tennessee and California (with a specialization in Mechanical Engineering) to support my engineering work in those states.

In the early 1990s, I was also recognized by the National Council of Examiners for Engineering

Based on my work in multiple states I worked to get certified by several engineering governing boards to ensure my P.E. was nationally recognized.

and Surveying for my engineering work and was admitted to Who's Who in Engineering. I also sat on the Board of the American Society of Mechanical Engineers (ASME) code committee for the design of high-pressure vessels. Additionally, I gave expert witness testimony to the California Safety Board as part of one of GP's client's requests for an exemption to the State's safety orders. These two opportunities were the high point in my career as an engineer.

This all might sound a little boring to you. That can't be further from the reality of being a consulting engineer. The projects that I worked on all required innovative thinking and very diligent application of engineering principles, codes, and standards and always addressed the Federal or local regulations that governed project completion.

So, where did I perform this work? I worked at most of the commercial nuclear power plants in the U.S., Kennedy Space Center, the Jet Propulsion Lab, the Air Force Eastern Space and Missile Center at Cape Canaveral, the Air Force Edwards Air Force Base, the Air Force Arnold Engineering Development Center, and Goddard Space Flight Center.

I witnessed Space Shuttle launches and landings, rocket launches, and worked on giant wind tunnels and space simulators. One launch was particularly memorable. I was working at Kennedy Space Center with our on-site team, and a night launch of the Space Shuttle was scheduled for that day. I was staying in Titusville, FL across the river from KSC. I had an excellent view of the launch which was incredible. We were listening to the launch controller on the radio and were able to watch the launch, the solid rocket booster separation, and follow it all the way to the point when the launch controller said it had reached orbit. These are the experiences that make the hard work worthwhile.

I also had incredible colleagues throughout the engineering community, in the nuclear power and petrochemical industries, and at NASA and in the Air Force. Who would have guessed that I would have all these experiences when I decided to take that master's degree in engineering at UCF.

Our team at GP was one of the best group of professionals with whom I have ever had the opportunity to work. Many were registered P.E.s (a goal that I set for the engineers in my department), inspection and test specialists with decades of experience in the discipline, and an administrative and technical support team that was second to none. We were the best in the country, and our ability to consistently win and execute projects was a testament to the teamwork and commitment to excellence of everyone who worked for GP.

This is the seal/stamp of a Professional Engineer that is used to certify that the work was done to the highest ethical standards, integrity and accuracy required by the engineering community. The P.E. is personally and professionally liable for the work on which they place their seal even if done by dozens of other engineers under their direction.

Just in case you have never had the opportunity to see what a professional engineer uses to certify that the integrity of the engineering work was done to the Engineer's Code of Ethics, here it is at the left.

I have now been a member of the science and engineering community for more than 60 years, including more than 30 years as an active participant in all that makes science and engineering work: codes of conduct, commitment to integrity in everything we do, peer reviews, and a willingness to change our minds and position when new evidence/facts/knowledge are presented to us.

At the end of this book, I have included examples of what it means to be part of the engineering community. This list of papers and presentations are included not as reference but rather as examples of what is expected of one who is committed to being a scientist or an engineer and who is truly an active member of this community. Feel free to read them if you want!

When people talk about STEM, this is what they mean. The totality of those papers is almost like a work of art, a record of my contribution, or as Whitman puts it: my *verse*.

We, the scientific and engineering communities, are invisible to the general population although without the science and engineering community, we would not have the world we all live in today. I hope you take away from this book a little of what it meant to me to have been part of this incredible group of people. Where you lay me to rest, make sure it says: "Scientist and Engineer."

FIVE

Being a Business Leader

Consider this list of Jack Welch's (past CEO of General
Electric Corporation) six rules for business leaders:
"Control your destiny, or someone else will.
Face reality as it is, not as it was or as you wish it were.
Be candid with everyone.
Don't manage, lead.
Change before you have to.
If you don't have a competitive advantage,
don't compete."

—Noel Tichy and Stratford Sherman 1993
—Control Your Destiny or Someone Else Will

DON'T BE AFRAID to be a leader. Being a leader requires the
honing of leadership skills and building your leadership "muscles."
I started to build my leader muscles as a paperboy as a young

teenager dealing with my Newsday manager, my customers, my prospective customers, and my mother. This was followed by my work selling luggage in a department store when I was 17. I started as a stockboy bringing luggage from the stockrooms to the floor and making sure the luggage on the floor always looked good and was presentable. When it was sold, I supported the customers. I quickly knew the stock and the luggage better than my manager. He then asked me to help with, and then soon own, the re-ordering of depleted stock and the ordering of new stock. I was now interfacing with our vendors, writing purchase orders, confirming receipt of merchandise, and managing some of my co-workers. I was building those leadership muscles every day—people skills, organization skills, process skills, and management skills. A key skill that I learned early in my life was the skill to "step up" and "fill the vacuum." If there is a need for someone to lead, be that person.

This "fill the vacuum" attitude is a key muscle that many individuals never develop, and they are left behind or left out of opportunities to take on more responsibility. I saw this play out over and over again as a physics tutor, research assistant, adjunct lecturer, and naval officer. Stepping up and filling a vacuum in leadership became my standard mode of operation. By doing this, I was able to hone my leadership skills and build new leader muscles—people management (including subordinates, supervisors, and colleagues), operational management, project management, mission and goal management, and budget management. In most cases, stepping up did not involve a promotion, more pay, or even recognition. However, I was always on the top of my senior manager's list of "high potentials" and was routinely top in their minds as they developed their "succession plans." When there was an opportunity for promotion, I got it.

Joining GP gave me a whole new set of challenges and opportunities to step up: first, as a project manager (managing teams and complex projects), next, as a functional manager (managing teams of engineers and specialists), then, as a project director (managing project and task managers), and finally, as a functional director (managing multiple functional managers and several tiers of engineers, specialists and support personnel). Wow, I was building those muscles like there was no tomorrow—profit/loss management, people management, talent development and succession planning, sales management (we had no sales department), and client relationship management.

It is funny, but I had implemented a number of Jack Welch's rules long before they were articulated in Tichy's and Sherman's book. This just made good sense to me, so I did them. In particular, was the rule associated with competitive advantage. Credentials, experience, reputation, and client references are everything in bidding and winning engineering projects. We heavily invested in the team getting many of them registered as Professional Engineers and insisting if they were going to a conference, then they would be submitting a paper for presentation. We gave them the opportunity to work on multiple projects and clients to build their expertise.

We had one key direct competitor for all of our projects and several others that competed on a project-by-project basis. My goal was to win every deal by beating our competition based on our credentials, experience, approach, and client references offering a fair price for our services but not the lowest price. We wanted to win on value. We won all projects except for one in which our main competition had a previous, long-standing relationship. We were number one, and after a few years, our competition got out of this line of engineering. Our team all did well. They had many opportunities for promotion, worked on numerous interesting and long-term projects, and had the opportunity to live in different parts of the country, either in new offices that we opened or on our clients' sites in offices that were dedicated to our team. Ultimately, we addressed every one of Jack Welch's rules and dominated as the hands-down engineering leader in this field.

Guess what? I was still not a "Business Leader!" Not yet; so, what was missing? I was not really participating in the management and leadership of the Company—business strategy, planning, budgeting, decision-making, financial management, and governance. This came with my promotion to Vice President in 1987 at around 35 years old. Well, that only took around 20 years of building my leadership muscles to now be considered a Business Leader.

I was now running the Engineering and Applied Sciences Division (which would later become a Group) containing all of the company's engineering and scientific staff (with multiple officers, managers, directors, project managers, and engineering and laboratory staff working for me) and responsibility for all of our technical clients and offices located across the country, and ultimately worldwide.

We commissioned an artist to capture the essence of what we did as a company. This was the result—a tribute to our dedicated team in the early 1990s. Part of this is now contained on the cover of this book.

That was the easy part. Now the politics of working in a large organization became real. We would go through multiple restructurings, a breakup of the company into two new companies (one listed on the New York Stock Exchange), years of significant success and growth, and years of challenge and downsizing. I was able to navigate all of these events, all the politics, and all the organizational changes but not without quite a bit of stress and a lot of grey hair. It was now all about leading our people and delivering for our clients. The engineering and science were easy.

By 1994, I was one of the top two leaders in GP. I was an Executive Vice President, a Group President, and a member of the Board of Directors. At this point, it was all about leading the Company—strategy, planning, and road-mapping future changes to the organization while still keeping my hands on the day-to-day operations of my Group. It is worth spending a few words on what

Strategies

A meeting of General Physics' new executive team, from left, John C. McAuliffe, Robert Danna and Jerome Feldman.

General Physics Embarks on Makeover

With Training as Core Service, Firm Strives to Broaden Client Base

By Daniel Southerland
Washington Post Staff Writer

Yes, that is me being interviewed by the Washington Post about GP's plans to makeover the Company. Pictured is the Company's chairman and the two of us tasked to lead GP and all of the changes.

it means to keep involved as a leader. As a senior executive, it sometimes becomes easy to get distracted from the day-to-day "fires," initiatives and projects that go on at the corporate level. This is the time when I first read Tichy's book and completely embraced Jack Welch's rules and Tichy's 75-page *Handbook for Revolutionaries* that was contained at the end of the volume. It was extremely timely and healthy that I did that. I worked closely with my Group's senior leadership team, client leads, office managers, and many others, along with leaders in the other groups and Executive Management to drive our change and place the Company on a new trajectory for growth. This handbook contained the core elements of transformation that we used as a three-act drama: Awakening, Envisioning, and Rearchitecting. Keeping your eyes squarely on your people and clients is always key to success. If you lose that focus, you can easily lose everything.

P.R. Vagelos, M.D., the then Chairman and CEO of Merck, said of the book, "This book captures the essence of competitiveness, which is vision, leadership and a hunger to succeed. It contains essential lessons that need to be learned by all of corporate America." I agree. The book is entitled *Control Your Destiny or Someone Else Will* and was authored by Noel Tichy and Stratford Sherman in 1993. I have re-read and revisited the insights in this book many times during my career as a business leader.

The most interesting aspect of my leadership role was now being a member of the Board of Directors of GP which was listed on the New York Stock Exchange and governed by all the rules of the exchange and the Federal regulations from the Security and Exchange Commission. It was a very different world from my past deep immersion in physics and engineering; however, my core values, guiding principles and the commitment to integrity instilled in me from the military and engineering disciplines were core to managing my day-to-day life.

This is our executive leadership team (from GP's 1994 Annual Report). I am on the one on the far right. Yes, all white guys. I would try to change that as I continued to take on leadership roles in other companies.

I have an additional interesting side note to share (side note NOT sidelight). During this time, I assumed responsibility for GP's Asia operations with offices in Singapore and Kuala Lumpur. I had traveled extensively internationally before but was never directly responsible for teams made up of almost all locals working for local clients in the ASEAN region. I had the opportunity to have a lead role on a project for Tenaga Nasional Berhad (TNB), the national electric utility in Malaysia. Working directly with the chairman of TNB, and our incredible team of engineers and specialists, was one of the best experiences I had ever had internationally. I also had the opportunity to interact with our teams on a personal level, having dinner with their families at their homes and socializing with them where they would go with their friends.

Your mom, grandmother and I were living in San Diego in late 1992 getting ready for a relocation back to Columbia, MD where I was to assume the Executive Vice President position in one of two General Physics Corporation sister companies. The company just signed a global agreement with Avis Car Rental to be our primary car rental agency. All the employees of the company were doing an enormous amount of travel for our clients. So, this was a very big contract for Avis.

You probably don't know that most of the people who go to major sporting events, like the Super Bowl, are hosted by companies for their best customers. So, because GP was now one of Avis' largest customers, they invited our CEO, Dave, and his wife to the game. Dave told me about the invite and the fact that he was not really interested in going but might I want to go in his place? Let's see, go to the Super Bowl as a guest of Avis? It did not take me a millisecond to decide! "Yes, yes, yes, Dave, I would be happy to take advantage of the offer and represent GP!"

The other thing that you probably don't know is that going to an event like the Super Bowl as a guest of someone like Avis is not a "day" event. This is not just going to the Super Bowl on Sunday afternoon. It was a four-day experience! Well, that sounds like something that your grandmother and I would definitely want to do. So, we connected with the Avis folks who would be coordinating the experience. The Super Bowl in 1993 would take place on Sunday, January 31 starting at 3:00 PM at the Rose Bowl in

Face value of a Super Bowl ticket in 1993 was $175, but that is just the beginning of the cost of the experience that we had from Thursday, January 28 to Sunday, January 31.

Pasadena, CA. The halftime entertainment would be Michael

Jackson at the height of his career. "Now, that is the kind of experience I am talking about, Kiddos."

The plan came together. Your great-grandparents would come down to our home in Carlsbad and stay with your mom while your grandmother and I would head to Los Angeles on Thursday and plan to return home after the game on Sunday night. Avis invited a handful of other couples as their guests, and all of us would have a four-night stay at the Bonaventure Hotel in downtown Los Angeles. That would be our home base for the entire four days. On arrival on Thursday, we were shown to our rooms and then taken to dinner at an exclusive restaurant in Hollywood. Avis hosted the dinner. We were joined at dinner by the NFL football stars and mingled with them during a cocktail hour followed by dinner. The stars were strategically seated among us to stimulate sports talk over dinner. Your grandmother is a sports nut. So, this was perfect. What a start to the whole Super Bowl experience. Friday was dedicated to

The entire 1993 NFL Experience, brand new in 1993, was held right next to Rose Bowl, the site of the Super Bowl.

an exclusive, escorted, behind-the-scenes day at Universal Studios in Hollywood. Talk about "Jump-the-Line" tickets—what lines? *We don't need no stinkin' lines!* It was an unbelievable day followed by another sumptuous dinner.

You may have seen the experience on TV of being at a recent Super Bowl. These are now much, much, much larger in scope than the one we went to. Since the one we went to was much smaller, celebrities, movie and TV stars, sports and political luminaries, and other business leaders were everywhere—like right there; they were all around us. Do you want to chat with Bill Murray? Sure! "Hi, Bill!" Do you want to meet Lynn Swann? Yes, why not? Do you want to say hi to Jack Kemp? I guess! We were right there. Thanks,

Dave. Oh, you remember Dave at GP who decided not to go to the game as a guest of Avis?

We started Saturday morning with a day at the NFL Experience. This was a single location and brand new to Super Bowl Weekend. We had a close-up look at the Vince Lombardi Super Bowl Trophy and the Pete Rozelle Most Valuable Player Award. We also saw an NFL locker room, the NFL quarterback challenge, the NBC Sports Broadcast Area, the NFL Films Theater, and the NFL main stage with music, team mascots, and NFL players. We wrapped up mid-afternoon and headed back to the Bonaventure to get ready for the highlight of the day—the NFL Party that evening. You could not walk 10 feet and not see a recog-

Sure—the Super Sunday Super Bowl Bus Pass—what could that be?

nizable celebrity. In 1993, there was only one of these parties; now, there are dozens. All I can say is wow, and it is still only Saturday. Now it is Super Bowl Sunday. After breakfast, we were told that we would be transported to the Rose Bowl for the Super Bowl XXVII Tailgate Party that would start at 11:00 AM, four hours before the start of the Super Bowl. We had been to tailgate parties before, so it would be interesting to see this one. We were given bus passes and told where we could find our bus. There must have been around 10,000 folks staying in the hotels in downtown Los Angeles in and around the Bonaventure. When we got outside, the entire area was closed down by the police, and there were more buses than I had ever seen in one place. We found our bus. Luckily, Avis was still shepherding us. All the buses were starting to line up for the trip to the Rose Bowl in Pasadena, about a 30-minute drive. As we entered the freeway, we noticed something strange. There were no cars on the freeway, only buses. The highway patrol was closing all the entrances to the freeway as the bus caravan passed. So, we had the freeway to ourselves. Now, it does not get better than that. Have you ever been on the 110 with no traffic in the middle of the day, especially on Super Bowl Sunday on the way to the game? We have. So, we arrived at the Tailgate Party. Oh yeah! Now, this is what I call a tailgate party!

Once we got into the Party, we saw tables set up everywhere across a field adjacent to the Rose Bowl. There were gourmet food stations located all around the area and celebrities everywhere. A main stage was set up for the Tailgate Party's entertainment. Well, how about Glenn Frey from the Eagles topped off by Fleetwood Mac, which is one of my all-time favorite groups. So, this is how the other half live. We definitely need to do this more often. There was Bill Murray again, sitting at the next table, and Magic Johnson, and, and, and. I do not go ga-ga over seeing celebrities, but this was pretty spectacular, especially since we were actually there with all of them. I wonder if they were saying, "I wonder who these folks are? I don't recognize them. Maybe they are the voices of the characters in a Disney movie." No. It was just your grandmother and me, guests of Avis. Nice.

The Super Bowl Tailgate Party was so far over the top that we could not believe what we were seeing. Here is the ticket.

Now, it was about 1:30 and time to start to make our way to the Rose Bowl, just next door, to find our seats for the game. The Rose Bowl held around 100,000 for the game. When we got to our seats we found a seat cushion, a battery-powered radio, a bunch of NFL pins and cards, and a large placard with one color on one side and a different color on the other side. This was very strange. There were some pre-game announcements and entertainment, and then an announcer came on to tell us about the game. We would all be part of the halftime entertainment. The placards were on every seat in the Rose Bowl—100,000 of us. Michael Jackson was the halftime headliner, and we would be part of a "card stunt." The audience members would each hold up one side or the other of the placard and form a mosaic of children from around the world. You can still find a video of the halftime performance. It was one of the coolest things we have ever participated in. We practiced it several times before the game so we could seamlessly pull it off during halftime. During the halftime, about 3,500 local Los Angeles kids came onto the field and sang "We Are the World" and "Heal the World" with Michael Jackson.

Now, for the game. Garth Brooks sang the national anthem. There were five blimps circling above the Rose Bowl and at least 10 small planes all with banners advertising something. I am sure they needed air traffic control just to manage all the air traffic around the stadium. The game started and immediately turned into a blowout. The Dallas Cowboys killed the Buffalo Bills 52 to 17. No one at the game really cared who won. The game was an incredible experience. The Tailgate Party, the NFL Party, the NFL Experience, all of the dinners and activities that Avis hosted were the "experience," and it was wonderful beyond words.

This is a picture of RWD's annual report. As an executive in public companies, I routinely appeared in the annual reports as an officer of the company.

We bought Dave a very nice limited-edition sweatshirt. I gave it to him when I saw him the next week in Columbia at the GP headquarters. I have never had the opportunity again to be hosted at a major sporting event by a company like Avis. By the way, Avis is still my go-to car rental agency.

I have been to numerous major sporting events on our own. They have all been great experiences, but they all paled in comparison with these four days in Los Angeles and Pasadena.

Late in 1995, after 16 years with GP, and an unbelievable learning experience in engineering, management, and leadership, I decided I needed to make a change. Two of us were candidates to take overall leadership of the company. My colleague was selected for that position, and I decided to accept an offer to join another company headquartered in California. To this day, I have nothing but warm feelings for GP, all the amazing people that I worked with, and all the incredible leaders that I had the privilege of working with and learning from.

I was 44 years old and ready for a new challenge and some new experiences. The company that I joined in California was not that. Their executive management team and I did not share the same vision, values, and principles and after a year, I left them.

Luckily, I was able to quickly join several members of the original team from GP who had started a new company, RWD Technologies, and I was off and running again.

As a side note, the RWD in RWD Technologies is Robert W. Deutsch, Ph.D., P.E., the original founder of GP in the late 1960s, a physicist and a registered professional engineer. Dr. Deutsch, along with John Beakes (a registered professional engineer and a navy submariner), brought me into GP in 1980. In 1996 they again brought me into RWD to assist them with the expansion of RWD to the West Coast and ultimately to Asia-Pacific. They were incredible human beings and a lot of who I am I owe

Officers of companies take a personal responsibility for the actions of the company. Both RWD and GP built companies on integrity, curiosity and teamwork.

to their leadership, vision, and adherence to core principles. They were also committed to technology at GP and RWD, including early pioneers in full-fidelity nuclear power plant control room simulators, computer-based training, and the commitment to a technology-based office environment for all team members.

Joining RWD in the mid-1990s was quite a good move for me. The internet was moving to the center of technology-based solutions, and most businesses were trying to address concerns associated with the turn of the millennia (Y2K). Enterprise resource planning (ERP) software was happening everywhere. RWD placed me in a one-person temporary office with a laptop, a printer, a fax machine, and a mobile flip phone and turned me loose. Working for another incredible person, Debbie Ung, my first woman boss and 10 years younger than me, I was able to leverage relationships with SAP, PeopleSoft, Price Waterhouse Coopers (PwC), and Business Objects to build a multi-million-dollar operation of dozens of clients, two new offices, and nearly 70 people in under three years. Additionally, working with Debbie, we developed and launched a joint venture with SAP called SAP Learning Solutions (51% owned by RWD) that I would lead with key offices in Singapore, Tokyo, and Sydney. Almost all the ERP experts we hired were locals. Again, I had the opportunity to socialize with our teams at their local restaurants and will be eternally grateful for their friendship and hospitality.

I turned 50 in 2001. I had experienced all the trappings of being a successful business leader—big corner office, nice salary and bonuses, stock options, company car, dedicated executive assistant, first and business class air travel, five-star hotels, and time to take lots of incredible vacations. I also came to discover that I had what is now called a Renaissance Personality: I prefer variety over a single-minded focus; I enjoy a work style that doesn't follow a linear, predictable process; and, I define success by challenges mastered. So, it was time for a change.

Building something from the ground up was what I decided to do. For the next four years, I joined a ".com" (which shut down during the early 2000s ".com bust"), started my own consulting firm (which was pretty successful but not what I wanted to do), and co-founded and co-funded a knowledge management and training software company (which still exists today). I also realized that I did not need the trappings of business leadership to be a business leader. Working from a home office and being able to deliver value at the executive management level could be achieved. I was one of the earliest examples of a successful "remote" worker and leader, and it felt fantastic. I still was putting in 10 and 12-hour days, but I had a lot more control over my "destiny."

In late 2005, I landed at what would turn out to be my final full-time executive position at a small company. I was a senior executive at a startup research and analyst firm headed by Josh Bersin, a globally recognized expert in the area of human capital management (HCM). The company was virtual (no offices) with our small team scattered across the U.S. In fact, our leadership meetings (four or five of us) met in Josh's dining room at his home in Oakland Hills, CA. I had found what I wanted to do with the rest of my career—help

Working in partnership with Accenture, I delivered a number of presentations and participated in several panel discussions on Learning Transformation in New Delhi, Chennai, and Mumbai, India.

Josh build Bersin & Associates into a globally recognized leader in HCM industry research and thought leadership. We built the company to more than 70 professionals with worldwide recognition for the quality and integrity of our research and thought leadership. I was ultimately promoted to executive vice president (EVP) and chief operating officer (COO) of the company. Josh decided to sell Bersin & Associates in 2012, and I assisted in every aspect of that transaction which ultimately resulted in the acquisition of the Company by Deloitte.

I was asked to join Deloitte as a senior managing director in their Human Capital practice. I served in that role for almost five years before retiring from full-time employment in 2017 at the age of 66. During my time with Deloitte, I got to work with an incredible group of professionals from young people coming into the firm as business analysts directly from college to seasoned consultants and business leaders. Two of my most rewarding roles were as thought leader and Transformation Lab facilitator. As a Managing Director in the Human Capital Practice, I presented Deloitte's research and thought-leadership at numerous offsite meetings hosted by Deloitte's clients—chiefly sponsored by Deloitte's clients' Chief Human Resource Officers. Additionally, I conducted numerous transition and transformation labs at Deloitte University for senior HR executives from Deloitte's largest clients. This, combined with all the normal duties as a Managing Director, made my time at Deloitte one of the best experiences of my life—definitely a capstone for my long career.

I now continue to stay engaged by investing in, advising, and supporting startups in HCM, as a member of boards of directors, advisory boards or as a limited partner in a venture capital firm. In all these part-time positions, I have a real ability to manage my own time and effort level for any of these ventures. I plan to do this for the rest of my life with no expectation of complete retirement from the professional community.

I want to make one final remark on something that I continually heard about my work as a business leader. "But you went on all of those great trips to interesting places, had great dinners, drank fine wine and obviously must have had a great time doing all of that." As I have told a number of folks, "Please don't mistake me doing a great job for me having fun. There is a difference." Always remember "work is work" and "fun is fun." Unfortunately, they never seem to coincide. Business dinners are just that—business. After a full day of intense business conversations and discussions on solving short-term business problems, developing long-term strategies and plans, and addressing a million other issues, we are ready to decompress over a nice dinner. So, what do we talk about? Business, of course! Well, that was relaxing. Not!

But, that was not the worst of my experiences with business dinners. It definitely gets bad when you need to speak at the business dinner as a business executive discussing the state of the business or other business initiatives, or, worse, as an invited "thought leader"—the entertainment for the evening. In either case, dinner was not going to be part of what you will be focused on during the evening. I can recall numerous times when the evening was wrapping up and the waitstaff, who noticed that I had not had the opportunity to eat dinner due to my presentation and follow-up discussions, offered to wrap up a dinner for me to bring back to my room. As usual, these folks were terrific, and I usually accepted their offer. So, there I am, sitting alone in my hotel room, eating a cold chicken dinner with a nice bottle of water, finally getting a chance to relax after a full day of work—thinking about having fun when I get home.

PART 3

Curiosity and Knowing Oneself

What Does it All Mean?

SIX

Heritage and Knowing Where You Came From

> "Heritage encompasses many things. It's about our ethnic roots, of course, but it also includes cultural teachings and personal experiences. It's about who you are and where you have come from to get to where you are today."
>
> —*Dr. Cen Huang, University of Alberta,*
> *What Does Heritage Mean to You? 2021*

I HAVE BEEN thinking about your heritage for several years. You have four grandparents. So, I will be describing one quarter of your family tree. I hope your other three grandparents do the same since what they will uncover for you about where you came from will be extremely valuable for you (when you grow up) to convey to your children and grandchildren as well as help you put into perspective your position in the flow of history, both in the world and the United States. I can now comfortably trace my heritage back more than 300 years to my fifth great grandparents (your seventh great grandparents). That is back nine generations for you! I have a few branches of the tree that go back to 1650.

Before I start to tell you about what I found from my genealogical research, I would like to tell you a story about what I learned as a scientist about our cosmological heritage which is

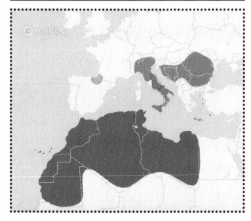

One quarter of your genes, those that I am passing to you, mostly come from Italy and the Aegean Islands. (source: Ancestry.com)

actually much more interesting and exciting. Based on extensive evidence and observation, we have good reason to believe that all the matter and energy in the universe came into existence a bit less than 14 billion years ago. Actually, time itself came into existence at the same time. So, all the quarks (which make up protons and neutrons) and electrons, that make up you, me, everything on the earth, in the solar system, in the galaxy, and in the entire universe are just a bit under 14 billion years old.

So, when someone asks how old you are, the answer is actually "I am a bit under 14 billion years old"—wow. That is one exciting way to look at your heritage, isn't it? We share our atoms with everything that came before us. One of those carbon atoms in your body could have been in a dinosaur 100 million years ago. It also could have been part of a wheel on a chariot in a race at the Circus Maximus in Rome 2,000 years ago. Or, it could have been created in a star 10,000 light years away and eight billion years ago. Consider this: A year ago, that carbon atom could have been in a little skin that flaked off your arm, in the air you exhaled, in your pee, or in your poop. Next year, it could be in the palm tree in your backyard or in a blade of grass in Africa. We are part of the universe just borrowing and returning atoms every day throughout our entire life. It is more incredible and beautiful than you can imagine. Okay, take a breath. I will wait a moment.

A very famous astrophysicist, Neil Degrasse Tyson, said "We are stardust brought to life, then empowered by the universe to figure itself out—and we have only just begun." So, atoms in your bodies were formed in the stars (and probably not the sun), have traveled here from around the galaxy to form you, and now you have the opportunity to actually understand the universe itself! The universe is understanding itself. Now, that is a heritage I want to learn more about and deserves a wow—wow—wow! This is the realm of the astronomer, the physicist, the astrophysicist, with maybe a touch of a philosopher. This is why you need to study hard, never be afraid of science or math, and continue to be curious. I hope you inherit my curiosity genes. They will go a long way toward you understanding your heritage and ultimately your place in the universe.

Now, back to the last hundred and fifty years and the genes from your mom, me, my parents, my grandparents, and the multitude of generations from Italy that have contributed all that they were to who you are. My ancestors (a quarter of your ancestors are also my ancestors) migrated to this country in the late 1800s and early 1900s. They primarily came to the East Coast (New York, Boston, and Philadelphia) from Naples, Italy. I have been working on my family tree as a gift for your mom and you. You can find it

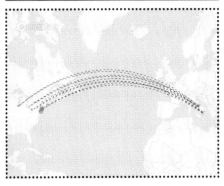

In the late 1800s and early 1900s, most of your second great-grandparents arrived in New York City, Philadelphia, Boston and Chicago.

as the Danna Family Tree on ancestry.com with over 800 members of my tree dating back to 1650, to Pietro Marsella, your ninth great grandfather. He was born in Messina, Italy and has a coat-of-arms in the records. It looks like we may not all be descended from peasants. I have subscribed to Ancestry and its global database of records for the past few years since being given a trial subscription by Taylor, Laci's oldest daughter. I have spent hundreds of hours researching my genealogy. It is totally fascinating what you can learn from this research. I hope you take this tree, combine it with the trees from your other three grandparents and enjoy the knowledge of the real "Circle of Life" and the contribution that your ancestors made to create you and your world.

It appears you may have a distant relative with a coat-of-arms. This is pretty funny. I'm not sure it is real since it is 12 generations back.

I hope to tell you lots more stories about the generations who lived in Southern Italy and help you build your own tree. So, now you have a better understanding of where you came from, from the very matter in your body (billions of years old), to "recent" history over the past more than 350 years. Perspective is wonderful.

SEVEN

Knowing Your Personality Traits and Developing a Great Attitude

"Two words attitude and personality are used interchangeably but there is a key difference between these two words. Personality is basically a combination of quality or the characteristic of any individual. On other hands, attitude refers to a way of thinking, belief or an emotion of an individual.

There is a very thin line of difference between personality and attitude. Though, we can say that personality is all about who we are and attitude totally depends on you and the environment where you reside. Personality is basically static while attitude is dynamic."

—*Urja Pandya, Technical Content Writer, LinkedIn, 2017*

HAVING MY PERSONALITY accurately assessed is probably one of the most significant insights I have had over my lifetime. The earlier you understand your core and your inherent personality traits, the better off you are. At the writing of this book, you are five and seven years old, and Laci's grandkids are three and four years old. I can already see the different personalities emerging in each of you.

I have taken multiple personality assessments and learned a lot about myself and how I interact with others with very similar and dissimilar personalities. Knowing this has been extremely insightful and valuable to me in interacting with others, both personally and professionally.

You probably remember, from earlier chapters, my descriptions of three personality assessments I participated in over the past 30 years. I participated in six: a tailored assessment conducted by The Marlin Group in 1993, Myers Briggs in 1997, the Predictive Index in 1998, the Harrison Assessment in 2010, Deloitte's Business Chemistry in 2014, and the Curiosity Diagnostic in 2021. They all had the same results, although each described the traits and characteristics in slightly different terms since they were each created by different organizations based on a different set of research data. When they described how these traits manifested themselves in my interactions with others, they were all spot on. That was me they were describing. My conclusion was, and is, that your core, inherent personality will be with you for your entire life because that is who you are—from birth to death—unchangeable.

So, if my conclusion is correct, then you really need to work on your attitude, your guiding principles, and the way you establish and manage relationships with others. You can control all of these and the result of you successfully developing and living these should result in a happy life. There is also chance and luck that you will need to deal with, but those are out of your control—or are they? Well, maybe.

I would like to share the results of one of my personality assessments in detail, the Deloitte Business Chemistry Assessment, and reflect on what it means to truly know oneself, and to put that into practice as a business leader, a colleague, a friend, and a family member. Deloitte defines "Chemistry" as "That hard-to-define, yet impossible-to-ignore elixir of great relationships and effective group dynamics." They describe their personality system as having four patterns: the driver, the pioneer, the integrator, and the guardian. One is generally made up of a combination of these patterns, the percentage of which drives the traits that everyone sees in you every day.

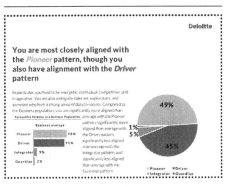

This is the summary page from the assessment. Wow, it is pretty pointed. I am not sure I want to meet this guy, let alone work with or for him. My nickname for years was the Ayatollah.

In fact, I am an extreme Pioneer and Driver, almost in equal measures and definitely to excess. I am not an Integrator (one who likes personal connection and enjoys seeing how the pieces fit together), and I am not a Guardian (one who likes concrete details and stability and respects what is tried and true). Wow, that is a pointed reality check. Okay, I can live with that. I have been living with that for over 70 years. All the other assessments said the same thing in their own way.

generous helpful networked experimental spontaneous
exploratory imaginative quantitative
expressive logical
methodical driven technical contextual
adaptable pattern-oriented intuitive
intellectual impatient leader trusting
restless competitive energetic visual optimistic
empathic creative dutiful ambiguity-tolerant
tough-minded tech-savvy inclusive
relationship-oriented collaborative big-picture even-keeled

A word-cloud was developed from my assessment data to provide someone an understanding of who I am and what to expect from me in personal interactions. This is the machine's view of me, not generated by me or any other human.

Well, I feel a little better looking at the word-cloud developed for me based on my assessment results. I am generous, helpful, expressive, trusting and dutiful—nice! A lot of the other stuff sounds a bit harsh. Yes, that is definitely me. It is funny that a lot of my stories can be summarized by this word-cloud. Remember that the word-cloud was generated by a machine based on an assessment when I was over 60 years old when I had most of my adult life behind me. You might say that my experience during my life developed this personality. My guess is this is who I have always been from birth, and no experience has done anything to change me. My personality came out in my life decisions, choices, and actions. Whew. That is a heavy thought. A few more elements of the report would be useful in learning more about how others probably see me. Remember that I can't change this. It is just my default personality. I would need to work very hard to be someone else, to exhibit a different personality. I actually don't have the energy or desire to do that.

Remember that I am extreme in both my "pioneer" and "driver" personality traits, and you get them in equal measure, whether you want it or not and like it or not. I often say that "I am, in fact, not an A-hole." Lots of folks probably disagree with me on that point and could make a strong case that I can be an A-hole on some, maybe a lot, of occasions. But I think we will leave it there for now. As I said at the beginning of the book, I will leave it to you to decide who and what I actu-

Likes variety, possibilities, and generating new ideas

DID YOU KNOW?

Pioneers are the chameleons of the personality spectrum; they are so comfortable changing their approach that they can be hard to identify – and can even have a hard time identifying themselves.

Me as a Pioneer.

Likes logic, systems, and laser focus on goals

DID YOU KNOW?

Drivers have two common sub-types. The Commander is more outwardly focused and directive in their working style, while the Scientist is more inwardly focused, concentrating on their ideas and inventions. Your Driver sub-type percentiles relative to a business population:

YOUR PERCENTILE

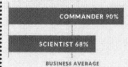

COMMANDER 90%

SCIENTIST 68%

BUSINESS AVERAGE

Me as a Driver.

ally am. I try to live to my values and guiding principles (driven by my attitude), but I am obviously burdened with a pretty strange personality.

Okay, I have one more major insight from the Deloitte Business Chemistry assessment. Yes, we are still gaining more insights from that assessment. Since I am an extreme Pioneer and an extreme Driver, the Business Chemistry machine-generated algorithms came up with a number of mottos that I can use in my day-to-day life in dealing with other people who I know, love, work with, or otherwise interact with. Yeah, thanks, very funny Mr. Machine. Am I limited to one from column A and one from column B?

> **EXTREME PIONEER MOTTOS**
>
> "Carpe everything."
> "Why not?"
> "Rules were made to be broken."
> "Have fun - it's just work!"
> "Challenge the status quo."
> "Dream big, brainstorm often."

> **EXTREME DRIVER MOTTOS**
>
> "Sugarcoating is for cupcakes. This is business."
> "Be quick. Be smart. Be gone."
> "We're competing. I'm winning."
> "My project, my rules."
> "What's your point?"
> "Enough schmoozing. Get back to work."

I want to spend a moment reflecting on attitude which is equally important to how successful we are in relationships, business, and life in general. So, I understand I can work on my attitude and use it to moderate my inherent personality traits. I try, every day, to use a positive attitude to manage my extreme personality traits. I, and people who I care for deeply, describe it as "managing the Bad Bob." Yes, there is a delicate balancing act involved in this effort, and I truly apologize when the Bad Bob pops out because of extreme stress or other complicating issues. My recommendation to you is to understand your personality traits as early as you can, hone your attitude every day, and manage your unique self as well as you can. We are all just living our individual journeys through this incredibly complicated world.

EIGHT

Some Thoughts on Relationships

"Developing relationship-enhancing habits is an excellent way to protect it from deteriorating. The three A's for increasing relationship happiness include expressing appreciation, admiration, and affection. Consistency in conveying these will increase your individual and your relationship happiness. In addition, these habits will infuse your relationship with positive energy and help fortify it against the frustrations and problems that every relationship encounters."

—*Susan Derry, Bridge Counseling, 2022*

WE ARE EACH on our own individual journeys through our amazingly complicated lives. Your journeys will probably never touch the journeys of most of the humans in this world. My guess is my journey has probably touched several tens of thousands (maybe hundreds of thousands) of people over the past 70 years in which I have had a single interaction (maybe picking up a pizza at a local restaurant), or a lifelong relationship (with my brother who is about 11 months younger than me). In every case, a please, a thank you, a hello, a goodbye, holding open of a door, a nod, a smile, or other expressions of "I recognize that you are here" and "I appreciate the opportunity to interact with you" goes a long way to ensure that the touching of your two journeys leaves a positive feeling between the two of you. I think of this as "Living Aloha."

In case you don't know, Aloha is a Hawaiian word that means "the presence of breath" or "the breath of life." It is an attitude and a way of living and treating each other with love and respect. "Alo" means face to face, and "ha" means breath. Think of it as I see you and even share the air we breathe. By just saying Aloha, we convey love, affection, peace, compassion, and mercy. Wow, pretty cool— with just one word. You know I love Hawaii more than any place in the world, and, ahhh, that native Hawaiian culture and the native Hawaiian people—there is nothing that can compare.

Living Aloha becomes a deeper and more important "attitude" as your journeys touch more often, or actually become intertwined with another person—your sibling, mom, dad, grandparents, children, friends, lovers, colleagues, schoolmates, teammates, and lots of others with whom you will spend days, weeks, months, years or a lifetime as part of your journey—sharing much, while still having their own journeys to live.

Living Aloha is really hard because it is not what those pesky, inherent human personalities tend to create in you. Most personality traits result in lots and lots of "me, me, me" and "mine, mine, mine" and "I can't win unless you lose." I certainly have experienced my lack of adherence to Living Aloha over my lifetime, sometimes without regret, but often with a desire to do better next time. Additionally, don't expect anyone to respond in kind to your "Aloha" attitude. Just try it during your day. Hold the door open for some, and see if they say "thank you" as they pass through the door that you are holding open for them. Most of the time, you will not even get a nod, let alone a "thank you." I will always hold the door open for someone and, without fail, will say thank you if they do it for me. It actually takes a real effort. That is the easy example. The longer-term, deeper relationships are a lot more complicated. My longest relationship, and the place where our two journeys have touched often, is with my brother, Al. Currently, at more than 70 years, we share many common experiences, especially as young children and teenagers. You can probably expect to have a close relationship with each other, and based on today's life expectancy, you could be together for more than 100 years. You definitely need to be good to one another. I am still a great friend to my brother after all these years. I respect him, love him, and always look forward to the next time we can spend time together. I hope you have the same long relationship with each other.

After my brother, my mom (and for a shorter period, my dad, because of his sudden and early death) and I had a more than 50-year relationship. This was first when I was a baby, toddler and small child, and then as a teenager, young adult and adult. This was probably the most complex relationship I, and probably you, will have—from totally being dependent on your parents for everything, to starting to show your independence as a child and teenager, to finally experiencing a time when you are both adults and "peers." A child's relationship with his parents is quite complicated on all parts—your mom and dad, you, and your evolving and changing relationship. Add all the "baggage" that all of you develop during your lives together, and it generally becomes quite messy. The goal is for it to all come together and end well before you part ways on this earth. I feel that definitely happened with my mom and probably was the case with my dad.

My next longest relationships are with your grandmother and your mom. After almost 40 years in a familial relationship—your grandmother as a wife and ex-wife—and your mom as our only child, it is a complex intertwining of our journeys and our lives.

At points it was hard to separate us into individual journeys since we shared so much. However, I am sure that each of us saw what we were experiencing from their own unique points-of-view based on filters constructed from each of our individual personalities and attitudes. I believe that we are in a very good place right now—probably in no small part due to the two of you, my grandkids—and hope to maintain this great relationship for the rest of my life.

As my young grandkids, it is now all about you. You are the next generation, our legacy, who will be responsible for carrying our collective journeys forward. You have your mom and dad, and your grandparents, there to love and support you, and numerous others who love you and help to nurture you, including Laci, your teachers, your coaches, family, friends and dozens and dozens of others that surround you in a network of relationships that you probably don't even realize exists today. Just tell them Aloha when you see them, "please" and "thank you" is also always nice, and remember that your journey and theirs will probably be tightly intertwined for as long as we are together on this earth.

For more than ten years, my and Laci's love, lives, aspirations, and our individual journeys have become tightly intertwined. We kid each other that we are the male and female versions of the same person—same personalities and attitudes toward life (not sure that is optimum based on what I shared with you about my personality—haha)—and trying to Live Aloha every day. Each day, month, and year gets better. Along with my, and our, ability to keep everything in balance, and working to keep everyone happy, is now my primary focus. I am hoping to still have many years left on my journey and plan to Live Aloha to the maximum extent that I can.

With that said, I wish you all Aloha.

NINE

Growing Up in a Low Income Home

> "Growing up, I never knew what "low-income" meant. Sure, I had probably heard the term before as simply not having a lot of money, but when I was young, those were just words."
>
> —*Amariyah Callender, Low on Funds, High in Spirit: Being in a Low-Income Family Does Not Define Me, 2018*

MY FATHER, YOUR great-grandfather, starting in the 1940s, was a carman on the Long Island Railroad (LIRR). His job as a carman involved the inspection, maintenance, and repair of the brakes on passenger rail cars operated by the LIRR. This was a dirty job physically as my dad spent his working hours in pits under rail cars in hot conditions during the summer and cold conditions during the winter. He was a union man being a member of the Brotherhood of Railway Carmen (and a union shop steward). Without the Union, I would not be who I am. I never forget that.

I found a write-up about the union from the 1930s that was very interesting to me. The Brotherhood of Railway Carmen's objectives were "to advance the moral, material, and industrial well-being of members" and "to secure for members a just remuneration in exchange for their labor and to shorten the hours of labor as economic development and progress will warrant, eight hours per day in the workday desired, and 44 hours per week, in order that members may have more opportunities for intellectual development, social enjoyment, and industrial education." They also worked to establish a railroad retirement system separate from the social security program which my dad enjoyed for several years before he died, and my mother continued to enjoy until her death. Needless to say, the words ring very true for me since my family did experience a stable and fair remuneration for my dad's work as a mechanic and, more importantly, the opportunity for his and our intellectual development and social enjoyment.

We lived in a working-class community on Long Island (South Farmingdale) in a small 900 square foot, four-room house, with few material comforts that you are accustomed to today. All our neighbors, my friends, all of my cousins and almost everyone we knew, lived as we did. We had one car. My mom would drop my dad off at the railroad station in Farmingdale every morning at 6 AM for his trip to Jamaica where he worked at the Morris Park shops. My brother and I would go with my mom to the station. We would love to see the trains coming and going. She picked him up around 5 PM, and they came home. My dad would do all the maintenance on the house and the car, and I can never remember someone coming in to help him. He was quite a good mechanic. I had no talent in that regard.

Getting back to the Union, I do not believe my dad would have been able to afford even this modest life and provide for his family if not for the ability of the union to negotiate a good contract for the workers with livable wages, health benefits, paid vacation time, free train passes for family trips and the first couple of years of my college transportation (from Long Island to Manhattan), and his retirement. It taught me the value of hard work and the power of organizing to achieve power in numbers.

There is something to be said about coming from humble roots. I believe that everything had to be hard earned by him and then, as his son, by me. Where does an internal desire to work hard come from? How about grit? Also, can you teach humility, integrity, desire to learn, marshalling internal energy, and the need to succeed and please? Or is that part of growing up without much, if any, discretionary income? I believe it is. We have talked about personality traits and attitude. That is the "nature" part of the "nature-nurture" debate. The "nature-nurture" debate is the debate about the contributor to a person's path through life. Is it shaped by genetics (nature) or the environment in which we live (nurture)? Despite what your nature component is, without being nurtured in a challenging environment, you may find it hard to be resilient, innovative, patient, and hungry for growth and success.

I want to share a quick aside with you. I believe I shared with you that my dad was very good with his hands and valued one's ability to work with their hands above everything else. I was not that child or young adult—kind of a klutz and definitely not good with my hands. A major contributing factor to developing my overall attitude may have been that I was both continuously denigrated and only indirectly encouraged by my dad. I was denigrated because of his perception of my lack of mechanical skills. I was reminded and ridiculed by him that I had better excel academically. Otherwise, he said I would never succeed in this world if I needed to rely on my hands and utter lack of mechanical aptitude and skills. The reverse side of this coin was probably the unintended consequence that I turned these negative criticisms into a positive by working hard, possessed of true grit, and excelling intellectually and academically. By the way, children should never be denigrated, only encouraged. On one final note, before I get back to my story, when my dad died, I inherited most of his tools. I have actually used the tools to do work around the house and on my cars. I am still quite a klutz and not very mechanically inclined, but I do seem to get it done when I need to. I plan to give his tools to the both of you when I get a little older. My dad, your great-grand-father, would have been very happy to think that his tools would be passed down to his great-grandchildren.

I lived on Willard Avenue in Farmingdale on Long Island from 1956 to 1971. Our home pictured here was a 900 square feet, one bath, two bedrooms, plus a living room and a kitchen. I shared one of the bedrooms with my brother for 15 years.

As a young kid, I watched my mom manage the family money. My dad's job, initially as the sole breadwinner, was to go to work and make the money. Once my brother and I were in school on a full-time basis, my mom went to work in the elementary school kitchen to make and serve lunch to the school children, earning a few more dollars to supplement my dad's paycheck. I never knew how much money came into the house other than it was enough to pay for our very frugal life.

The most important lesson I learned in growing up in a low-income home, in addition to working hard to make money (which we have already talked about), was the critical need to plan and budget your expenses. Back in the 1950s and early 1960s, almost all things were paid for with cash, including loans, utility bills, clothes and food shopping, and everything else. So, when my father got paid, he would show up at home with a pile of cash, usu-ally lots of small bills—$1s, $5s, and $10s. In fact, I am not sure that I saw a $50 or $100 bill until I was a teenager.

My mom would let my dad keep a few bucks for himself to bet on the "numbers" with his bookie. In case you have never heard of "playing the numbers," this was an illegal game in the U.S. in which guys, like my dad, would place bets on combinations of numbers that appeared somewhere in the local newspaper, in this case, the Daily News in New York. We knew when he won because he would come home with Italian pastries in the evening. I can still clearly remember how good those were and the smile on my dad's face for having the winning number that day. There was always a story about how and why he picked the number that day. There was always a good story even though it was totally random. I realized this from an early age.

Since my mom made lunch for my dad in the morning to take to work, and the fact that the LIRR provided him a free pass to get to and from work on the train, he did not need much more. My mom kept a small steel box in the closet in their bedroom and had lots and lots of envelopes in the box labeled for each expense that they had. She would take the cash (all those small bills) and divvy them up among the envelopes based on what she needed to save to pay the bills.

That was her planning and budgeting. She had it all in her head and in those envelopes. There was also savings for Christmas, birthdays, our trips, clothes, and food. Everything had an envelope. When the bill was due, she would take the cash and pay it. When sufficient cash was not available, often when shopping for clothes at a local clothing store (Robert Hall) in Farmingdale, she would put the clothes on "lay-away" which entailed paying a small amount weekly until the total bill was paid. Then, the items were brought home. You can't get any closer to managing your money than that. We got a small allowance—a few cents per week until we started to work ourselves. Then, we became part of the earning, saving, and managing spending routine that my mom had taught us.

My brother and I had a great childhood. Stickball in the street, riding bikes for hours and hours with friends, taking long hikes along a stream that ran through South Farmingdale to a series of small ponds, playing hand ball at the school with a pink, Spalding high-bounce ball (called a Spaldeen), all-day snowball fights with our friends during the winter, and hundreds of other things that cost almost nothing to do. How we played when I was a young kid was way different than what you are experiencing growing up today.

We only occasionally went out to a hamburger joint (Wetson's Hamburgers) for "dinner." Only once per year we went to a nice restaurant (an Italian white tablecloth restaurant called Caruso's Levittown) for my mom's and dad's wedding anniversary in June. Caruso's had linen napkins, silverware, china plates, matching glasses, and the best veal parmesan on earth. Every time I smell olive oil, this restaurant pops into my mind. Wow, that is pretty amazing when you only have experienced eating in one nice restaurant for your entire time growing up. We also went to lots of drive-in movies. They were cheap, and my mom could bring cookies and snacks that she made for us. We went to the movie theater in Farmingdale a couple of times a year. That was a really big deal.

So, would I trade this experience for anything else? Looking back, I would say no. It was a very frugal life, but we did not know it. We had little, but we did not really know it. It was an incredibly full life, an authentic life, a genuine life filled with family, friends, and lots of lessons I learned. I kept my eyes wide open and took it all in, every bit. It actually was a big part in making me who I am, the environment that nurtured me and my attitude to adulthood.

TEN

Living Your Values and Guiding Principles

"When we think about the big questions, such as who we are and what we want to achieve in life, we often ponder things like our personality traits and goals. We try to figure out if we are introverts or extroverts, if we are agreeable or not, or how many of our New Year's resolutions we have managed to tick off our lists. But how about personal values? The truth is, we rarely think explicitly about our moral standards and how they influence our character and life."

—Evelyn Marinoff, a wellness advocate, How to Define Your Personal Values and Live by Them, LifeHack, 2023

AT A SUMMIT of Nobel Peace award winners in Warsaw, Polish Nobel Peace laureate Lech Walesa called for a "secular Ten Commandments," a guide for universal values that transcend religious beliefs. The response has been a heated debate among secularists about what could constitute such a guide. While some have criticized the idea for being too dogmatic, others have embraced the notion of a set of rules which might bridge the gap between evangelicals and nonbelievers. I am one of those who embraces the idea of having such a list of shared values. If we can post the Abrahamic Ten Commandments on the wall in a U.S. Courtroom, a State Assembly or a schoolhouse, why not a Humanist Ten Commandments, or at least Ten Commitments.

THE HUMANIST TEN COMMANDMENTS

1) Thou shalt strive to promote the greater good of humanity before all selfish desires.

2) Thou shalt be curious, for asking questions is the only way to find answers.

3) Harm to your fellow human is harm to humanity. Therefore, thou shalt not kill, rape, rob, or otherwise victimize anyone.

4) Thou shalt treat all humans as equals, regardless of race, gender, age, creed, identity, orientation, physical ability, or status.

5) Thou shalt use reason as your guide. Science, knowledge, observation, and rational analysis are the best ways to determine any course of action.

6) Thou shalt not force your beliefs onto others, nor insist that yours be the only and correct way to live happily.

7) If thou dost govern, thou shalt govern with reason, not with superstition. Religion should have no place in any government which represents all people and beliefs.

8) Thou shalt act for the betterment of your fellow humans, and be, whenever possible, altruistic in your deeds.

9) Thou shalt be good to the Earth and its bounties, for without it, humankind is lost.

10) Thou shalt impart thy knowledge and wisdom gained in your lifetime to the next generation, so that with each passing century, humanity will grow wiser and more humane.

Christian Hagen, *from the American Humanist Association*, proposes such a list, a Humanist Ten Commandments. He proposes that the list might serve to aid those questioning the moralities of the universe regardless of their religious belief or non-belief. Many of the ideas behind these commandments are inspired by the tenets of humanism as outlined in the Humanist Manifesto and by the Humanist Education Center's "Ten Commitments."

As you know already, I have completely rejected the tenets of organized religion and its position that the tenets of organized religion represent the moral high ground. They don't. So, what is a possible alternative? Let's look to the secular humanists, and ask why this approach is not significantly better than the religious dogma politicians, leaders of the church, government leaders, and others who force us to subscribe to the notion that "to believe" is our only option.

I call myself a Secular Humanist—a label that I proudly embrace. The religious right in the U.S. has NO moral high ground in this regard, not one bit. This would make a very good plaque in any courthouse, the congress of the U.S. and State houses, and in all our schools.

I shared my values and guiding principles with you at the very start of my story. At that time, I asked for you to listen to my reflections on my life, and my stories, and to judge for yourself whether I have actually lived those values and principles. You can keep it to yourself; no need to share your thoughts with me. At over 70 years of age, I have done it or not, and for the most part, I can make only the slightest of changes in who I am. So, we will just leave well enough alone.

Finally, I will leave you with a challenge. Develop your own list of values and guiding principles. Then, revisit them often, and try to live by them. It is hard. You will often stray from living them to the extent you hopefully want, but they will be your guidepost. Use this guidepost to inform your choices in life, your decisions, your relationships, those that you support and oppose, where you contribute your time and money, how you vote, and ultimately how you live a full life.

ELEVEN

What Makes for a Happy Life and Overcoming Challenges

> "A calm and modest life brings more happiness than the pursuit of success combined with constant restlessness."
>
> "In the middle of every difficulty lies opportunity."
>
> —*Albert Einstein*

I BELIEVE THAT I have experienced what it means to have a happy life. This is not a Pollyanna and privileged life free from stress, challenge, and heartache tied up in pretty ribbons and bows. On the contrary, most days were long, complex, filled with work and life challenges, and always requiring that extra bit of grit and energy to power through the myriad situations I routinely faced.

For more than 50 years, this included having a partner that I loved and supported (my first wife, Janice), your grandmother (also Janis), Laci, a great daughter (your mom), incredible life experiences (both personal and work), and an amazing network of relatives, friends, and colleagues who all give me energy. You notice I did not list *things* as a source of happiness.

Although I have been financially successful during my lifetime, I continue to live modestly. Although, I do enjoy surrounding myself with fine art that means something to me. Vacations, travel, cruising, and experiences are worth more than things. Supporting social causes and educational institutions are more important than things. Enjoying the arts, museums, theater, live music, live comedy, live sports, live scientific events, actually almost anything live, is more important than things. One other item: I tend to enjoy activities that make an impact on me and have an emotional edge to them. I do get choked up when I experience "it"—the Arizona Memorial in Pearl Harbor, the Wall at the Vietnam Memorial in Washington, a total solar eclipse, or a particularly moving play.

Happiness is the combination of people and the experiences. Everything else is what you need to live comfortably. One other item that is very ephemeral for me is thinking about what you, my grandchildren, will tell your children, grandchildren, friends and colleagues about your grandpa. What will you say? First, I hope you say I had a full and happy life. Second, I hope you say that I left the earth better than I found it. I hope you tell your kids and grandkids that I lived my life well and that you are here because I took the road "less traveled" by others. That is probably a good lesson to take away from this book. I would be happy with that.

The Road Not Taken by Robert Frost, published in 1915

> Two roads diverged in a yellow wood,
> And sorry I could not travel both

And be one traveler, long I stood
And looked down one as far as I could
To where it bent in the undergrowth;

Then took the other, as just as fair,
And having perhaps the better claim,
Because it was grassy and wanted wear;
Though as for that the passing there
Had worn them really about the same,

And both that morning equally lay
In leaves no step had trodden black.
Oh, I kept the first for another day!
Yet knowing how way leads on to way,
I doubted if I should ever come back.

I shall be telling this with a sigh
Somewhere ages and ages hence:
Two roads diverged in a wood, and I—
I took the one less traveled by,
And that has made all the difference.

"The Road Not Taken" is a poem that is an appropriate description of my life, focused on the importance of our choices, both big and small, since they shape our journey through life. I, too, "took the one less traveled", and "it has made a difference." I have had a very happy life.

From an early age, I loved to experience new things. I was not a shy child and never resisted going to a new place or doing something that I had not done before. In fact, even though we did not have much money, my mom and dad figured out how to set aside a few dollars each pay period to fund short trips around Long Island, to New York City, to New Jersey, and to Washington, D.C. We always drove or took the train. As I told you, I did not get on my first plane until 1970 when I could afford to pay for it with the money I had worked hard to earn.

There is one important experience that I would like to share with you. We would always go to the annual Shinnecock Indian Pow-wow on the Shinnecock Reservation in Southampton on Long Island. It was my first exposure to Native Americans and the Native American culture. In the late 1950s and early 1960s, "cowboys and Indians" were everywhere in the American culture, on TV, in the retail stores. Dressing up as a cowboy as a kid was common. The Indians were always portrayed as the aggressors, savages, uneducated with no real reason for existing other than to be a foil for the "good guy," gun-slinging, cowboy. I had a cowboy outfit that my mom would dress me up in. I definitely was immersed in the American cowboy culture. The Pow-wow was really different. These were people with families and a deep culture they were sharing with us. I loved the experience and took in everything that there was to see and experience during these events. I took away a lot from these Pow-wows that stayed with me through today, mainly an appreciation for the Native American history and culture and what we, as immigrants to this country, did to them.

My dad would take us all to New York City to take the circle tour boat ride around Manhattan and up the Hudson to West Point. This was a real eye-opener. I loved to go to Manhattan and visit the museums, especially the American Museum of Natural History and the Planetarium. I could not get enough of that. Science, astronomy, history, and on and on, all interested me, and I remember saying to myself that I needed to be part of all of this.

Next, I will tell you about Washington, D.C. We would always do this in a day since my dad could get a free train pass on the Long Island Railroad and the Pennsylvania Railroad for the day. We would get up before dawn, get on the train on Long Island, go to Penn Station and change trains to D.C. By mid-morning, we would arrive at Union Station in D.C. and walk to the D.C. Mall and the museums and sites in D.C. We would walk everywhere until our feet hurt and were so tired that we could not walk another step. My favorite was seeing all the airplanes (including the actual Wright Brothers' plane), other technology and tons and tons of U.S. history. This would set the tone for so much of my life, and I am still reflecting on everything I saw then as a child.

My more adventurous life began one morning in the early 1970s when I was a physics student at Hunter College. The Physics Department set aside a small room to serve as a study lounge for physics majors. I still remember the number—room 1313, on the 13th floor of the main building at 695 Park Avenue—how appropriate for a non-superstitious group of science geeks. Well, anyway, a group of us would always gather there in the morning as we were getting ready to take our classes. We made coffee, brought in the daily newspapers to read, and had lots of scientific magazines like Physics Today (yes, there is such a thing) and other science stuff to read, many provided by the Physics Department.

There was an article in the newspaper that caught our attention. It was about what was going on at the Rhinebeck Aerodrome in upstate New York. The article was talking about static-line parachute jumping using army surplus gear. We had never heard of such a thing. The article said that you could actually go up to the airfield in Rhinebeck, get some training, go up in a small, single-engine plane and jump out. We now had a small group of us gathering around to hear more about it.

The article went on to describe the experience. What really got our attention was at the end of the article: a short description of an incident that happened to one of the jumpers. They usually took two or three jumpers up at a time. The plane was a small, high-wing aircraft with a strut connecting the wing to the body of the plane and a small step to stand on before you let go. You would fall a few hundred feet as the static line pulled the parachute out and it fully opened. You would then descend a couple of thousand feet or so to the ground.

So, now the incident occurs. A plane went up with the jumpers. The guy assisting the jumpers connected the static line for the next jumper to exit the aircraft. The pilot pulled back on the throttle to feather the propeller to reduce the air speed of the airplane to lower the force of the wind that the jumper would experience when exiting the plane. The jumper got out on the step and was holding onto the strut. The next step is to let go of the strut, arch your back and fall away from the plane.

That didn't happen this time. The jumper froze and refused to jump, and worse, refused to get back into the plane. The plane cannot land with a jumper on the step outside of the plane. So, what to do? The next line totally got everyone's attention. The article ended with the fact that the solution, wait for it… was to go full throttle, bring the propeller to full speed, and blow the jumper off the wing! It worked.

We were sold. We all agreed. We needed to go to Rhinebeck and do a parachute jump. We started the planning process, and five of us agreed to jump with another eight or 10 of the group agreeing to come along to watch. We finalized a date and arranged for the reservation with the Rhinebeck group that would be taking us up. About three weeks before the scheduled jump, a bunch of us went over to Central Park to play touch football, something that we often did. Unfortunately, during this game, I fell hard and broke my collarbone. Now, that could be a bit of a problem. Well, not really. I was around 20 years old, a bit of a fool and not one who was going

This is a stock photo of a static line parachute jump. It is not me, but I can still remember every detail of that experience.

to wimp-out. So, I did not tell anyone and still planned to jump out of the plane with a pretty major injury. What could possibly go wrong?

On the day of the planned parachute jump, we organized ourselves into four or five cars and all went up to Rhinebeck: five jumpers including me and a big bunch of watchers and supporters including my brother.

We arrived in the morning to ensure we could get trained for the jump. The training consisted of listening to them speak about the process we would follow: processes for entering and exiting the plane, watching the parachute packing procedure, practicing landing by jumping off a box, bending our knees and rolling on the ground, and other safety instructions including the use of the backup parachute. By the way, the "jump off the box" part was pretty easy even for someone with a broken collarbone. Actually, thinking back on it now, it was as insane as it sounds from this description. Remember that these were army surplus parachutes used by paratroopers. They planned to take us up on two separate flights since we would not all fit in the plane together.

So, we got on our parachutes and walked out to the plane. The plane took off and climbed to a couple of thousand feet. It was now my turn to jump. I shimmied over to the open door. They hooked up the static line. The pilot pulled back on the throttle, and the propeller feathered. I reached out and grabbed the strut, stepped out onto the step, positioned myself, and when they said go, I arched my back and jumped. I still can remember the feeling of falling and me saying ohhhhh shittttt. A few seconds later, I looked up and could see the plane disappearing in the distance.

Stock photo—you can see the static line, the step and the guy assisting the jumper—nice arched back!

The chute opened, and I was now floating. I could see the target, a gravel pit in the center of the field. I steered the parachute with toggles and enjoyed the ride down. *Pretty cool, looks like I made it unscathed.*

As I approached the ground, something did not feel right. Jumping off the box and bending my knees and rolling looked pretty straightforward. I was coming in fast—seemed *too* fast. Yes. Before I could think another thought, I crashed into the target. My face plastered into the rocks on the target, and my right shoulder (the one with the broken collarbone) slammed into the rocks. Whoa, now I was hurting. Jumping with that broken collarbone was, in fact, a bad idea.

I was not done. The last part of the instruction was that I needed to gather up the parachute and bring it back to the prep area where the parachutes were originally packed. I did that. I was not a wimp even though I was a science geek. I was the only one to land on the target. It took me months before I could use my right arm without feeling like it was about to fall off. You can still see the bone sticking out of the right side of my collarbone. Every time I look at it in the mirror, I think of this day and the wonderful feelings of jumping out of a plane on my own.

I learned to fly in the Piper PA-28 Cherokee Warrior. This was an incredible aircraft.

I learned to fly in Orlando, FL in 1978. In 1977, one of my Navy buddies at Nuclear Power School, a Lieutenant and experienced nuclear propulsion plant operator, and I had been talking about our interest in getting a pilot's license and flying all over Florida. It seemed like a cool thing to do. Our wives took note and decided that a couple of flying lessons would make a great Christmas gift. They went to Showalter Flying Service, at what is now Orlando Executive Airport, and bought gift certificates for a couple of initial lessons with an instructor. That was one of the nicest gifts I have ever received.

In February 1978, Andy and I decided we would give it a go and scheduled our first lessons. My lesson was fabulous. My instructor introduced me to the plane, a Piper PA-28 Cherokee Warrior. The Piper was a four-seat, single-engine, low mounted wing plane with a tricycle landing gear. I got into the pilot's seat. My instructor was going to let me fly the plane. He gave me a few more minutes of instruction on the operation of the plane including throttle, yoke, ailerons, elevator and rudder, plane motion through three axes, roll, pitch, yaw, radio and navigation systems, and the basics of takeoff and landing. I was totally overwhelmed but ready to give it a try. So, on February 25, I was ready to take off. With his incredibly detailed instruction, we taxied to the end of the runway, held for the tower's permission to take off, put on the flaps, received permission from the tower that we were cleared for takeoff, turned onto the active runway, throttled up, and started down the runway. He had me watch the speed. At around 70 mph and 3,000 feet down the runway, we were ready to fly. He had me pull back on the yoke, and we were in the air. I had just taken off. I really liked it.

We now needed to climb and get to an altitude to do a little flying. He guided me step-by-step through the process, and we flew around for about 10 minutes. Now, we were heading back for a landing which was about 1,000% more difficult than the takeoff. Remember there are way more controls than in a car. You are flying in three, not two, dimensions. So next, he has me setting up for a landing: do this, then that, and do this again. I was totally confused about what all the controls were doing. Then he said, yes, that is it. I said, "I have no idea what I just did or what effect it had on the plane." He knew that but was just having a bit of fun with me. He took the controls and easily landed the plane. The Hobbs meter (the device that measures the time the aircraft was in use) indicated that the whole thing only took 30 minutes—from starting the engine, to taxiing, to taking off, to a few minutes of flying, to setting up for the approach, to landing, and to taxiing back to the hanger—30 minutes! I got out of the plane and immediately signed up for a longer flight the next day with my flight instructor who would be my flight instructor for my entire time for me to get my pilot's license at Showalter.

This is a copy of the first page in my flight logbook. It shows my first flight and my first solo flight about one month and 8.2 hours of instruction after my first introduction to flying.

I also signed up for ground school training. A big part of learning to fly was not just having your hands on the controls of the aircraft. I also needed to learn everything about the aircraft systems, use of the radio for communications with control towers, navigation, use of flight charts, weather, winds, developing flight plans, and a million other things about the technology and math of flying. This included evening and weekend classes, lots of home study, and putting it all into practice while flying under instruction, and during solo and cross-country flights around the area or between airports in Florida, all as part of the qualification process for the pilot's license. Luckily, I had my buddy with me during the four months that it took us to get our private pilot's licenses. We studied together and when we were flying under instruction, one of us would sit in the back seat of the plane so we could hear all the things that our instructor was telling each of us. One of us would be in the pilot's seat (the left-hand front seat), the instructor in the co-pilot's seat (the right-hand front seat) and one of us in the back seat. This definitely accelerated the process of getting qualified.

You actually did not know when the flight instructor thought you were ready to go solo. He had me practice touch-and-go's numerous times—take off, get into the pattern, ask permission to land, get on approach, land (never an easy task), and then accelerate while still on the runway and go around again repeating that over and over again until it was just your muscle memory that was flying the plane. The challenge came when the wind was coming at an angle to the runway. This is what makes flying and landing extremely complex. You need to "vector" your way down to the runway, and just at the last moment, straighten the plane and place the wheels down on the runway. I got very good at landing including navigating some really challenging wind conditions.

This is the Flight Computer we used to help navigate when flying from one airport to another.

I was scheduled for a lesson on April 1 which was about eight hours into my training. I was still under instruction and expected this day to be like every other: touch-and-go's, a little flying around the area, and then back to the hangar. It started as expected with the touch-and-go's. About 20 minutes into the lesson, my instructor said, "I think you are ready." Is this an April 1 joke, or is he going to let me solo? It was not a joke. He asked me to taxi off the active runway. He jumped out. He told me to do a couple of touch-and-go's on my own. I got on the radio and asked the tower for permission to take the active runway and received it. I accelerated down the runway, and that muscle memory just took control. I took off, got in the pattern, asked permission to land, got on approach, landed, and repeated it once for good measure. I came around, landed and taxied off to find my instructor waiting for me with a big smile. He had gotten another would-be pilot to solo. The only happier guy than him was me. Whoa! I had just soloed. That moment is burned into my brain. I can remember every minute of those 15 minutes of my life.

Ground school, along with my training and solo flights, went well for a couple of months. Training with the instructor involved numerous flights to practice emergencies, including stalling (when the pitch of the plane prevents adequate airflow over the wings to support the plane in flight), loss of power (requiring you to find a place to land the plane—on one occasion on a grass field), and maneuvering around transmission towers and other air traffic especially jet planes. The turbulence around jets is incredible.

As part of the qualification process, I needed to complete several "cross-country" flights. A cross-country flight required a three-leg trip—leave from Orlando, fly to one airport a distance away, land, take off, fly to a second airport again some distance away, land, take off, and then fly back to Orlando. This generally occurs close to the end of the training process as a capstone before scheduling the FAA examiner's final check ride prior to issuance of the license. The cross-country involves quite a bit of planning (navigation, weather checks, filing flight plans, etc.) and is the biggest test of your ability to actually fly a plane as a private pilot. This was all done to Visual Flight Rules (VFR). This means that you need to see where you are going.

My first solo cross-country, which was a bit less aggressive, went well. Now, I was ready for a more challenging solo cross-country. I would fly towards Tampa and land at an uncontrolled field east of Tampa and then fly to Stuart (north of Palm Beach), a controlled field just off the St. Lucie River. I planned to leave in the morning and be back by mid-afternoon. Everything looked great, and the weather appeared to be cooperating—just some possible showers predicted near Stuart, but I had flown through showers before—no big deal. With my flight plan filed, I took off for the uncontrolled field. Everything went well with my navigation, and I arrived at the airport. I checked for traffic in the pattern. I entered the pattern and landed without an issue. Remember that this is 1978. No cell phones and no good weather updates. I then took off for Stuart.

By the time I arrived in Stuart, the weather conditions had definitely deteriorated. My navigation system said I was here but because I was a new pilot and flying VFR, and it was raining pretty hard, I could not find the airport. Luckily, I was in contact with the air traffic controllers, told them I was a student pilot and that

I was in trouble. They could see me on their radar, but I was now disoriented and could not tell where I was or how I could get to the airport. They instructed me to start to fly an east-west zig-zag pattern and try to find the St Lucie River. After around five minutes, I could see the river through the rain. They then instructed me to fly south down the river, which I did, and the airport appeared in the distance. Luckily, the rain started to let up, and I was able to get priority to get into the pattern and permission to land. I taxied to the tower, and one of the controllers came out to meet me. I was a bit shaken and frazzled and still needed to get back to Orlando. The air traffic controller was great and was able to get me to relax a bit and get ready for my trip home. To this day, I have enormous respect for our air traffic controllers and the level they go to in order to keep us all safe. After a short stay, I was able to get back in the plane and take off for Orlando.

Well, the return flight went well until I approached the Orlando area. As I approached the Orlando Executive Airport (my home base) from the south, there was a little issue that I forgot to take into account. It's called the Orlando International Jetport. I was still a bit frazzled, and I did not obey the rules for overflight of the airport. I was definitely too low and flew into restricted air space. That is not good. By the time I got back to the Executive Airport and asked for permission to enter the pattern and land, the air traffic controllers were already pissed at me for a major infraction. They told me once I landed and had secured the plane, to come up to the tower. They needed to speak with me. Well, they actually needed to yell at me. I made no excuses and was given a stern talking to and a warning. All and all, not a bad result to the day. I completed the most complex cross-country that I have ever done and made it back alive. I recalled a quote from Chuck Yeager: "There are old pilots and there are bold pilots, but there are no old bold pilots." I will do a much better job in the future and will not get myself into that kind of trouble again. I didn't.

So, I was ready for the FAA examiner to conduct the exam and determine whether I was qualified to receive my private pilot's license. I had completed 43 flight hours—20 under instruction, 23 solo, almost 16 cross-country, and three flying at night. The exam was one hour, all in the plane, going through a series of standard maneuvers, emergency procedures and other "unplanned" situations. As you can see, I passed on the first try.

On July 2, just 4 months after starting my training to qualify as a private pilot, I completed my check ride with an FAA examiner and received my private pilot's license.

So, now I am a private pilot. We flew a lot around Florida for fun. My most exciting day was when I took my first wife, Janice, who got me started flying with the Christmas gift, your great-grandmother and great-grandfather on a flight over Walt Disney World. It was fabulous.

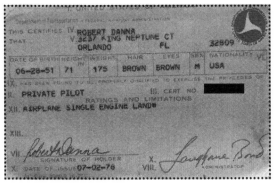

This is a picture of my private Pilot's License. It is dated July 2, 1978.

In case you have never seen a pilot's license, I have included a photo of mine. I am really proud of the fact that I was able to qualify for the license in four months and still remember every detail of that experience and the time that I had as a pilot. After a few years, I no longer had time to fly for pleasure. The demands of my work did not permit me this opportunity. I hope you will find a time when you can do something like this for yourself.

It's amazing to challenge yourself with something that appears very hard and then succeeding in achieving it. I became a private pilot. There are a multitude of things you might do. Just go for it.

PART 4

Continually Curious

Technology

Art and Music

My U.S. Travels

My World Travels

Politics

Religion

Reason, Logic and Being a Skeptic

TWELVE

Let's Talk About Technology

"Have you ever watched a cartoon snowball roll down a hill? It usually picks up snow on its way down, getting larger and larger, before inevitably running over someone. In many ways, the advancement of science and technology since World War II (WWII) has acted a lot like that snowball—out of a few small technological developments and breakthroughs has come even more innovation and new devices which seem to come to market at a faster pace every day. It's how we can go from adding machines the size of an apartment to handheld computers in barely a half century."

—Lesson presented by Christopher Sailus entitled "The Advance of Science & Technology Since 1945: Developments & Impact." Study.com, 25 January 2014

BORN IN 1951, I became aware of technology in the mid 1950s—vacuum-tube AM radios and black and white TVs with only three network channels (NBC, ABC and CBS), "party-line" land-line and live operator-managed telephones, Lafayette Radio Electronics Corporation (in Syosset, New York) and their hundred-page catalog, nuclear weapons (and hiding under our desks), rockets, and satellites (including Sputnik 1). My life in the 1950s would be almost unrecognizable to you today.

During the entirety of the late 1950s and 1960s, we lived in a 900-square foot, four room (not four bedroom), one bath home in Farmingdale where we did not have a clothes dryer. In fact, the only appliances we had were a refrigerator and a stove. We had no microwave oven, no dishwasher, no sink food disposal, no air conditioning, no wi-fi or internet, no cable TV, no coffee maker. Well, we

That is me at around 4 years old in our Levittown home with a small black and white, wall-mounted TV in the background. The back of the TV was in a closet so we could access the tubes and other components as they routinely needed replacement. The antenna was on the roof of the house.

really had nothing. They did not exist for the general population at that time.

We used a clothesline to dry our clothes outside, even in the winter. During the winter, the clothes would often be brought in by your great grandmother (my mom) frozen solid. We would defrost and dry them on the radiators inside the house before we could put them away. We did have a clothes iron to get the wrinkles out of the clothes. My mom would iron most everything.

We also never had a color TV. We got a small stereo record player in the mid 1960s, and my dad would play songs recorded by Perry Como and Frank Sinatra and an orchestra called "One Hundred and One Strings." He loved that music and could not understand why we did not love it as well. My brother and I would introduce folk and rock and roll music to the home in the mid to late 1960s, a pretty radical change to the music that my mom and dad had introduced to us.

The one rotary dial phone in our home sat on a telephone table in the middle of the house between our small living room and the two bedrooms just across from our one small bathroom.

Our heat was provided by an oil-powered furnace in the basement. An oil truck would show up periodically to fill two big oil tanks in the basement. The furnace would boil water in another big tank and then circulate steam to radiators located throughout the four rooms in our house. There was no central heating or air-conditioning as you know it today. To stay cool in the hot and humid summers on Long Island, we would open the windows and have window fans blowing air throughout the house. Sounds awful? Actually, we had nothing to compare it to. So, it was just our life, and we lived quite well with it.

We only had one rotary dial phone in the house. It sat on a "telephone table" in the hall. When you picked up the handset on the phone, you might hear one of our neighbors speaking to someone. You would say, "Sorry, I will try back in a few minutes to see if the line is open." In fact, we shared the telephone line with several neighbors, and only one home at a time could use the line. So, you would need to wait for the line to be open before you could use it. Also, you would need assistance to connect to someone outside of your immediate calling area. You would need to speak to an operator to help you connect to that person. There would also be two big books on the telephone table containing the phone numbers of all the folks that lived in your local area (the "White Pages") and the businesses in your local area (the "Yellow Pages"). The Yellow Pages would also contain lots of ads for the businesses in your town. There was only one provider for all of these services

"Ma Bell"—the name we used to refer to the Bell System who had a monopoly over all telecommunications in our area. Ma Bell today is known as AT&T, but is much, much different from what I knew as Ma Bell when I was growing up.

The 1960s encompassed all the dreams about the future (including *The Jetsons* cartoon show premiering in 1962): robots, telecommunications, jet planes, manned space flight and giant rockets, computers, fission and fusion energy, modern automobiles, the transistor, electric guitars, home technology and appliances, and hundreds and hundreds of other things that are available everywhere today and totally taken for granted. At that time, none of it existed for the lower and middle classes and was only available in early-stage forms for the upper class. Also, my recollection of John F. Kennedy's speech outlining the challenge to the Country to land on the moon by the end of the 1960s was one of the most exciting parts of my memories of that time—wow.

Each year I would wait for the updated catalog from Lafayette and dream about what I could buy with what I earned from my paper route and retail jobs. It could be a birthday present or a gift under the Christmas tree from Mom and Dad.

In the 1970s and 1980s, I would have the opportunity to see numerous rocket launches at Kennedy Space Center and the Air Force Cape Canaveral Air Force Station (Delta, Atlas-Centaur, and Titan) as well as day and night launches of the Space Shuttle. I also saw one of the first landings of the Space Shuttle at the Edwards Air Force Base in California.

I lived with the Lafayette Radio Electronics Catalog at arm's reach at all times in the early to late-1960s. It was my "wish book" for anything technological that I could hope to have at home—portable transistor radios, tape recorders, cameras, other electronics, my own hi-fi stereo turntable, amplifier and AM-FM tuner, or any of thousands of other items to wish for. I did ultimately own the amplifier-tuner, reel-to-reel tape recorder and portable transistor radio pictured on the cover of the 1967 catalog.

My brother and I listened to hundreds and hundreds of hours of WNEW-FM 102.7 progressive radio which certainly changed my life. I will have more to say about how having a stereo radio in the bedroom that I shared with my brother and access to WNEW-FM was a life-changing time for us. We still speak about it today as old men.

I have another funny story to share. My mom (your great grandmother) always asked my brother and me to join her and my dad (your great grandfather) in the living room to watch TV together in the evening. Most of the programs that they watched did not interest us. When I was 16 or so, I bought a Motorola solid state (no tubes), stereophonic (two speakers), high-fidelity combined receiver, turntable and separate speakers. My dad hung the speakers from the ceiling in the bedroom that I shared with my brother. Since my mom wanted us to sit with them in the living room, I bought a set of headphones with a 25-foot extension cord that could be plugged into the stereo in our bedroom. Since the house was so small, it all worked perfectly. I could listen to my progressive rock and folk station, was with them in the living room, and we were all happy. Well, at least I was happy. I am sure that my mom intended for me to speak with them, but that was just a detail to me as a 16-year-old. Sound familiar? I have watched the two of you do it to your mom and dad today. The only difference is you are scrolling your iPads. Technology changes; kids don't.

The state of technology available to kids in science classes was quite rudimentary including lots of calculating by hand: log/sine/cosine/tangent paper tables, interpolation, and slide rules. My first exposure to computer languages and programming occurred by using the new FORTRAN computer language for science. I probably walked away with as deep an understanding of math as I could imagine. Algebra, trigonometry, geometry, calculus and probability and statistics were all done by hand. No, calculators were not available. I computed everything "by hand" manually.

In other words, I added, subtracted, multiplied, and divided with paper and pencil and plotted answers by hand on graph paper. I got totally immersed in mathematics.

I was always asking myself: Does my answer make sense? That is how close I was to the math. Our labs were all hands-on with a substantial dependence on truly understanding what was going on during the lab "experiments." In fact, when I graduated high school in 1969, there was still no technology in the schools that were part of the science curricula.

Probably the most significant element of technology introduced during the 1960s that impacted my life was the transistor and the portable transistor radio, first AM only and then radios containing both the AM and FM bands. In the early 1960s, everyone had an AM radio and would be allowed to bring them to school during the Baseball World Series. I can still remember having this transistor radio the size of a book to listen to the game during recess, lunch or on the way home from school.

The early 1970s changed everything. The Wang Lab was introduced. This was the first desktop scientific calculator. Next, the Hewlett Packard and Texas Instruments hand-held, battery-operated calculators were introduced. We could do complex calculations on an electronic calculator including log functions (sine, cosine, etc.) and numerous other math functions that took forever to do in the past were now instantaneous. There was no more need for books of paper tables and slide rules. We were ready for the eye-popping growth of computers, calculators, and associated electronic devices in the 1970s, 1980s, and through today. Additionally, in the late 1960s and early 1970s, the main-frame computer became available for use by students. I used an IBM 360 which was so large it filled a college classroom. You would write out every line of a program to solve a problem or simulate a physical situation—like an object moving through space or a vibration on a spring. It would contain decision logic, if-then statements, branching and "do-loops," and other items built to lead the computer through the actions and activities it would need to address and complete. Each line would then be punched onto individual punch cards using the FORTRAN language which was designed to program formulas and mathematical logic statements. You would have the deck of cards run through a card reader and into the computer. In general, the computer would tell you that there were "syntax" errors that prevented the program from executing. You would need to correct them, and once all the syntax errors were removed, the program would execute. Now the question is, "Are the results logical?" "Do they make sense?" This is where those years in the 1960s became valuable. You really needed to debug the programs based on a real feel for the math, expected results, and the ability to "see" the potential discrepancies and errors in the results. Once all of this was completed, you would then be able to continue to evolve, modify, and expand on the programming to address more and more complex problems and simulations which I did throughout undergraduate and graduate school. I would still be modeling the situation, developing the decision logic, writing down all the equations and logical statements, punching those never-ending cards, and debugging, debugging, and more debugging. Now that was early computing! Today's computers and programming languages have little in comparison to those very early days.

I carried this Compaq portable personal computer for project work. Notice the green screen. It was only useful for engineering work at this time.

I was an early adopter of technology in the 1980s. General Physics (GP), my employer, allowed me to have cutting-edge technology to support my client and project work for a wide variety of engineering and technical contracts. Until having access to the "portable" Compaq computer, all the work was done at the home office or on the client site mostly doing calculations using hand-held calculators and pencil and paper. This now gave us the opportunity to have a bit of automation introduced to our engineering processes and the ability to show up at a client site with computing capability that we never had before. In the late 1980s, Toshiba introduced the first laptop computer that I quickly incorporated into my day-to-day business activity. I would now do word processing and presentation development on my own using the WordPerfect software for the IBM PC. This is before we adopted Microsoft Word at GP in the early 1990s. I became really good at generating my own proposals, presentations and could handle complex spreadsheets to manage both engineering and business data. This would all seem archaic to you now, but it was totally revolutionary at that time.

I was also an early adopter of business technology including pagers, mobile phones, the BlackBerry assistant, and finally the smart phone. Before the pager, we would need to call our secretaries back in our offices and ask to be read all the messages that came in while we were away from the office, either on a plane or in client meetings. We would then need to find a pay phone and use coins or phone charge codes to make the call to follow up on the messages. This was incredibly inefficient, and it could take days to follow up on a message and close the loop with a colleague or client to get a question answered. How long does that take you today? The answer is probably minutes, maybe even seconds.

The BlackBerry Assistant was the immediate precursor to the smart phone—really the first modern business productivity tool

I loved my BlackBerry. I was one of those committed users who would go everywhere with it. It was just part of who I was. I used every function on it and awaited every upgrade, both new devices and new software updates. There was nothing like it. I could actually get and answer email, messages and see my business information in real time. It was almost as we experience it today on our smart phones. When the Apple iPhone was introduced on June 29, 2007, it was not embraced by the business world. We were all totally committed to BlackBerry.

Within a few years, Apple changed our minds, and I moved to being a committed iPhone user embracing all the applications available for business as well as for personal use. In fact, as EVP and COO at Bersin & Associates, I went totally mobile. I could see all our sales activities and drill down to client-by-client intelligence on my mobile, smart phone. I could see our financial performance, manage and approve expense reports, and literally see every aspect of the business on my mobile device. I have never looked back or considered another option to the iPhone and will probably die an Apple fan. My iPhone now seamlessly communicates with my MacBook Pro, my Apple Watch, the Cloud and hundreds of business and personal applications.

Wow—we have come a long way since the late 1960s and early 1970s, and I was there every step of the way. I can't believe I actually have experienced the entirety of this technology revolution. It has been quite a ride. I can't imagine what you, and the generations who follow you, will see in your lifetime. The future still looks bright. Never fear STEM. Embrace it. Use it. It will be good to you.

THIRTEEN

Let's Talk About Art and Music

> "Music constructs our sense of identity through the direct experiences it offers of the body, time, sociability, experiences which enable us to place ourselves in imaginable cultural narratives."
>
> —*Identity Through the Eyes of Music—Music and Identity in a Globalized World, diggit blog*

AS YOU PROBABLY realize at this point, I love art and music and try to surround myself with both as much as possible. Although I am neither an artist nor a musician, I get great pleasure from experiencing art of all kinds and can listen to folk, jazz and rock and roll music for hours on end. I find great meaning in both. There is nothing like experiencing these in person—live and up close. That

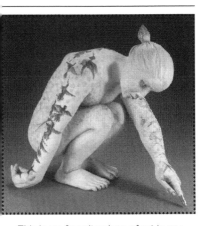

This is my favorite piece of art in my home. It is a sculpture created in 2018 by Magda Gluszek entitled "From Dark to Light." I look at it multiple times a day to remind me of the power of enlightenment.

is not where I started. The art we had growing up was probably purchased at Sears and hung on the wall to fill an empty space; or, at least, that is how it felt to me. As a child, my mom and dad took us to the Metropolitan Museum in New York City, and we were encouraged by our teachers to check books out of the library on art to get an appreciation for artists throughout history. We did. So, we got to learn about fine art at an early age, although none of it could be found in our home, neighborhood or local museums.

Every piece of art now in my home was created by the artist, signed, with a history and meaning for the artist and me. I bought most of the artwork at auction or in a gallery and can tell you where and when I bought it and why I felt it spoke to me. I also love to go to public art galleries and museums and appreciate a very wide variety of art. My favorite galleries and museums are the Louvre and Rodin museums in Paris, the Academia and Uffizi galleries in Florence, the Kunsthistorisches museum in Vienna, the National Gallery in London, the Metropolitan Museum in New York City, and the National Gallery of Art in Washington, D.C. I

hope you have an opportunity to spend time in each of these and also immerse yourself in the magnificent cities that contain these wonderful art galleries.

Although it will be fun to talk to you about art and what I love about seeing it and having pieces important to me continually around me, it is the music that truly reaches to the inner depths of who I am and speaks to me in a way that nothing else can. My earliest memories of music, real music, beyond the childhood songs that were played on a cheap record player playing scratchy 45 rpm kids' songs, were 33 rpm long-playing records that my dad bought and would play on a small stereo system in the living room in the early 1960s. Frank Sinatra, Perry Como, and the 101 Strings Orchestra were standard fare in our house when my dad was home. In hindsight, it was actually a good introduction to music for a 10-year old: a little classical, a little jazz, a bit of Hawaiian music, the Blues, some Broadway tunes, Camelot, Duke Ellington, and a million seller hits from the 1930s, 1940s, and 1950s. You get the idea. All the music was played by a full orchestra, and the cost for each record was a couple of dollars per record. They probably got played hundreds of times each at our house. I got exposed to dozens of different musical styles with songs played by a 125-piece orchestra. This was a great foundation to build upon.

Pop music in the mid-1960s was driven by the rise of the new generation, the baby boomers, of which I was part of the early wave of children and young adults in this generation. Two elements of this "new" music really resonated with me—folk and rock and roll—both reinvented to reflect the major cultural changes that were taking place in the late 1960s: antiwar, environmental awareness, rejection of the older generation, need for racial equality, social awareness, and of course, "Sex, Drugs, and Rock & Roll." Although I did buy my first cheap AM-FM radio in the mid 1960s, I did not really have a "good" transis-

This is a picture of my first AM-FM multi-band portable transistor radio from Lafayette Electronics that I bought with my Newsday paper route money. The cost of this radio represented about two months of work at that time.

tor radio until around 1968 when I bought the Starfire VI pictured in the Lafayette catalog. Wow, now I was really there. What did I listen to? Well, I listened to WNEW-FM 102.7 in New York City, of course. I had started to listen to this station on my cheap radio, but the quality was horrible. The Starfire VI was amazing in comparison. WNEW-FM was one of the earliest progressive rock radio formats. I found it in 1967 when it first started as a game changer with all-female disc jockeys. This was followed in late 1967 by a mixed staff that became the only station that was played in the bedroom that I shared with my brother. The station, which I knew as the place "Where Rock Lives," was hosted by disc jockeys including Bill "Rosko" Mercer, Johnathan Schwartz, Scott Muni, Alison Steele, Dave Herman, and Pete Fornatale—all of whom were not afraid to push the boundaries of what was acceptable to be played on the public airways. We were totally into this music which continually evolved during the late 1960s and into the early 1970s.

Janis Joplin was amazing. She sang the Blues combined with Rock & Roll like I had never experienced before. I must have played this album a thousand times and still have it on my playlist on my iPhone more than 50 years after hearing it for the first time.

I could not afford folk or rock & roll albums at that time, so most of my listening came from WNEW-FM, other than a handful of 2-song 45s including the Beatles and a number of other very popular groups. This music provided the underlying fabric for my life and spoke to me like no other music I had heard before. This was also the time when I got my first retail job as a stockboy in a department store on Long Island. I could now afford to buy a long-playing (LP) stereo record. The first rock album I bought was Cheap Thrills in 1968 by Janis Joplin and Big Brother & the Holding Company.

"Summertime," "I Need a Man to Love," "Piece of My Heart," and "Ball and Chain" were fabulous songs. She had great passion, and the virtuosity of the Big Big Brother Band was like OMG! As a 17-year-old, it could not get better than that.

Please find this album online, and listen to these four songs in the order above. You will know who your grandpa was in the late 1960s when music was much more real than it is today. This is just my opinion, but this is my story, so I get to make the call. This is the kind of music you could find on WNEW-FM—really? Yes, really.

Although I was listening to progressive rock on WNEW-FM radio, this got me started buying albums and getting involved in the whole live music scene. My first live concert was Jefferson Airplane in 1969. The concert took place in Stoneybrook, Long Island, on an open field at the State University of New York. The concert was incredible as you might imagine. I was an 18-year-old, missed going to Woodstock and now could see a live concert from Grace Slick, Marty Balin, Paul Kantner, Jorma Kaukonen, Jack Casady and Spencer Dryden—the San Francisco Sound which I was now totally in love with. I can still remember the psychedelic projection on a screen behind the band. The evening has stuck with me for more than 50 years. I still listen to "Somebody to Love" and "White Rabbit" (two of their original songs) as if I just heard them yesterday. Still today, I will always look to experience a live concert. There is nothing like it. It just becomes part of you if you really love the music.

In the early 1970s, I attended an incredible number of live events including:

- Jethro Tull during their "Thick as a Brick" tour
- Blood, Sweat and Tears with David Clayton Thomas at Philharmonic Hall at Lincoln Center
- Simon & Garfunkel at the Forest Hills Tennis Stadium
- Iron Butterfly (doing a very extended version of "In Agada Da Vida") at the Wollman Rink in Central Park

- Procol Harum at the Fillmore East in Greenwich Village
- Multiple other folk and rock singers and bands at the Wollman Rink during the Summer concert series in Central Park
- The Concert for Bangladesh at Madison Square Garden

The Concert for Bangladesh needs its own description! It took place on Sunday, August 1, 1971 at Madison Square Garden (MSG) in New York City. This was the first benefit concert of this size ever organized. You can find a video recording of the concert on the internet. It was historic, and I was there somewhere in the crowd of 20,000. I had just turned 20-years old. The concert was organized to increase international awareness and fund relief for refugees from East Pakistan following the Bangladesh Liberation War-related genocide. This is what "woke" looked like in its most basic manifestation. I loved it. It represented awareness of and support for the marginalized, the poor and oppressed, the under-represented and the unrepresented. The concert was organized by George Harrison (former Beatles) and Ravi Shankar (Indian sitar player). They brought together Ringo Starr, Bob Dylan, Eric Clapton, Billy Preston, Leon Russell, Klaus Voormann, and the band Badfinger. I want to give a shoutout to my brother who attended the concert with me. Concert tickets were in extremely high demand and a line formed to buy the tickets when the date was announced. He spent hours and hours in the line waiting to buy the tickets for us. He got two tickets to the afternoon show. In fact, if you see the video of the prelude to the concert, including the line of kids queued up to buy tickets, he is the kid in line reading a book. Thanks, Al.

The concert stage was filled with about three dozen musicians including George Harrison. This was Harrison's first appearance since the breakup of the Beatles. Bob Dylan was more amazing than I could have imagined. He performed "A Hard Rain's A-Gonna Fall," "Blowing in the Wind," and "Just Like a Woman"—just three of the many songs he sung that day. Harrison closed the concert with "Hear Me Lord," "My Sweet Lord," and "Bangla Desh." My brother and I walked out of Madison Square Garden mesmerized, transformed by what we had just experienced. Ultimately, through the sales of the album recorded at the concert, along with the film and other items, more than $12 million was generated by the concert and donated to Bangladesh for the refugees. Rolling Stone Magazine said that the concert was "a brief incandescent revival of all that was best about the Sixties." That was exactly how we felt when we left MSG and how I feel about it today. It was the best event I have ever attended in my entire life. Since the early 1970s, I have attended hundreds of live concerts and will continue to do so until I am dead. Over the years, I have attended live events with Billy Joel, Elton John, Meat Loaf, Pat Benatar, Fleetwood Mac, Spyro Gyra, Billy Ocean, Cheap Trick, Emerson, Lake & Palmer, The Moody Blues, O.A.R., Smash Mouth, and many, many, many others.

The Concert for Bangladesh was the first, and maybe the greatest, benefit concert in human history. I am incredibly grateful to have been part of it. It raised awareness and money for a population that would have otherwise been totally ignored. This is, in fact, the real meaning of "woke." I hope you grow up to be people who understand and embrace this kind of thinking.

Of all these artists, my favorite one, by far, is Meat Loaf. From the mid-1970s when he made his movie appearance in "The Rocky Horror Picture Show" and his first album "Bat Out of Hell," I have been a diehard fan of his music seeing him perform live multiple times over the years. My favorite songs include "Paradise by the Dashboard Light," "Everything Louder than Everything Else," and "Out of the Frying Pan (And Into The Fire)." This is Rock & Roll at its finest: passionate, loud, in your face lyrics, delivered in a no-holds-barred unique singing style. I have listened to his music continually over the past 50 years. It never gets old, and when I need a little pickup to my spirits, I listen to Meat Loaf.

Our largest piece of artwork is a framed, stage-played guitar, signed by Meat Loaf and his lead guitarist, Paul Crook, from the Bat out of Hell III tour. It also contains a number of Meat Loaf guitar picks, a poster, picture and CD, all signed by Meat Loaf, and a picture of Paul and the backdrop from the show— by far the best gift I have ever received.

In 2013, Laci wanted to give me a special birthday present. She knew of my love of Meat Loaf's music and live performances along with my love of unique pieces of art.

She decided to combine that all into one gift and experience. Meat Loaf had a short residency at Planet Hollywood on the Strip in Las Vegas. She thought that a signed, stage-played guitar that we could frame and hang on the wall in our living room would be an amazing gift. She was right. She researched the band and discovered that Paul Crook, Meat Loaf's lead guitarist, lived in Las Vegas and was selling his stage-played guitars from the Bat Out of Hell III tour. The most famous of his guitars was his "Star Guitar." You can still find it on the internet by searching the phrase "Paul Crook Star Guitar."

Laci visited Paul at his home, and he told her the history of the guitar including the bullet hole sticker that is on the guitar. On tour with Meat Loaf at a truck stop for dinner, they saw the bullet hole sticker, for sale in the gas station's convenience type store. Meat Loaf kidded him that he should buy it and put it on the guitar. He did, and it was there during the next show.

Buying the guitar, signed by Paul, was just the first part of her plan. Since Meat Loaf had the residency in Las Vegas, she bought tickets to the show. She didn't just buy concert tickets, but she also bought a two-person table right at the foot of the stage. She worked out a detailed plan with Paul to have us bring the guitar to the show and then get it signed by Meat Loaf while we were there. Wow—the plan worked out flawlessly. In addition, Meat Loaf actually came to the front of the stage and sang to us. Well, what can I say—it does not get any better than that. The stage-played guitar, signed by both Meat Loaf and Paul Crook, with the bullet hole sticker now sits as a centerpiece of our artwork in our living room. Music meets art, art meets music, and they are now united as one. Thank you, Laci, so much.

As you can guess by now, I am defined by the music I love. I ask you, can you give me a list of five or six songs that if I listen to them, I would know who the authentic "you" is? I have done a lot of thinking about that for myself. The following are *six songs that help define who I really am—revealing my authentic self.* Listen carefully to these six songs to know everything about me. The complete lyrics to these six songs are contained in Appendix A.

Imagine (1971) and *God* (1970)—by John Lennon— these songs express my beliefs as a Secular Humanist.

Sniper (1972) by Harry Chapin—this song captures the nightmare that we continue to live every day caused by the unrestricted availability of weapons of war in our general population and why we need to ban them all.

The Great American Eagle Tragedy (1972) by Earth Opera— this song, written during the Nixon Administration and at the height of the Vietnam War, captures the passion of the anti-war movement in the 1960s and early 1970s. We should never lose the passion to oppose war.

In Held 'Twas in I (1968) by Procol Harum—this song speaks to our inner struggles with self and self-discovery, the absurdity of many things in our daily life, and the need to rely on one's self to ultimately navigate this difficult world.

Everything Louder Than Everything Else (1993) by Meat Loaf—this song speaks for itself. I am still young and wasting my youth—enough said!

FOURTEEN

Let's Talk About My U.S. Travels

"Traveling helps you grow through hands-on, reallife experiences. It can be hard at times, but every challenge you face will make you even more prepared for the future. You can only learn valuable lessons from traveling, and you'll gain some unforgettable memories along the way."

—*Worldpackers website—6 ways traveling encourages self-development*

MY EARLIEST MEMORIES of travel were either in my dad's Mercury Monterey or on the Long Island Railroad (LIRR). My dad did love that car and because he worked for the LIRR, he could periodically get free passes on the train for us to travel to NYC or

Washington, D.C. He also had a wanderlust. So, we were always going somewhere on the weekend, mostly local places and mostly by car.

My dad's two-door white Mercury Monterey—whitewalls, rear fender skirts, headlight covers, no seatbelts, no A/C, AM-radio, and as much chrome as you can get on a vehicle. That screams the 1950s.

My mom, brother and I went to the AAA office in Farmingdale to plan our trip across the U.S. My brother and I, at 12 and 13-years old, would be the navigators for the trip. We were about to get a geography lesson of a lifetime.

We visited relatives throughout Long Island and in Queens and Camden, NJ. We went to Jones Beach, crabbing on Long Island, drive-in movies, historic sites and local parks. The visits were nothing special other than they started to build in me a love of getting in the car, or on the train, and going to do things, see things, and experience things. Generally, it cost little or no money, other than the gas, and was always great fun. I can remember eating in a restaurant (Caruso's Levittown on Hempstead Turnpike) only one time a year for my parent's wedding anniversary in June. We never stayed in a hotel. Every trip was a day trip. If it was an overnight trip, we stayed at someone's house.

That all changed in the early 1960s. My dad started to talk with us about planning a major road trip across the U.S. from NYC to Southern California. It would be by car; we would stay in motels every night, and we would stop and see as much as we could while driving through the states: New Jersey, Pennsylvania, Ohio, Indiana, Illinois, Iowa, Nebraska, Colorado, "The Four Corners,"

Arizona, California and then back through Arizona, New Mexico, Texas, Oklahoma, Arkansas, Tennessee, Virginia, Maryland, back through New Jersey and home to Long Island. Thank goodness for the AAA! Back then, they provided the best maps, tour books, hotel directories, and could develop step-by-step travel directions in something called a TripTik. You will also need to remember a few things about the early 1960s. There were no interstate highways to speak of. Most were just in the planning or early construction stage. There was no GPS, just paper maps. There were no mobile phones. Who needs a phone when you are driving cross-country on your own? There were no rest stops, just the occasional roadside restaurant, truck stop, Howard Johnson's, or Stuckey's for lunch and a bathroom break. So, we had this thick book of page-by-page directions, custom-created for us by the AAA travel counselor based on our meeting to discuss what we were planning to do. She advised on places to stop, things to do and see, police speed traps, road construction, detours, and places to stay. We would not actually have any motel reservations because we had a general plan of where we would stop, but that could change during the day as we drove across the country. We would pull into town, look for the "vacancy" signs in the motels and pick the one that looked "acceptable"—typically the cheapest in town since we were still doing this on an incredibly slim budget.

To a young kid growing up on Long Island, the country looked very different from state to state and town to town. I knew of the differences and what to expect, but seeing it in person and up close was a real eye-opener. The way people spoke, the way they looked and dressed, what they ate, and how they lived was all fascinating. Although somewhat different, there was one common denominator—they were generally all white. This was definitely a segregated country with Blacks located away from the main streets and thoroughfares that crossed towns, states and the country. We never saw a Black person in a motel or restaurant. Thinking back, that should have felt weird to us. It did not because that is basically how we lived our lives as well.

Also, there were often long distances between towns and cities, and you would see the sometimes drastic change in all of these cultural elements. This was one country, true, but made up of lots and lots of distinct cultures and ways of life—certainly not the "melting pot." In just about ten days, we saw a lot: farms to cornfields, cornfields to ranches, ranches to Rocky Mountains, the Rockies to the Mohave Desert, the Desert to southern California including Hollywood and Disneyland. We saw all this in about 10 days. Memorable parts of the trip included the endless corn fields in Iowa; our stop in Ogallala, NE, where we saw all of the cowboys and cattle; driving on the Million Dollar Highway between Silverton and Ouray in Colorado (my mom cried most of the way—she was deathly afraid of heights); standing at the Four Corners Monument (with my arms and legs in four states at the same time—AZ, NM, CO, and UT; visiting Mesa Verde and seeing the 700-year-old Pueblo ruins; seeing the Grand Canyon (and walking the rim trail); visiting Las Vegas (and seeing all of the lights—more glitter than I had ever seen in my life, even in Times Square in NYC); driving through the Mohave Desert in the middle of the summer in an un-air-conditioned car (gotta love those early 1960s—I thought I was going to die); and finally seeing Los Angeles (wow, Hollywood and Disneyland).

We picked up a number of souvenirs along the way. My favorite was a bullwhip that I got in Nebraska. I became quite adept at cracking that bullwhip. I have one additional thing to tell you. I took a ton of pictures along the way and not just pictures but slides, too. When we got home, my mom paid for all the pictures that I took to be developed into slides, and we bought a slide projector, slide carousel, and a screen. The hundreds of slides were assembled to tell a story of our travels, and I presented the trip multiple times to our relatives in New York and New Jersey. My brother and I got really good at telling everyone everything that we experienced on our cross-country travels. I am sure everyone was bored to death, but they said they loved it. We definitely learned more during the trip than words can express.

We would do two more big road trips when I was a kid, one to Florida and one to Canada. We took the same approach as the cross-country trip. My mom, brother and I planned the trip. We went to AAA to get the TripTik, hotel Directory and Planning Guides. We were off on two additional adventures adding North and South Carolina, Georgia, Florida, Tennessee, Ontario and Quebec to the list of states and provinces that I visited before I was 18 years old. On all three trips, we did not follow the same route to and from California, Florida, and Canada allowing us to see more of the countryside and experience as many different places and cultures as possible.

One thing that I distinctly remember growing up was my curiosity about flying in a plane. When they flew over our home, I would always look up and say to myself that I definitely wanted to go somewhere by plane. This was totally out of reach for us. We never had the money for plane tickets and certainly could not afford a vacation away from the New York area in other than our car. I would have to wait until 1970 when I was 19-years-old to pay for a flight to Daytona Beach in Florida for a week's summer vacation with two of my friends from college. The flight, on Eastern Airlines, was amazing. I know you have no idea what I am talking about since you have been traveling on airplanes since you were babies and flying as routine as getting in the car and going to McDonald's for a happy meal. For me, growing up with very little, my first experience was something to savor. I was committed at that point to not make this an exception. It would not be until 1980 that flying commercially and experiencing the country and the world became the norm and not the exception.

I have now had the opportunity to visit and/or work in 48 of our 50 states. I have not visited North and South Dakota. Most of the other states that I have visited were a result of business travel for General Physics Corporation while working at commercial nuclear power plants, NASA and Air Force rocket launch and research facilities, and other manufacturing and process plants.

I have met some incredible people and still marvel at different cultures and histories that make up the United States. I have concluded that we are not a melting pot of immigrants and races but more likely a conglomerate of regional cultures and histories that are trying to function as one country. An example of this would be the European

This is a view of the Pacific Ocean from the back of the Koko Head crater on Oahu during a hike in the early 2010s. You might be able to see Laci and me under the arch.

Union which is made up of distinct European countries with their own histories and cultures (rather than Japan with its long, homogenous culture and history). What makes us even more unique is our history of immigration and discrimination. Put this all together, and we have continual tension and stress in our "American" culture as we continue to evolve as a people and a nation.

I would like to spend a few minutes with you chatting about my favorite place on earth—the Hawaiian Islands. In aggregate, I have spent over two years of my life there since 1987 when your mom—age 18 months—your grandmother, and I visited for the first time. I hope this will be your favorite place to visit as well especially since you, too, have been visiting the Big Island since you were toddlers. Hawaii feels like a second home to me. These days we go there for six to seven weeks per year having bought timeshare weeks from Hilton Grand Vacations on Oahu, the Big Island and Maui. These two-bedroom resort units are each incredibly unique, and each island has its own distinct vibe and feel.

During times that we have visited, we have experienced flowing lava at our feet, "doors-off" helicopter rides over erupting volcanoes, authentic luaus, long hikes through rain forests and into incredible tropical valleys, visits to multiple gorgeous waterfalls, time at the top of Mauna Kea (seeing the multiple huge telescopes and our spectacular universe at night—the view of the night sky was breathtaking), walking on black sand beaches and seeing sea turtles in the wild, tasting Kona coffee and touring the coffee farms, seeing hundreds of wild chickens everywhere, witnessing the "green flash" on the beach at Hanalei on Kauai, walking the beach at Waikiki, and seeing rainbows beyond description. I could go on and on for hours.

The beauty of the Islands and its native Hawaiian culture are wonderful and should be experienced by everyone. You will walk away understanding what it means to Live Aloha—one of my core principles. As a visitor on the various Hawaiian Islands, there is a pledge that has great meaning to me, and the pledge goes something like this: "I pledge to travel responsibly by respecting the land (aina), sea (kai) and traditions of the Hawaiian people. I will embrace Hawaii's "aloha spirit" by expressing the same warmth, kindness and care to others that I give to my family and friends."

We started to plan to attend the 1996 Summer Olympics in Atlanta in 1995. We needed to buy tickets for the various events, get reservations for a place to stay, and decide when we would arrive in and depart from Atlanta. Your mom was an aspiring gymnast. So, we definitely wanted to see the women's Olympic gymnastics event. That was going to be the cornerstone of our planning. We built the rest of our plans around seeing the finals of that event on July 23rd, 1996. That year was an intense year for me in business. I was leaving GP in Columbia, MD and joining another company in Sacramento, CA. We planned to relocate during the summer to allow your mom to start the new school year in El Dorado Hills in California where we were building a new home. We had a lot going on. We decided to stay in Maryland until after the Olympics and then get to California in August to make sure your mom started school at the beginning of the new school year.

We bought tickets to a number of events surrounding the July 23rd date. We also decided to try a new program being offered at that time. We could rent a home for the time that we would be in Atlanta, close to the Olympic venues. We did this. This is long before Airbnb. We paid our money up front to the company coordinating this and received confirmation of the reservation. We were set. We drove to Atlanta in July, and everything seemed to be playing out as planned. When we arrived at the reservation company's designated location, we found that the company was not going to be able fulfill the reservation commitment. It was chaos since they had committed to hundreds of people to have houses to stay at in Atlanta for the Olympics. Luckily, because of all my business travel, I was a Diamond-level customer of Hilton Hotels making me one of their best and most loyal customers. I found a pay phone (no cellular phones at that time), called Hilton and was able to secure a room at the Hilton in Marietta, GA for the time we planned to be at the Olympics.

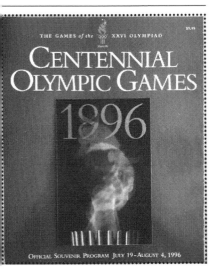

The Olympic Games in Atlanta celebrated the 100th anniversary of the Modern Olympics. This was a very big deal.

Being around the Olympic venues was absolutely electric. You could feel the excitement at every turn. People were coming out of, and heading for, one event or another. You could hear them all speaking about what they saw, what they experienced and what they planned to see next. We were in and out of the Centennial Olympic Park in the middle of the Olympic venues on a regular

When you grow up it might be fun to take your kids to Atlanta and find the brick that was placed in our name at the Centennial Olympic Park. We stood there in 1996 when we attended the Games.

basis and actually bought a brick with your mom's, grandmother's, and my name on it. You can probably still go and find the brick if you are ever in downtown Atlanta. Now that would be very cool.

On a very sad note, on July 27th, only a couple of days after we stood at the same location, a bomb killed one person and injured 111 others. It was the first of four bombings committed by Eric Rudolph in a terror campaign against what he called "the ideals of global socialism" and against "abortion on demand." That could have been us. That is what we believe in, so he was actually trying to kill people like us. I think about that often

I took this picture. There they are—the U.S. 1996 Magnificent Seven warming up for the event. Talk about sitting on "pins and needles." How would they do?

and the poor people who were killed and injured. It is still going on today for the same reasons! When will we ever learn? We were at a gathering to celebrate the coming together of people from around the world to participate in something that is amazingly peaceful and beautiful, and this ugliness was thrown in our faces. This is so, so sad. Will we ever be able to rise about this insanity?

On July 23rd, we attended the women's gymnastics event at the Georgia Dome. Your mom was 10 years old and a young and aspiring gymnast herself, so going to this event was very exciting for all of us. Our Magnificent Seven were Shannon Miller, Dominique Moceanu, Dominique Dawes, Kerri Strug, Amy Chow, Jayce Phelps, and Amanda Borden. You may have seen the videos of the famous ending of the event. Although individually the gymnasts did well, their team performance won the gold medal. It showed the U.S. and the world that working for the success of the team is as important, and probably more important, than working for individual success at the detriment of the team. This is a great lesson for all of us.

This is a sampling of the tickets we used for the Olympics in Salt Lake City.

Six years later, we had the opportunity to attend the Winter Olympics in February 2002 in Salt Lake City. We were living in El Dorado Hills in California, and your mom was 15 years old. We started planning for these Olympics in 2000. We would drive over to Salt Lake City, stay in the Salt Lake City area and get tickets to events in the city and in the Park City area. This time, everything worked exactly as planned. One difference between the summer and winter Olympics that I observed: although the summer Olympics were very exciting, everything is human sized. The winter Olympics are very different. The venues are super-sized. The ski jumping hills are very big. The competitors are doing things that are extraordinary—almost super-human. They are going 80 miles per hour on a sled down the luge, or they are flying through air on the ski jump. The conditions can be brutally cold, icy, snowy, or worse. The two events that have stuck in my mind are the luge finals and the big hill ski jumping. Both of you have now been at the luge and bobsled track in Park City. That is the same one your mom, grandmother and I were at in 2002. We were able to walk the entire length of the track. It was all a viewing area during the Olympics. This luge was terrifying. The competitors were going so fast when they passed you that you could hardly see them. You would need to move your head while they passed, pick them up on the left and, like a TV camera, turn your head to the right at the same speed as they passed you. Now there they are. Like I said, this was super-human. Over the past few years, the Utah Olympic Park has opened the track to the public to experience a bobsled run which I was able to do with Taylor, Laci's older adult daughter. Wow, it was as exhilarating as it looked, and I loved it.

The big hill ski jumping was even more amazing. We arrived in the early morning for the event, even before the sun came up. It was frigidly cold, and everyone was gathered at the bottom of the hill. Then the competition began. Unbelievable is a total understatement. It seemed like they were in the air forever, so graceful, so quiet, so practiced, and so incredibly super-human. When the jumper landed, the crowd went wild. It was wonderful.

We were able to get tickets to the medal award ceremony for the men's halfpipe event in snowboarding. The Americans swept the event. For the first time since the 1956 Winter Olympics, three Americans were on the medal podium: Ross Powers (gold), Danny Kass (silver) and Jarret Thomas (bronze). Your mom, grandmother, and I were there to see them receive their medals. It was so cold that evening that I thought we would freeze to death while we were waiting for the medals to be awarded. Looking back, it was worth it, but during the ceremony, I could not wait to get someplace warm.

I will let your mom tell you about the other events that we saw and how she felt being there. As for me, I would do it again in an instant. It also gives a whole different feeling when you watch it on TV. We were actually there, in the incredibly electric atmosphere of the crowd experiencing the super-human effort of the competitors and the excitement that was everywhere.

FIFTEEN

Let's Talk About my World Travels

> "Moving around the world and travelling to different places means discovering new and beautiful cultures, learning about ancient belief systems and hearing fascinating stories about life in different environments from the people who actually live there."
>
> —*EF Education First—10 reasons why travel is the best education (and why life without it would be dull)*

IT ACTUALLY TOOK me a long time before I made my first overseas trip. In fact, it was not until the Spring of 1985 that I was able to afford to pay for a vacation from work outside the U.S. (except for Canada). I was 33 years old. Additionally, at that time, my work at GP was all domestic. I would not start to do international travel for GP until the late 1980s. In comparison, your mom did her first overseas travel at the age of 13 when she accompanied your grandmother and me on a two-week trip to Europe in 1999. I am sure that you will probably be younger than that when you take your first international trip.

Your grandmother and I were married in December 1984. We decided to plan a honeymoon in the spring of 1985 that would be very different and very memorable. Since neither of us had been to Asia and both of us were interested in experiencing new

This is a photo of a traditional ryokan (not the one we stayed in), but it is a good example of the room we had at Mt. Fuji.

cultures, we decided to book a two-week trip to see as much of Asia as we could. In the early 1980s, doing this on our own would be pretty difficult, so we worked with American Express (AE) Travel to find a tour that fit our personalities and interests. We found one itinerary that seemed perfect. We would fly from Maryland, where we lived, to Tokyo and connect with a tour originating there.

The approach of the AE tour operator was to get you from city to city and country to country around Asia, give you a half-day orientation to the city and then leave you on your own to explore. There would be periodic get togethers for dinner and cultural immersion, and then on schedule, they would collect your bags, get you to the transportation to the next city, and accompany you on that mode of transportation—the Bullet Train between cities (Tokyo, Kyoto and Osaka) in Japan; a plane from Japan to Taiwan; buses around Taiwan; a plane from Taiwan to Hong Kong; ferries (including the Star Ferry), buses and the Victoria Peak tram in Hong Kong; a hydrofoil to Macau; and a bus to Guangzhou in mainland China. We also took a train on our own in Japan from Tokyo to Tsukuba to visit the 1985 Expo which I talked about in an earlier chapter. The trip came off flawlessly, and we experienced multiple countries and got an incredible feel for the local people which was a big part of what the tour promised—that is, for us to meet the people.

Although the entire trip was incredibly memorable, two stops stand out. We spent a day at Mt. Fuji and in the evening spent the night in a traditional Japanese ryokan (an inn). When we arrived, we traded our shoes and clothes for slippers and a yukata robe. We were shown to our tatami-mat room with rice paper walls and had a nice cup of tea. The entire experience could not have been more different from a stay in a traditional Western hotel. The small group of us who were on the tour got together for dinner that evening for a taste of very traditional Japanese cuisine known as Kaiseki. In this case, we were also treated to a geisha ceremony—the ceremonial tea ritual. While we were at dinner, our sleeping room was set up with sleeping mats for us. The entire experience was incredible. I had the opportunity to return to Japan many times over the next 20 years because I had a local Japanese consulting team from RWD reporting to me. Unfortunately, in Tokyo, it is very difficult to find a traditional ryokan. So, this experience was a once-in-a-lifetime opportunity for me.

I have one additional item I would like to share with you regarding our experience entering China in 1985. At that time, the country had just started to open to Westerners for tourism, but entrance was very controlled and very restricted. The AE tour had arranged for a day tour crossing the border from Hong Kong (which was still a British Colony at that time) into the People's Republic of China (PRC). We would get to meet an "entrepreneur" starting her new business, visit a family at their new home, and see the construction of the new cities that were rising from the dirt in southern China. The construction was the thing that I have talked about many times since this trip. All buildings and structures were erected by hand—tens and tens of thousands of hands. They manually constructed high-rise buildings, roads and highways, plants and retail shopping centers, and water piping and sewers. They were all hand-built using Bamboo scaffolding and a small hand-operated "tractor" that they used to power everything. It was the most amazing thing that I would ever see—talk about the possibilities when you marshal hundreds of millions of people to change their world!

We were able to experience the stark differences between Japan, Taiwan, Hong Kong, Macau, and mainland China. We saw the modernization and Buddhist temples in Japan, the Huaxi Street Night Market (Snake Alley) in Taipei, Victoria Peak, and the Jumbo Kingdom floating restaurant in Hong Kong, the Macau casinos, and the cities under construction in south China (in Guangzhou and Shenzhen). The people were all amazing. They were all different from one another. They were all welcoming to your grandmother and me. I felt very different coming home from this trip. I felt changed. I realized the possibilities we have available to us if we just work together. We could minimize the politics and bravado and just try to see everyone as a citizen of this very small planet. We actually have so much in common.

Since this trip to Asia in 1985, I have visited or worked in almost 50 countries over the past 40 years. Most interesting to me were my visits to, or work in, Japan, China, Singapore, Malaysia, India, the Philippines, Italy, Spain, England, France, Russia, Venezuela, Australia, and Turkey. I have also taken more than two dozen cruises, have well over 4 million air miles on a variety of airlines, and probably have a few thousand nights that I have spent in hotels worldwide.

CHINA

GP started to look to China in the late 1980s and early 1990s to expand their international consulting services both in the areas of process systems safety and automobile manufacturing. I led several delegations and initiatives in this regard. That got me to Beijing and Shanghai a number of times. Since I was there for a few weeks at a time, on weekends I took the opportunity to visit some of the major historical sites. On March 27, 1993, I spent the day walk-

I bought this engraved medallion at Badaling, a town on the Great Wall, about 80 km northwest from Beijing.

ing on the Great Wall of China. It was breathtaking. Additionally, I was able to spend days exploring the Forbidden City, Tiananmen Square, and a number of other important historical locations in Beijing and then in Shanghai. At the beginning of my time in China, I experienced a number of restrictions to my travel. By the end of my travels there, I saw a new China open with a welcoming of Europeans and Americans to help in their continued growth and expansion of their technology, manufacturing, and overall involvement in the global economic community. It was very nice to have a small role in this.

SINGAPORE AND MALAYSIA

GP founded a wholly owned subsidiary, headquartered in Singapore, to manage its operations in Southeast Asia including a large office in Kuala Lumpur (KL), Malaysia. When I was promoted in the early 1990s, the division that contained this operation fell within my responsibility. That gave me the opportunity to spend a lot of time traveling to the region and working closely with the team (almost all of whom were locals) to help develop new business and support a wide spectrum of existing clients. But since I was, again, spending a couple of weeks at a time in the region, I had a chance to experience the culture firsthand. The best part was that the incredible folks I was working with often took me to their favorite spots, like Sentosa Island (where the monkeys acted like they owned the place, which they probably did), the Hawker Centers (where the stalls sold all of the local food and drinks and probably did not get going until 11 PM at night), Orchard Road (where I usually stayed—it had the best shopping in the city at that time) and the Dragon Boat Festival. Since we also had most of our staff in KL, I also spent quite a bit of time there. On visit after visit, I watched the Petronas Twin Towers being built (ultimately having the opportunity to walk across the sky bridge between the two towers). I also had a chance, guided by our local office manager and lead staff, to venture outside of KL to see the countryside. Malaysia is one of the most beautiful countries in SE Asia.

PHILIPPINES

In the early to mid-1990s, I was able to get to the Philippines several times on projects for both GP and RMI. Initially, the work focused on assisting General Motors in assessing possible locations for their planned expansion into Asia to manufacture their vehicles in that region. Most of that work was in the area surrounding Manila. I spent a lot of time in the city and at local businesses.

This is a picture of Unit VI of the Hydroelectric Complex, a 200MW plant. It was located at the base of the 320-foot-high Maria Christina Falls—one of the most beautiful locations for a power plant that I have ever visited.

Those businesses built parts for locally manufactured automobiles. Although it might be interesting to chat about Manila—a big Southeast Asian city that many folks have visited with lots of things to see and do—it is not what I would like to talk to you about.

In the mid-1990s, GP got involved in project work focused on the privatization of electric utilities and the burgeoning private power industry. We got involved in a large project in the

Philippines to explore the potential of privatizing the Agus River Hydroelectric Complex including their seven hydro plants on the Agus River in Mindanao. I would travel from Maryland to Manila and then connect to a local flight to Cagayan do Oro in Mindanao where we were met by a car and driver. Then, we took a drive to Iligan City where we stayed in a small hotel. This location was the base of operations for the project. Surprise, surprise—there was an armed guard at the front door to the hotel. The seven hydro plants stretched from Unit 1 in Marawi City on Lake Lanao down the river to Unit 7 in the north on Iligan Bay. At that time, Units 1 and 2 were located in the Autonomous Region in Muslim Mindanao (ARMM) with the balance of the Hydroelectric complex located in the Christian zone of the island.

Since this was a newly established autonomous region, there was still a lot of tension in the area in which we would be working. I was responsible for assessing the integrity of these plants and addressing issues associated with the integrity of the facilities as part of our due diligence for the project. So, I needed to get to all the plants and spend time inside each to do the required assessment. The drive from our hotel in Iligan City to Unit 1 in Marawi was quite problematic. Five of us would get into our Mitsubishi Pajero: the driver, one of my colleagues, me, and two heavily-armed escorts. Units 1 and 2 had heavily armed guards everywhere. We were able to get the work completed but were told by the escorts that we were fired upon during one of our trips to Unit 1. This was nothing like the tension that is felt every day, for decades and decades, across the world between Muslims, Christians, and Jews. Frankly, I would never like to experience that again. Oh, and by the way, the countryside that we saw and the people we met were all incredible, as usual. Everywhere I went, I always found people with common desires to do a good job at raising a family, to work hard, and (for the most part) to be honest and forthright in their dealings with me.

JAPAN

In the late 1990s, I led an effort to establish a joint venture (JV). The JV was called SAP Learning Solutions, and it was established between RWD Technologies and SAP to provide Enterprise Resource Planning (ERP) software training and tools across Asia-Pacific. We accomplished the formation of the JV with our headquarters placed in Singapore and one of our offices in Tokyo (inside of the SAP Tokyo office). One hundred percent of our team in Tokyo were Japanese nationals. They delivered all the training in Japanese. The software and tools were created primarily in Kanji (the Japanese written language). Our general manager was a gentleman named Suita-san. I visited the team in Tokyo often and spoke to Suita-san at least weekly and often more frequently. Having experienced Japan before, I was attuned to Japanese culture and the norms of doing business with Japanese teams and executives.

You have started to experience some of this at your martial arts classes—bowing, formality, respect, honesty, keeping one's word in everything you did, and most importantly always ensuring that everyone was given the opportunity to "save face" in all interactions, both personally and in business dealings. Suita-san was used to dealing with a lot of Americans who did not try to understand the Japanese culture or work with the team on their terms. Initially, our interactions were quite formal with Suita-san feeling obligated to "entertain" me during the evenings by taking me to Western-style restaurants.

I felt quite comfortable at Japanese restaurants and quickly told him that although I greatly appreciated his taking me to western restaurants, I would really like to join him for dinner at restaurants that he would go to with his friends and family. I am not sure if he had ever been asked that before. He loved it. We became close friends as well as colleagues. I always enjoyed our time together. I was informed a few years ago that he passed away suddenly from a heart attack while he was on business travel. That saddened me greatly, and I will always have a warm feeling for the time we spent together and the opportunity to truly experience the Japanese culture with a gentleman that still I admire today. Thank you, Suita-san, for your fellowship and friendship.

INDIA

The most memorable part of my visit was the day I met with the head of HR for the Tata Group at Bombay House, their world headquarters in the middle of Mumbai.

During the late 2010s, Bersin & Associates had established a close working relationship with Accenture, a management consulting firm with a very large global presence. I was leading Bersin's advisory services work along with several other parts of the business. Accenture was planning a major push in India to establish their brand in human capital management and talent development and asked us to support them as a subject matter expert in business forums, at a conference, in press interviews, and in one-on-one meetings in New Delhi, Chennai, and Mumbai. Having never been to India, I immediately volunteered to support them and worked to plan all the activities needed to make the two weeks in India as impactful as possible.

This was definitely a working trip with business sessions, forums, conferences and meetings and little time for sightseeing. We did have business dinners each evening, and I did get a chance to interact with hundreds of business leaders. Additionally, traveling from one venue to another gave me the opportunity to see the drastic differences in the culture and environment that make up modern India—ultra-modern buildings, interspersed with Colonial-era buildings, streets with Mercedes Benz, buses, tuk-tuks, and cattle-drawn carts all competing for space on roads of various states of development, upgrading and repair. You could easily tell that this country had a lot of people, more than a billion at that point, and was growing everywhere you looked. I have one quick aside to share with you. The day I flew from New Delhi to Chennai was the same day they opened their new, ultramodern airport in New Delhi. So, I arrived days before at one international airport (the old one) and flew out of the brand new one.

My last stop in India was in Mumbai to support a conversation with the head of Human Resources for the Tata Group with two colleagues from Accenture. This was special because it would take place at Tata's historic headquarters, the Bombay House. The Bombay House, built in 1924 during the colonial period, is a four-story building that screams the history of the 1920s when Sir Dorabji Tata oversaw the building of the structure and the focused expansion of the Tata Group. Our discussions went very well with the head of HR of the entire company and left me with a new-found realization of the power of the Indian people and the degree to which they would continue to be a major driving force in the increasingly interconnected global economy.

ENGLAND

Having visited England over a dozen times—mostly to London—I have seen almost all the sites that most people see when they come to this great city including attending the theater in the West End, eating at numerous ethnic restaurants (the Indian food is possibly the best in the world on Brick Lane), and actually getting into Buckingham Palace for a tour when the queen was

After 400 years, Shakespeare's Globe Theatre was rebuilt on the bank of the Thames River. We saw Antony and Cleopatra there as it would have been played in the 1600s.

out of town during her August holiday. With that said, the best thing that I did took place in 1999 when your mom, grandmother and I were there on an extended vacation in London. We attended a performance of Antony and Cleopatra as it would have been performed 400 years ago.

The cast was all male (including Cleopatra), bawdy (not in the highbrow manner Shakespeare's plays are delivered to us today), and in a setting that is fitting of Elizabethan England—in an open-air theater on the Thames.

The theater had just opened in 1997. So, we were fortunate to catch a play in their third season. We sat on the second level to the left of the stage and had an incredible view of the performance. There were over 500 members of the audience standing in front of the stage. They were referred to as the "groundlings." Historically, "groundlings" would be the poor who paid a penny to stand in the "pit" in front of the stage and in front of the Queen's Box. By the way, as you can guess, the "groundlings" paid more than a penny to enjoy the performance in 1999. Since the play was performed for such a wide spectrum of society, it needed to be funny, bawdy, risqué with multiple double entendre and meanings for everyone from the peasant to the royalty to enjoy. Wow, the performance was so far over the top and enjoyable that I can almost not attend another performance of Shakespeare without thinking about how it should really be performed—as written and directed by the Bard himself—in the early 1600s.

Twenty years later, in October 2019, London felt a little different. Laci and I arrived in London for a few days before we planned to board an 11-night cruise to Portugal, Spain and the Canaries. Most of the city was shut down due to a massive Climate Change protest. Most of the streets around central London and the bridges across the Thames were closed. People were camping on the streets, and it was almost impossible to get anywhere other than on foot. Almost all the historic sites were closed or had restricted access. We spent most of the time mingling with the crowds who were peacefully protesting against government policy on environmental and climate issues. We actually felt quite at home. We never expected to have this experience but walked away from the three days in London with a renewed appreciation for the power and value of protest. This was a nice way to complete an understanding of what this great city has to offer a visitor.

RUSSIA

In the early 1990s, National Patent Development Corporation (NPDC), the then owner of GP, was committed to the expansion of GP globally. NPDC had always been focused in this regard, especially in new markets including China and Russia. When Russia came on their radar screen for GP, I had the opportunity to represent the company's leadership in meetings there. This was shortly after Gorbachev's resignation, Yeltsin's rise to power, the dissolution of the Soviet Union, and the transition to what we know today as Russia. Needless to say, Russia (at that point) felt like the wild west with numerous factions and people vying for power and money. In addition to all the meetings, one of which was in the Kremlin, I spent time with Russian colleagues of NPDC, in business and science, and got to see the changes going on in the Russian society up close. As usual, once you were past all the politics, the people were all friendly, interesting, and loved to drink their Vodka. Working in Russia was an entirely different matter, especially for GP. Navigating the corruption, barriers to entry, and the bureaucracy would have been almost impossible for a technical services company doing consulting projects, and GP would do very little work in Russia in the 1990s which was actually my specific recommendation.

MEXICO

Over more than 30 years, I have visited Mexico multiple times. I have traveled there by cruise ship. I have stayed for one week and for multiple weeks at several of the timeshares in the programs I

The timeshare on the Playa La Ropa had no elevators, no glass windows, outdoor showers, outdoor eating areas, hammocks, and a feeling like no one was there but you.

participate. I have stayed on both the Caribbean and Pacific coasts. All of them have been terrific. I always have a great time and partake in the wonderful food and interact with the wonderful people. I have experienced whale watching, zip lining through the jungle, visiting ruins, and everything this great country has to offer. The most beautiful of these places is probably somewhere you may have never heard of. It is called Zihuatanejo, and it is in Guerrero on the Mexican Pacific Coast. Maybe you have heard it mentioned in a famous movie called the Shawshank Redemption. The two main characters (prisoners at the Shawshank Penitentiary) talked about this town as part of their dream after leaving prison. In the movie, you never saw the beach or the town itself. Even at the end of the movie (spoiler alert), the beach was in the Virgin Islands. Andy Dufresne, one of the main characters, says "Zihuatanejo. It's a little place in Mexico on the Pacific Ocean. Do you know what the Mexicans say about the Pacific? They say it has no memory. That's where I want to live the rest of my life—a warm place with no memory." That was how I felt every time I was there.

Over a period of around 15 years, I was able to spend multiple weeks enjoying Zihuatanejo with Laci, your mom, your grandmother, and friends. The small fishing village (fishing boats would bring in their catch into the docks in the morning, and we would be enjoying the fish for lunch and dinner), the restaurants right on the beach next to the condo (you could sit at a table on the beach and watch the tide come in at your feet—yes, right at your feet—you could expect to have your feet get wet while eating dinner—so, no shoes please), and the charm of Mexico and the Mexican people were all around us.

One morning, Laci and I walked into town for breakfast at a small coffee shop that we routinely visited, and to our surprise, a Mexican film crew and a group of actors were there for a shoot in the market right in front of us. We were literally in the middle of the filming—totally surreal. The fishing boats were coming and going, dropping off their catch, people milling about in the shops and restaurants, and cameras, sound equipment, directors, actors, support crew and everything else needed to film a scene were all mixed together, including us. Zihuatanejo was definitely a lovely, warm Mexican village. I am also sure it has no memory of us, but I have nothing but fond memories of it. I can tell you lots of additional stories about this incredible country and this "little place in Mexico on the Pacific Ocean."

ITALY

I have never had the opportunity to work in Italy but have visited as often as I could. The thousands of years of history, beautiful countryside, incredible things to do and see, and the people (my and your heritage) made this a go-to vacation on multiple occasions. Although I do love all the places that I have been in Italy (including Rome, Pisa, Cinque Terre, Naples, and Pompei), my favorites are Florence (for its history and art) and Tuscany (for its beautiful hill towns and amazing red wine). We visited Siena,

The hill towns in Tuscany all have very narrow streets and lots and lots of shops, restaurants, wineries and wine tasting. The most interesting part is visiting the barrel rooms which are located at multiple levels under the street.

Montepulciano, Montalcino, and numerous others on wine-tasting visits and fell in love with the Tuscan countryside, the historic Renaissance hill towns, and the Sangiovese wine.

One of my favorite things to do is to visit the wineries in these towns and then go under the street level to the barrel rooms with the maturing wine in row after row of oak casks. The scent of the maturing wine is still chiseled in my brain. Every time I go into a barrel room at any winery, I am immediately transported back to Tuscany and the fantastic experience of being there where most of today's best red wine varietals originated.

SPAIN

The art and architecture of Gaudi is unmistakable. It is so original. Once you see it, you will immediately recognize his work (or the work of those who have adopted the Gaudi style).

I only worked in Spain one time but have visited it many times on vacation. Like India, while I was at Bersin, Accenture sponsored me to chair a panel discussion at a conference in Barcelona in the early 2010s. I had been to Barcelona before, and there was really nothing memorable about the business trip—just one more fly in, work, and fly home.

I love Barcelona, though. I have been there for multiple extended stays with both your grandmother, and after my divorce from her, with Laci. Barcelona is a lovely Mediterranean city with incredible beaches, art, architecture, history, delicious food, wonderful people, and Antoni Gaudi, the greatest exponent of Catalan Modernism. His architectural and artistic touch is seen everywhere in the city. It is so different from any other architectural style that once you have seen it, you just want to see more. We have visited numerous locations where his architecture overwhelms you including La Sagrada Familia, the lampposts at Placia Real and Pla del Palau, Casa Batllo, Palau Guell. Oh my! Park Guell is beautiful. I would definitely live there or in any of the other buildings that he designed before his untimely death (he was run over by a trolley) around 100 years ago. Gaudi is an original and helps to make Barcelona one of the best places to visit in the world.

TURKEY

In 2008, your grandmother and I took an 11-day cruise to the eastern Mediterranean out of Rome. Although the entire cruise was filled with highlights including two days in Istanbul, one stop was particularly memorable, a day in Ephesus.

You probably never heard of Ephesus, the second largest city of the Roman Empire, and probably one of the best-preserved ruins from the ancient world.

Ephesus was one of the largest and most important cities in the ancient world. Located on the west coast of Turkey on the Aegean Sea, it had paved streets, large squares, beautiful homes with frescos and mosaic tile floors, a coliseum, a library, a forum, baths, eating stalls, and all the trappings of one of the most powerful Greek and Roman cities in the world. The ruins were recently excavated after being buried for more than a thousand years. Having visited Rome (the Forum), Athens (the Acropolis), and Pompei, Ephesus puts them all to shame. This is a site that should not be missed. We spent the day walking through the city only a portion of which was then excavated and made available to the public. The homes and buildings could have all been lived in by any of us when they were first constructed if we were rich and powerful enough at that time. For 2,000 years ago, they were ultramodern.

PANAMA

Laci and I booked a one-day, small-boat tour on the Panama Canal allowing us to be right next to the ships transiting from the Atlantic and Pacific Oceans. The highlight was feeding the "wild" monkeys!

In May 2015, Laci and I decided to get away on a trip to a place that neither of us had been to before. We had been talking about different options for a while and one of us said "how about Panama?" I said great and booked a flight to Panama City and made a reservation for seven days at the new Waldorf Astoria. Panama City was a joy. It was totally walkable with a very modern center-city and was adjacent to the Pacific Ocean and oceanfront—walkways and great restaurants. The people were incredibly friendly. The Panama Canal and the Miraflores Locks and Casco Viejo (old Panama City) were nearby, too. We took advantage of it all. Our highlight was the time we spent at the Locks watching the ships transiting. The process was amazing and probably far exceeds actually being on a cruise ship going through the locks. We were able to watch multiple ships enter and be raised or lowered to adjust for the differences in sea level between the Atlantic and Pacific Oceans and the numerous lakes in Panama between the two oceans.

That was not the best part of our visit to the canal. We booked a small-boat tour on the canal itself. We were right up next to the cargo ships in the lakes adjacent to the Locks visiting a jungle island populated by wild monkeys. They were obviously waiting for us! On multiple approaches to the island, the monkeys (including the babies) jumped onto the boat and were hand-fed by us. That was a wow experience. It was totally amazing!

AUSTRALIA

When I was with RWD, I led the establishment of SAP Learning Solutions, a joint venture with SAP, that was headquartered in Singapore. This allowed me to visit Australia and New Zealand multiple times with extended stays in Sydney (where our office and team were primarily located), Brisbane, Melbourne, Canberra and Auckland. Since the majority of our team were Australians, I was again able to get immersed in the culture and really get to know the people. As usual, I enjoyed everything about the opportunity and experience. I will end this chapter with one funny story that I recently shared with folks that I have known for 20 years and who actually took part in this little adventure—another example of my curious life.

On one of my trips in the early 2000s to Sydney to visit our folks, we decided to do a team-building exercise: a fun day sailing on Sydney Harbor—a little sun, a little wine, some great food, and lots of camaraderie. A yacht was rented for the day. It had a white hull, white decking, white leather seats. It was just gorgeous. We brought on lots of food and a nice supply of white and red wine. Two of our team were experienced sailors (not me). With their leadership, we were off for a fun day in Sydney Harbor.

We were cruising through the harbor. We were all having a great time. Then, someone suddenly yelled "watch out!" The light-house in the middle of the harbor passed us by a couple of feet. Well, we actually passed it by, but it felt like the lighthouse just jumped out from nowhere. Whew—good thing we missed it. We continued with the day all having a great time. Then, it was time to get back to the dock to turn the boat in. It looked like we might be a few minutes late. In our haste to get back, we evidently cut the corner a bit close on a rocky outcrop in the harbor. In an instant, we were on the rocks. That boat pitched over. Food, white wine, and more red wine than I thought existed on earth were all over the cockpit. Yes, you remember. The white leather interior, the white seats, the white deck, the white everything were all covered in red wine.

I am not sure I have told you, but I do not swim! (Although the Navy did make a valiant try to teach me when I was at the Officer Indoctrination School in Newport, RI, they were way more interested in my ability to teach physics than my ability to swim across a pool). No ability to swim was not a problem since, at that point, we were in only a few inches of water—since, of course we were on the rocks. Once I was told that and everyone had a good laugh, we got into action to try to get the boat off the rocks (by this time, we had attracted the attention of lots of other folks in their boats trying to help pull us off the rocks). That accomplished, we now needed to clean up the mess that was created by the boat being on its side—rolls and rolls of paper towels and all of us washing down the seats and deck and bagging the food, bottles and every-thing else was our focus for the time we had between the rocks and the marina where we would return the boat. During this tran-sit, we noticed that the bilge was wet, and yes, we were taking on water and had damaged the hull. We were able to get the boat back, almost all cleaned, a bit worse for wear and a story that we have been telling for 20 years. By the way, it was probably the best team-building exercise I have had in my entire career.

SIXTEEN

Let's Talk About Politics

> "And what sort of lives do these people, who pose as being moral, lead themselves? My dear fellow, you forget that we are in the native land of the hypocrite."
>
> —*The Picture of Dorian Gray by Oscar Wilde*

DISCLAIMER!

MY DEAR GRANDCHILDREN, these next two chapters focus on politics and religion. It's often said those topics should be avoided in polite conversation, but that ship has sailed. Plus, this is my book, so I refuse to pull my punches. Throughout my career, I often have had to bite my tongue or hold my nose. I know people look at me and make assumptions about what I must think and believe, but in these next chapters, I'm simply going to let it rip. You probably haven't seen this side of Grandpa before, and you probably won't be ready for these chapters for several years. Hopefully, by the time you do read these chapters, the human species will have evolved to a kinder, wiser place. I won't hold my breath, though, and I offer these broadsides as a way to prepare yourself for the onslaught of lies and falsehoods in both realms.

My first awareness of "politics" was probably when I was in first or second grade. I knew that our president was Dwight D. Eisenhower. I knew he had established NASA and the whole space program which was a very big deal to me as a 7 or 8-year-old. I am sure that I did not get the whole Republican-Democrat thing but shortly would with the 1960 election cycle and the Nixon-Kennedy fight for the presidency. I was in fourth grade and was definitely paying attention especially since my dad loved Richard Nixon and was always talking about him and the election. He hated John Kennedy. So, it begins.

John Kennedy won the election. The Republicans, especially the conservative branch of the party, leaned more conservative. My dad, your great grandfather, started to read more books from the far-right John Birch Society as well as a host of arch-conservative pundits and leaders. By the way, in the early 1960s, the Republican and Democratic parties each had liberal and conservative branches of the party and associated leaders who leaned right and left. As you know the parties now, the Republicans lean almost exclusively conservative, and the Democrats lean liberal with a number of centrists still in the Democratic party. So, getting back to my dad, he gave me very conservative books to read and was always talking about how bad the Kennedy administration was and that we would be so much better with Nixon and the Republican party leading the country. He was also an antisemite, a bigot and a racist. The home conversation was filled with derogatory comments about these people, and the use of racial slurs was rampant in our home.

Interestingly, in school, I was exposed to different thinking. I was starting to be taught about our government in 5th, 6th, and 7th grades. Since John Kennedy was our president, he, his family, his history and his politics were everywhere. I liked him a lot more than Nixon on a visceral level and gravitated to wanting to learn more about him and his politics. He was inaugurated on January 20, 1961 when I was 9 years old and in 4th grade. I can remember his inaugural address. In fact, I probably memorized sections of the address and recited it in class: "We observe today not a victory of a party, but a celebration of freedom—symbolizing an end, as well as a beginning—signifying renewal, as well as change." Then, at the end of his address, he presented a challenge to us—to the next generation. It went like this: "And so, my fellow Americans: ask not what your country can do for you—ask what you can do for your country. My fellow citizens of the world, ask not what America will do for you, but what together we can do for the freedom of man." Yes, I was sold, and I got it. So, who was this guy?

Robert Donovan wrote PT 109—John F. Kennedy in World War II. I remember reading the first edition in paperback in 1962.

I tried to learn about John Kennedy. In 1962, I read *PT 109* about his time as a Naval officer in World War II (WW II). It was inspiring to a 10-year-old. I think I started to contrast what I was seeing with John Kennedy, his history, and his administration's activities with what I heard at home from my father and the books that he was giving me to read. Wow—there was a real difference, and it forced me to start thinking on my own and asking what actually made sense—a pretty heady task for a little kid.

One additional politician who is worth mentioning at this point is Jacob Koppel Javits, our New York senator from 1957 to 1981. He was Jewish, born in New York City in 1904, a Republican, a Liberal, and a WW II veteran. I was becoming aware of politics and our society in the late 1950s and early 1960s, and he was the senator that I routinely saw as our NY representative in Congress. He was a supporter of labor unions, the Great Society, and civil rights, and played a key role in passing civil rights legislation. He was also an opponent of the war in Vietnam. I liked Jacob Javits. He was also not my father's Republican far-right conservative.

The Civil Rights Movement was raging across the country, and Dr. Martin Luther King, Jr. (MLK) was the clear leader in the movement. His March on Washington and the "I Have a Dream" speech on August 28, 1963 at the Lincoln Memorial set the tone for our generation. I thought the speech was incredible. My dad thought it was horrible. I was definitely a liberal and believer in civil rights for all. My dad was definitely a racist and a "zero-sum game" guy. If the Blacks were going to gain rights, he was going to lose his rights. It is amazing how little has changed in this country over all these years. This is so sad.

In 1963, when I was in 7th grade, I was elected by my class to the Student Council and started to learn a lot more about how government worked. The world changed on Friday, November 22, 1963 at 1:30 PM ET. John F. Kennedy was assassinated in Dallas, TX while in a motorcade passing through Dealey Plaza. I was 12 years old. I had just started to participate in the Student Council meetings. The principal came on the public address system in my middle school and told the school that the president had been killed. Our teachers were all crying. Some of the kids were crying. We were told the school day would end early. The buses would be here shortly to pick us up and take us home. We were all devastated.

This is a picture of JFK's original gravesite in Arlington Cemetery in 1964.

The buses showed up, and we got on board and were dropped off at our usual bus stops near our homes. I got home, and to my surprise, my mother was in tears and totally beside herself. I thought that she and my father would be happy. They hated John Kennedy, his administration the Democrats, and everything they stood for. I was so confused. The whole country was confused, scared, outraged, and very, very sad. I can remember seeing Walter Cronkite on the news talking about what had happened and followed every update that day, for the next few days and during the weeks that followed. Lyndon B. Johnson (LBJ), as vice president, immediately assumed the presidency. The assassin was captured and then was assassinated himself. The funeral and the burial at Arlington Cemetery were televised live. Everything in my very young life seemed to be different after that. One thing did not change. My dad was still an arch conservative.

1964 was a presidential election year. LBJ was running now for re-election, and one of the leading candidates was Senator Barry Goldwater from Arizona. My dad took me to several rallies where the teachings of Phyllis Schlafly and other John Birch Society members were addressed. I was also taken to one rally at which Barry Goldwater spoke. I was definitely taking it all in and starting to understand the differences between liberal and conservative and Democrat and Republican. Wow, it was really complicated. LBJ, with deep roots in Texas, won the election by a landslide and went on to put in place some of the most progressive programs in the history of the United States. Remember, it was all mixed up at that time including differences between how the parties worked in the North and the South. It was also the year that the Student Council took all the council members, around 50 of us, to Washington, D.C. for a week to see, firsthand, our federal government. It was my first time away from home without my parents.

The trip to Washington was by bus. We stayed in a cheap hotel on New York Avenue just outside of downtown with four kids to a room. We really had a busy schedule. First, we got to Jacob Javits' office in the Senate Office Building. He gave us a copy of Kennedy's 1961 inaugural address. Then, we toured the Capital. Next, we went to the White House and the Smithsonian Museum and the National Archives. Finally, we had a multitude of other stops including the Washington Monument and Jefferson and Lincoln Memorials.

This is a picture of July 4, 1970 on the Mall in Washington, D.C. for Nixon's Honor America Day at the height of the anti-war protests and the conservatives' silent majority. It turned out that, in fact, they were the vast silent majority! This collage was captured from photos from the various photographers.

One of the most memorable stops was at the original Kennedy gravesite at Arlington Cemetery. It was surrounded by a low, white picket fence. The experience was stark, solemn, sad, and very quiet. Looking back on these few days in Washington, along with my dad's attempts in 1964 to get me to be a far-right conservative, my thinking as a liberal and more open-minded person was solidified. Remember that the Southern Democrats were chiefly conservatives and anti-civil rights for African Americans. From 1963 to 1968, MLK and the Civil Rights Movement were continually in the news, and the country was confronted with the injustices that were rampant: opposition to integration, segregation, protests, riots, the lynching of Blacks, the KKK, and a myriad of other horrors that were in the newspapers and on the evening news. Add to that the growing commitment of the government to fighting the war in Vietnam and the whole atmosphere was crazy. The poor whites and minorities bore the burden of fighting the war. On April 4, 1968, the unthinkable happened again. Martin Luther King, Jr. was assassinated in Memphis, TN. As a junior in high school, this was crushing. The country felt like it was completely coming apart. It actually was about to get much, much worse.

Since the Republicans and Democrats still had Northern liberal and Southern conservative wings, it was not until the run-up to the 1968 presidential election that I steered solidly towards the Democrats chiefly because I was supporting Robert F. Kennedy's candidacy for President even though I was too young to vote. Bobby Kennedy was a New York Senator. He was young, energetic, an advocate for civil rights and was the leading candidate to run for president in 1968. He probably would have won the election. However, around midnight on June 5th, right after winning the California primary, he was assassinated. The news struck all of us like a thunderbolt. I was 16 years old just finishing my junior year in high school and barely recovering from MLK's assassination, and this happened. The country exploded with back-to-back assassinations. MLK and RFK were both dead. The Democratic Convention, held in Chicago from August 26 to 29, was broadcast live and devolved into a full-scale police riot on Michigan Avenue against the antiwar protestors who chanted "The whole world is watching." I was glued to the TV set and saw it all. The Democratic party fell apart. LBJ and Mayor Daley sold us out. Hubert H. Humphrey (HHH) was nominated. The peace plank was defeated. 1968 was going to be the worst year in my life. Richard Nixon was nominated as the Republican candidate for president and defeated HHH in November. So, the Vietnam War was set to rage on, and Civil Rights would continue to be a challenge for our country. Nixon was inaugurated in January 1969 with the words "We cannot learn from one another until we stop shouting at one another, until we speak quietly enough so that our words can be heard as well as our voices." Okay, good thought, but you need to be willing to allow the opposition to speak. I, for one, hated Nixon.

Soon after I graduated from high school in 1969, I was a full-fledged hippy—including long hair and a beard. I marched in anti-war protests in New York City and participated in the Moratorium to End the War in Vietnam in October 1969 which was a peaceful mass action to end American involvement in the Vietnam War. This followed Nixon's first year in office in which there were 10,000 soldiers killed in action. The majority were young draftees. This was the beginning of the pressure the young kids brought on the administration to stop the war—lots of marches, strikes, protests and anything we could do to have our voices heard. The Spring of 1970—my freshman year in college—went crazy with the killing of students at Kent State and the shutdown of colleges and universities across the U.S. including Hunter College.

My brother, a friend, and I participated in a major protest in Washington, D.C. on the 4th of July 1970. Nixon invited Conservative Republicans to D.C. for an "Honor America Day" to counter all the anti-war protests that were going on. Lots of Conservatives showed up but also lots of hippies to protest the war. Initially, they were separated; but, by nightfall, there was about 350,000 people gathered near the Washington Monument for the celebration including us. The police decided to break up the pro-testers and started to fire tear gas into the crowd. You can guess what happened. The police were not too accurate, and the wind direction changed. Everyone including, Conservative moms, dads, kids, hippy freaks, my brother, our friend, and me were all gassed. It was pandemonium. That is when I learned the key metric as to whether you were getting the attention of the people in power: Could you smell the tear gas?

I have one additional note to share with you. You may have seen the decorations that are used to celebrate the 4th of July including bunting all over and lots and lots of flags on lights posts all over the city. Well, we noticed one light post across the street from the White House with three flags and lots of bunting. We decided we needed to have those flags. I climbed up the light post and tossed the flags down to my brother. That flag hung upside down in my bedroom until the war ended. In case you didn't know, an upside-down flag is displayed on a ship to indicate it is in dis-tress. In this case, the ship of State was in distress under Nixon. By the way, I still have the flag if you want to see it. It flew across the street from the White House on the 4th of July in 1970. It is none the worse from a little tear gas wear and tear.

I have one more thing to tell you. We hippies had no money. So, the cheapest way to get from New York to Washington that day was on a bus chartered by the conservative group led by James Buckley. What? You gotta be kidding me. Yes, we rode down and back on the Buckley bus. They were skeptical when we came down to D.C. in the morning, and we definitely got some rude remarks on the way back to New York. That is the way it goes. We had our flags, smelled of tear gas, and got the cheap bus fare provided by the "Honor America" dudes. The Libs owned the Conservatives that day even if they did not know it. Nice!

The war continued. Our boys, most of whom were draftees, continued to be killed and maimed by the thousands. The Vietnamese, Cambodian and Laotian men, women and children were killed and maimed by the thousands. We continued to protest, march, strike and tried to get our voices heard as Nixon requested on the day he became president. The politicians lied to us on a continual basis with the Nixon Administration unwilling to end the war. The evening news programs started to show the body bags that were being returned to the U.S. from the war, and a reporting was provided routinely by folks like Walter Cronkite to the public on the number of dead and wounded Americans as a result of the war. The stories of atrocities became routine, and the pain inflicted on the country became unbearable. In 1972, Nixon ran for re-election based on a great economy and his foreign affairs successes against the Democrat George McGovern who ran on ending the Vietnam War and several progressive social programs. Nixon easily won. Actually, it resulted in a 520 to 17 electoral college vote—a complete blowout. Nixon carried 49 states. I was very, very disillusioned with politics and the ability to make a difference. I am sure you can guess—my dad was elated.

I have been a Liberal Democrat ever since never wavering for a moment. The Democrats ultimately became almost 100% liberal or centrist, and the Republicans became almost 100% conservative. Today, we have become a very polarized country.

In fact, it turned out that Nixon, his vice president, and most of his administration were totally and utterly corrupt. He cheated during the election and was found out. Senate hearings were held to address the "Watergate Scandal," and all of us were glued to the black-and-white TV in the physics majors' lounge at Hunter College (room 1313) between classes. The gavel-to-gavel coverage was the most amazing thing I could imagine. Nixon resigned in disgrace on August 9, 1974, and Gerald Ford assumed the presidency. That might have been the best day in politics for all of us who opposed Nixon and everything that he stood for—that S.O.B. got what he deserved. Well, maybe not. He should have gone to jail, but Gerald Ford, our new president decided to pardon him so he would not stand trial to face all his crimes. Ugh. On April 30, 1975, the North Vietnamese drove their tanks through the gates of the presidential palace in Saigon, and the war ended. It was ended because we lost the war. The protests and the anti-war movement had little effect on the outcome. It was a total and utter political disaster.

Our troops did what they were asked to do by their corrupt political leaders. They should have returned as heroes but were vilified for their actions in the war. Tens and tens of thousands were dead, maimed for life, addicted to drugs, and psychologically damaged. We destroyed hundreds of cities, towns, and villages and hundreds of thousands of lives of the Vietnamese, Cambodians and Laotians were lost. And for what? Nothing, really. This was a war to stop the Communist Chinese. My guess is that there might have been a few other things that we could have done that might have had a different, more positive outcome; but, history is played in only one direction, and once lived, it needs to be learned from and placed behind us.

I have now visited the Vietnam Memorial a number of times on the mall in Washington. I cry every time. The military should never be used to satisfy the desire to demonstrate the power of a political leader. The military as a deterrent is what we should focus on and not as a tool of a politician to wage a war of aggression on a mythical enemy. Unfortunately, we have seen a number of horrible examples with the worst of these being the two wars of George W. Bush—Afghanistan and Iraq. I vocally and vehemently opposed both wars. The same corruption, misinformation, lies, atrocities, and disastrous decisions that took place in the Nixon administration also took place in the Bush administration.

Over the years, I have supported a number of causes donating my money and time to try to make a difference. One in particular is important to note. On March 30, 1981, two months after he was inaugurated as president, Ronald Reagan was shot and wounded in an attempted assassination. The White House press secretary, James Brady, was also shot and severely wounded. I have been a gun control advocate for my entire adult life and have never fired a gun (yes, I was in the military for 13 years). Please listen to Harry Chapin's song "Sniper," written in the early 1970s. It says a lot about what I learned and believed in during my early 20s. Nothing, and I mean nothing, has really changed since then other than the exponential increase in the carnage in this country from gun violence.

With the attempted assassination of Reagan, the country started to coalesce around the idea that handguns, and especially rifles and assault rifles, should be much more strictly regulated and controlled. This manifested itself around James Brady as a person. An organization formed in 1974 as the National Council to Control Handguns, also known as the Brady Campaign to Prevent Gun Violence and Brady: United Against Gun Violence. I actively supported them contributing money and time to the cause. By 1994, we achieved a major success in the passing of the Public Safety and Recreational Firearms Use Protection Act which essentially banned assault weapons. The nation had come to its senses and started to realize that gun safety was a real thing and that all of us could benefit from this regulation.

Unfortunately, it had a 10-year renewal life, and in 2004, under the George W. Bush administration, the ban was not renewed, and the real start to the insanity and mayhem that we experience today began. Thank you, "W," for your personal religiosity and your caring administration. This is another reason why I believe the George W. Bush administration was the worst in American history. Destroying our economy was the cherry on the top of the disaster of his eight years in office.

I would like to give you one thought that you can use as an argument for those who tout "Second Amendment Rights" above all other rights that we, as Americans, enjoy in this great country. The "second amendment rights" folks, mostly white men, have won. The gun lobby has won. The NRA has won. The gun manufacturers have won. The compromised or feckless politicians have won.

The gun lovers and zealous gun owners have won. Yes, they have all gotten their way. America now has more than 400 million guns in this country including tens of millions of weapons of war in the hands of everyone who wants one. Now, for my point. All of these folks need to now own their "victory" and the results it brings to us: the annual and continuing carnage that we experience every day, the collateral damage resulting from tens of thousands of innocents killed, maimed, and otherwise affected by gun violence. Just think about a football stadium on January 1 filled with 60 or 70 thousand happy fans—women, men, children, babies, whites, blacks, Asians, Hispanics, old and young—happy, cheering, laughing, singing, just having a great time together. Now, think about that same stadium on December 31, with everyone dead, ripped apart by bullets, blood everywhere, or wounded and maimed and screaming for help. This is what the "second amendment rights" folks and all of those who allowed this to happen need to own. I will leave it here for now, but you will hear it from me again when we have an opportunity to chat in more detail.

I have one more thought about W. W is a devout Christian. We also know what he did—the untruths, the deceptions, the lies, the actions and the inactions. He was responsible for hundreds of thousands of unnecessary deaths in Afghanistan and Iraq. He was the cause of hundreds of thousands of unnecessary gun deaths in this country since 2004. He was responsible for a multitude of unchristian actions and activities across this country during and since his presidency. He knows he will be judged for all his sins by his God after he dies. I am sure that his God is saving a special place in Hell for him. W must be scared to death at night when he has the opportunity to think about his eternal soul and the suffering that is in store for him.

Luckily, he will have lots of company there. I do not fear death and sleep well—like a baby—knowing that I have tried to live a good life but, in fact, there is nothing for us after death. So, W has nothing to worry about—no heaven, no hell, no gods, no devils, no angels, no Jesus, no eternal reward, no eternal punishment—just all of us together in this world trying to live our lives in peace. How about we focus on that? I feel good thinking that W might be worried about what will become of his eternal soul when he dies.

So, let's go back to gun control. I continued to support Brady and really, really hoped for a different outcome, but no, the gun lobby, the corrupt politicians, and the feckless Democrats let it all slip away. By around 2018, when the Brady Campaign and several other gun control organizations called me for my annual contribution, I said no. You lost. Give it up. Put your money somewhere else. I never contributed another dime to this lost cause. I still vote for anti-gun candidates in attempt to get control and the Congress to try to enact laws that will finally end this madness—our only option. When you are old enough, you will need to vote, vote, vote as every vote counts.

We especially saw the value of every vote in 2016. By 2016, I thought I had seen everything in politics, religion, and governing in the U.S. I was wrong; Trump happened. His election in November of 2016 confirmed all my worst fears about what this country had become. Although he lost the popular vote, the Electoral College provided him the edge he needed to be elected president. Worst of all, more than 60 million of my fellow Americans voted for him including some of my best friends. One of my longest friendships, of more than 40 years, did not survive this election.

I felt this election brought out the worst of our society's racist, misogynistic, sexist, antisemitic, anti-democratic, dogmatic, hypocritical, anti-woman's rights, and religious-right-focused underlying tendencies. Nothing was off the table. Everything was fine if Trump said it. In addition, integrity, truth-telling, keeping one's word, and living up to high "moral" values were cast into the gutter. From day one, to be part of the new Administration and Trump's Republican party, the cost of entry included compromising one's integrity and values as well as outright lying.

The next four years, including the next presidential election cycle, were a nightmare. Tens and tens of millions of my fellow Americans loved this guy, what he said and did, and his Administration's policies and actions. The economy, tax policies, the way more than half the population was treated, the response to a global pandemic, and almost everything else was a disaster in my mind. Then, there was that "little" issue about the peaceful transfer of power when Trump lost the election to Joe Biden. Wow, Trump was the most anti-democratic, dictator-wannabe that I could ever imagine. Then, there was January 6 and the Trump mob. Was this really the United States of America? Yes, it sure was. It was all Trump and his over 70 million supporters who still think he won. It is a cult of personality, and almost all the Republican party has bought in to this guy as their leader. It is not over. It is just the beginning of a major inflection point that will determine the future of the American "experiment" which I fear will not end well for a large portion of our fellow inhabitants of the U.S.

One last thought before I get off my soapbox. I know you are thinking that I am just your crazy grandpa railing at the Thanksgiving dinner table. Maybe I am. Sorry. Let's go back to that one last thought. I was a very early supporter of Barack Hussein Obama including as an early contributor to his campaigns. In fact, when I was living in San Diego, he spoke at a Democratic gathering at the Convention Center. He was a Senator from Illinois at that time. Your grandmother and I were there to support his candidacy for the presidency even though he had not yet declared his candidacy. We got to shake his hand and tell him how much we wanted him to run. Now, that was thrilling. Could it even be possible that this man could run to be the President of the United States and win? Yes, yes, yes. He did. I still think he was one of the greatest presidents we have ever had and am so proud to have been a supporter of him from the very beginning. I would get to see him a number of times in person over his two campaigns for the presidency—always inspiring.

As a closing, here are some of the causes I now support. I hope this will help you understand who I am now and—for the most part—who I have always been:

> *Sierra Club*—Life Member, Wilderness Guardian, member of the *Sequoia Circle* for the preservation of our planet for future generations

> *Secular Coalition for America*—Lifetime Member and supporter for the separation of government and religion

> *Emily's List*—Member and monthly supporter for women's rights and getting Democratic women elected to office

> *Union of Concerned Scientists*—Member and monthly supporter to use science to solve our planet's most pressing problems

> *The Planetary Society*—Member and supporter to help increase awareness and curiosity for the exploration of our solar system and beyond

> *314 Action*—Monthly supporter to get Democrats with STEM experience elected to office

> *VoteVets*—Monthly supporter to get ex-military officers and enlisted personnel elected to the Democratic office

Hunter College of the City of New York—Alumni and monthly supporter to ensure public higher education continues to be available to all individuals

University of Central Florida—Alumni and monthly supporter to ensure public higher education continues to be available to all individuals

SEVENTEEN

Let's Talk About Religion

"Frederick Douglass told in his Narrative how his condition as a slave became worse when his master underwent a religious conversion that allowed him to justify slavery as the punishment of the children of Ham. Mark Twain described his mother as a genuinely good person, whose soft heart pitied even Satan, but who had no doubt about the legitimacy of slavery, because in years living in antebellum Missouri, she had never heard any sermon opposing slavery, but only countless sermons preaching that slavery was God's will. With or without religion, good people can behave well and bad people can do evil; but for good people to do evil—that takes religion."

—*Steven Weinberg, American theoretical physicist and Nobel laureate*

I WAS RAISED as a Roman Catholic. My mother was a devout follower of the faith and took us to church every Sunday. Following our CCD training, indoctrination, and first communion, we went to "confession" on a routine basis to cleanse our souls and to allow us to take communion every Sunday. Confession was a very strange activity for me as a young child. We would go to our church, St. Killian, in Farmingdale on a day when mass was not being held. We would line up along the wall waiting to enter the confessional.

Upon entering and kneeling in the confessional, the priest would slide open a small door with a screen that hid him from view from me. I was required to say this: "Bless me, Father, for I have sinned. My last confession was two weeks ago (or whenever it was)." I now needed to tell the priest of my sins. I was nine or 10 years old and a pretty good kid. What sins? Would my sins be sufficient for absolution? What if I had not sinned since my last confession (which was usually the case)? Would he believe me? Would he ask me more questions? Wow. This was kind of nuts for a little kid.

So, I always made something up: "I had some bad thoughts," or "I disrespected my mother" or something like that. It always seemed to be sufficient. I got a little worthless advice, penance to do and was then asked to say an act of contrition—"My God, I am sorry for my sins with all my heart. In choosing to do wrong and failing to do good, I have sinned against you whom I should love above all things, etc." I would then hear the priest mumble his piece. I made the sign of the cross, left the confessional, said my penance, and left the church with my mom and brother. By the time I was 11 or 12 years old, I was sitting through CCD classes getting ready for my confirmation. I was definitely questioning what this was all about.

There was at least one unintended consequence of my mom taking us to confession. It actually taught us to be deceitful and lie to a priest, the representative of God. I had no sins to confess. I had to make up some sins so the priest would not question my honesty in the confessional. So, the result is that I was forced to lie. This was not the intended outcome. To me, as a nine or 10-year-old, looking back, this was the only outcome for all the innocent kids that are routinely asked to confess their sins.

You are being raised by your mom and dad to believe in the Golden Rule and have a strong set of values that are not based on any religion or religious dogma. That is very good. You, however, will come in contact with a large number of "believers" who may challenge you with their beliefs or try to force you to do things that conform to their dogma or religious values.

I am leaving this chapter for you to read when you are a little older and can truly understand what I learned early in my life about religion and its significant shortcomings in helping to guide our lives and life choices. It is my most pointed challenge to the core of today's thinking about religion, what is good and evil, dogma, values, principles, integrity, hypocrisy, what the Bible teaches us about Jehovah (the God of Abraham), and what makes for a true purpose and value-driven life.

Additionally, charlatans, pedophiles, and grifters use the Bible to get their way with a trusting population who is looking for guidance and leadership to support their journey through life. I am saddened when I think about all the bad decisions people make based on the teachings of these people. I am sure there is some good you might be able to point to and say, "What about that?" It is my position that the evil done in the name of God far outweighs the good. This is just my opinion, but I need to say it so my voice does not go unheard. I do not ever want you to believe I support or tacitly agree with the teachings contained in the Bible. I do not.

I believe I can distill my difficulty with religion into a simple equation:

> *Money + Politics + Power + Religion = extreme corruption + outrageous hypocrisy + unbelievable atrocities*

The Bible was brought into the mainstream of society by Constantine I, Emperor of Rome, in around 300 A.D. With more "powers" and hopes, he wanted a religion that would provide the Roman Empire with the required social order across all of its subjects. Until then, the Bible and Judeo-Christian beliefs along with a myriad of other pagan beliefs, were not universally accepted. They were chiefly embraced in pockets of the Middle East or in other regional populations. It was one among many shared stories, myths and legends about the gods. For example, the gods of the Roman Empire included Jupiter, Minerva, Ceres, Mars, Juno, Vesta, Venus, Apollo, Neptune, Vulcan, Bacchus, Diana, Janus, Mercury, Zeus, Hermes, Saturn, Poseidon, Athena, Pluto, Aphrodite and Hera. This was way too complicated to fit nicely into the formula above for the "religion" factor.

Sylvester I was born in Southern Italy and had roots in Calabria. His appearance is interesting. His face looks a bit familiar. Picture me with a beard.

So, Constantine needed to find a religion that he could bring into the Roman Empire to help manage all the varied populations across the Roman world. Christianity was that religion. Christianity stood for one all-powerful god. It represented a solid set of stories, myths, and legends. It represented "hopes" and fears in those stories (about Christ, too) in the old and new testaments.

The persecution of Christians became illegal, and the liberty of the Church was declared by the signing of the Edict of Milan in 313. The government then bankrolled the building of churches around the empire (including the Basilica of the Holy Cross in Jerusalem and the Old St. Peter's Basilica in Rome), and councils of theologians were convened to decide on the religious doctrine that would be promoted by the Roman Empire. The 33rd Pope was named Bishop of Rome in 314, Sylvester I. Sylvester I served for almost 22 years and guided this whole process. He established papal supremacy and papal authority based on imperial power. The emperor then confirmed the Bishop of Rome as the primate above all other bishops. At the First Council of Nicaea in 325, the Nicene Creed was formulated, books of the bible were selected and modified, and others left out. A politically-sponsored religion was endorsed for the Empire and all of its subjects. Thus, Roman Catholicism is born. So, money and power, politics and religion are all seamlessly united. The madness now truly begins.

I have assembled some examples (see Appendix C) of my thoughts about several of the Bible stories that I was told by my mother, the sisters in CCD, and the priests in the church. My opinion is very unfiltered and direct. It may be difficult to read. I feel that considering a second opinion to the generally accepted dogma of our society is not a bad thing to do. I hope you consider this when presented with Bible stories in their usual forums.

In other sections of the Bible, evidence just repeats itself. The Old Testament says all you need to know about the God of Abraham and what his intentions are for mankind and the kind of being that "He" is. I have made my case in detail so there is no confusion about my logical and reasoned thinking on each of these core Bible stories. The teachings of the major Abrahamic religions have no real place in today's civilized society.

I came to this conclusion when I was a teenager: this all-present, all-knowing, and "loving" being can't be that at all. It, this "God of the Universe," is capricious, murderous, misogynistic, homicidal, infanticidal, democidal, genocidal, racist, homophobic, narcissistic, and an advocate of slavery, incest, rape, and childhood sexual abuse.

It's all in the Bible to see. You just have to ask the question, "Why did He do that?"or "Was that really necessary?" Did "He" really have to kill everyone—men, women, children, babies, innocent animals, dogs, cats, the bunnies in the field—like everything, indiscriminate destruction, murder, and carnage? Really? Why? To what end?

No, wait for a moment. You know that I do not believe in anything supernatural. I don't believe in any gods including the God of Abraham. So, God did not do all this stuff? The Bible is just a bunch of stories, myths and legends designed to steer. God wants the masses to do what the powerful want: to be subservient, to pay them homage, to pay tribute, to not ask questions, to not gain knowledge, and to do unspeakable evil at their direction. So, who then is capricious, murderous, misogynistic, homicidal, infanticidal, democidal, genocidal, racist, homophobic, narcissistic, and an advocate of slavery, incest, rape, and childhood sexual abuse? Well, the answer is the men who told the tales also wrote the verses in the old "testaments" and used the "Word of God" to maintain power over the masses of poor, uninformed, ignorant, and unquestioning people—for thousands of years—including today. Those who questioned the "teachings" and "party-lines" were ostracized, shunned, tortured, and killed. It is a fine line that you may have to walk to function in society at the same time as standing up for what you know to be right.

Please remember:

> *Money + Politics + Power + Religion = extreme corruption + outrageous hypocrisy + unbelievable atrocities*

Please, grow up to be a good person. Never take part in, lead, or be complicit in this corruption and hypocrisy. That would just be bad. Be brave, speak up, and oppose those who try to do anything based on religious beliefs, dogma, the unsupported party-line, lies, half-truths, and anything else that cannot be supported with real facts, evidence, and the truth.

You may ask: what is the alternative? Don't we need religion to lead a moral life? The answer is absolutely not! We will start our discussion on the core tenants of Secular Humanism—the obvious modern, civilized alternative to these ancient and incredibly barbaric religious teachings. I will not dignify the Ten Commandments by covering them here. They are more of the same. Remember the Humanist "Ten Commandments" I introduced to you earlier. Reread them and think about them. They transcend any religious belief or claim. Here they are again:

THE HUMANIST "TEN COMMANDMENTS"

1) Thou shalt strive to promote the greater good of humanity before all selfish desires.

2) Thou shalt be curious, for asking questions is the only way to find answers.

3) Harm to your fellow human is harm to humanity. Therefore, thou shalt not kill, rape, rob, or otherwise victimize anyone.

4) Thou shalt treat all humans as equals, regardless of race, gender, age, creed, identity, orientation, physical ability, or status.

5) Thou shalt use reason as your guide. Science, knowledge, observation, and rational analysis are the best ways to determine any course of action.

6) Thou shalt not force your beliefs onto others, nor insist that yours be the only and correct way to live happily.

7) If thou dost govern, thou shalt govern with reason, not with superstition. Religion should have no place in any government which represents all people and beliefs.

8) Thou shalt act for the betterment of your fellow humans, and be, whenever possible, altruistic in your deeds.

9) Thou shalt be good to the Earth and its bounties, for without it, humankind is lost.

10) Thou shalt impart thy knowledge and wisdom gained in your lifetime to the next generation, so that with each passing century, humanity will grow wiser and more humane.

EIGHTEEN

Let's Talk About Reason, Logic and Being a Skeptic

"Reason is the capacity of consciously applying logic by drawing conclusions from new or existing information, with the aim of seeking the truth. For many folks the phrase "common sense" speaks plainly as sound and prudent judgment based on a simple perception of the situation or facts. We live our lives for the most part as reasonable thinking creatures doing what satisfies us and society. However, it seems to take only a little encouragement to fall off the wagon down a deep rabbit hole."

—*Michael N. Searles, The Abandonment of Reason, April 20, 2022, The True Citizen*

FROM MY EARLIEST memories, I was a logical and reasoning kid. I was always asking the "5 Ws and an H"—what, why, when, where, who, and how. I did not know that is what they were called. I just did it. You should try to do this as often as you can. Asking the questions and getting the answers allows you to ask more questions and get more answers. That is the best way to learn anything. The knowledge you gain will then stick with you. I always say that my brain is filled with an incredible amount of useless information. Actually, it is useless only until you need to access and use it. At that point, it becomes the most useful bit of information that resides in that wild, cluttered place called your brain.

I had no inherent mechanical, physical, or artistic capabilities or skills. I could not do anything with my hands. My dad recognized this in me at an early age because his whole life was made up of working with his hands. He did manual work on the Long Island Railroad as a railcar brake repairman. He had a hobby as a woodworker. He had a general capability to build and maintain things around the house and maintain the car. In fact, at an early age, he told me this: "Bobby, you will need to make a lot of money by using your mind so you can pay other people to do things for you because you really can't do anything yourself with your hands." That conversation has stuck with me for my entire life. It was probably the best piece of advice that I ever received from him.

So, I went about my young life following his advice—developing my mind. This certainly involved being attentive to my studies at school, but that was not enough. Luckily, a big part of growing up in the 1950s and 1960s was exposure to science and technology, critical and logical thinking, and the application of these to everything in the world around us. The U.S. split and fused atomic nuclei to make, test, and use atomic weapons. Nuclear power plants were starting to be used to generate electricity. Submarines went nuclear and were surfacing at the North Pole. Test pilots traveled faster than the speed of sound in a new generation of jet airplanes. Rockets were launched—first in the atmosphere, next sub-orbit-ally, then in an intercontinental fashion, and finally into orbit. They had capsules containing monkeys, dogs, and then people.

We talked about computers, robots and automation, and an infinite number of new technologies and devices that were used in business, manufacturing, and in homes. Everything was new and needed the "5 Ws and an H" to understand what we were reading and hearing in newspapers and on TV. I think I mentioned to you, although you might not recall, that neither my mother nor my father graduated high school. They probably had a 7th or 8th grade reading level, knew nothing about science and math (past arithmetic), and generally could not answer most of my questions. We had a cheap encyclopedia that my mom bought book-by-book from the grocery store with "green stamps" and a number of other used books that we bought for 10, 20, or 25 cents from book sales in Farmingdale. My brother and I used the public school library and the South Farmingdale Public Library incessantly and insatiably. If we wanted to learn more, we could ask our teachers, check out a library book, or be a sponge in class. Our parents, grandparents, aunts, and uncles were of little, or no, help. They, too, had minimal high school education and, for sure, no college education. None of my grandparents even spoke English, only Italian.

In the late 50s and early 60s I also probably got my first taste of being a "skeptic." Although, at that time, I am sure I did not know it was a thing. Since I was a questioning kid, I got lots of answers from lots of different people and had sources of information that provided a lot of different points of view. My mother, my father, my teachers, the sisters and the priests at CCD and the church, TV news and programs, and newspapers all had an answer to my questions—most based on opinions and beliefs.

By 10 years old, I started to understand that facts matter. Evidence matters. One's ability to carry a conversation past the first level of questions with more facts and evidence mattered. Additionally, I started to understand that it was important to judge the credibility of the source of the answers to my questions, especially when answers differed widely from one another. Also, if what I was being told was not what my eyes were showing me, I might want to question the source. I was starting to build a muscle of skepticism that I would develop and hone for my entire lifetime.

If you do one thing as a child and young adult, I believe this may be the most important muscle that you need to develop and use often and on everything you see, hear, and learn to become a good person. Both of you participate in martial arts at Victory Martial Arts in Las Vegas. I try to attend as many of your classes as I can. I am struck by the Tigers Creed that you recite at the beginning of each session: "To be a good person, I must have knowledge in my mind, honesty in my heart, strength in my body, to make good friends, and to be a black belt leader. Sir/Ma'am! Hiyaaaa!" I hope that you are able to use this advice to be questioning, logical, reasoned and skeptical, to be that good person, and to always do the right thing when you become that black belt leader.

During the late 1960s, there was an explosion of interest in the paranormal, aliens and extraterrestrial visitation, the occult (ghosts), and claims of the supernatural. Needless to say, I, as a 15 or 16-year-old boy, was interested in understanding what was going on. Moving things with your mind, bending or distorting spoons and forks by concentrating your psychic energy into the objects, or other extraordinary feats, were being demonstrated all over the world. Many people believed that all of it was real. A small group of individuals, chiefly magicians, led by James Randi, set out to debunk these individuals as charlatans, liars, and frauds. James Randi (The Amazing Randi) was one of the best magicians of his time and could do everything that the psychics and paranormal purveyors claimed to do. Randi specially stated that these acts were not real. He said they were just magic tricks.

In 1973, I distinctly remember a demonstration that Uri Geller (the guy who claimed he could bend spoons and move objects with his mind) was to do on Johnny Carson's The Tonight Show. Carson, who did not believe that Geller was real, asked Randi to make sure Geller could not trick the audience but needed

I started to follow Carl Sagan in the 1970s. I l loved one of his best quotes: "We are made of stardust." Yes, we sure are.

to actually do what he claimed to be able to do. Obviously, he could not pull off the stunt if he did not set it up beforehand. It was just a magic trick. He was a fraud. Here was the result: any thinking person now knew he was a fraud. Everyone else continued to believe Geller was real, thought Randi was lying and just trying to tear down their superstar. What? Yes, you see this over and over again multiple times a day, even today. Being a skeptic, using science to understand what is going on with charlatans and liars is hard. Facts, evidence, truth, and the scientific method be damned. These folks just say "I want to believe what I want to believe, and you can't show me anything to convince me otherwise." Uri Geller went on to be a Paranormal superstar, and James Randi continued to lead the effort to expose as many of these fakes and liars as possible. There were certainly no shortage of them. I was now a follower of Randi's work and knew what I could call myself—a Skeptic!

In the 1990s, I started to actively read Skeptic Magazine, became part of the skeptical movement, and ultimately participated in the Skeptics Society, Center for Inquiry/Committee for Skeptical Inquiry, and the James Randi Educational Foundation. There is never a shortage of opportunities to practice your skills in skeptical thinking, investigation and inquiry, logic and reason, and doubt.

This is a very small community of like-minded, free-thinking individuals. Getting together with them is always energizing. The best gathering I have ever attended was one in which Laci and I participated in July 2013. It was a four-day conference in Las Vegas. Penn Jillette's No God Band (a rock band) also attended and put on a private, rock and roll "Bacon and Doughnut Party." In a word, it was AMAZING!

The entire conference is very engaging, thought-provoking, and snarky. Scientists, atheists, magicians, free-thinkers, intellectuals, academics, researchers, and debunkers were all there to exchange ideas and have some fun but no "Woo!"

I have one closing thought and comment about doubt to share with you. It is all part of the same questioning process. One key element is to always be ready to doubt your own thinking or position if someone presents a more compelling set of facts or evidence that forces you to reconsider what you believed to be true in the past. That happens quite a bit in science and all the time in the world around us. Once you start to hone your thinking in this regard, it is almost impossible to go back. I hope to help you to develop this muscle as you grow up. It will be a key to you having a fulfilling life.

This is a poster from The Amazing Meeting in 2013 in Las Vegas. Yes, there are signatures from both James Randi and Penn Jillette.

NINETEEN

Grandpa Sunday

"When I embrace my grandfather I experience a sense of richness as though I am a note in the heartbeats of the very universe."

—*Tayeb Salih, novelist (1929–2009)*

GOOD MORNING, SEAN and Kyle. Thank you, Beth and Erik, for dropping the kids off for another fun *Grandpa Sunday* play day. There is nothing better for a nice summer day in 2023 in Las Vegas. Whoa, whoa, guys, say bye to your mom and dad and not just run past me into the house. Okay, you are gone. I'll be right in. Your mom and dad and I chat for a minute. Then, I wave goodbye. I shut the garage door and follow you into the house to see what you are up to first.

You are already saying hi to Laci when I get inside. Okay, looks like we are going to start on some of the things that I set up on the kitchen counter to play science—magnets that Kyle loves and new fossil dig and crystal growing kits that I just got from National Geographic for both of you. Since you are only seven and four years old, the time we spend at the kitchen counter is pretty short, maybe 30 minutes, just enough to get things started. We'll be back later.

Before I know it, you are both headed upstairs to the loft and the area set up for the grandkids—the two of you and Laci's two grandkids, Parker and Carter, now four and three years old. You probably don't realize it now, but the three big, wooden toyboxes and the cabinets at the top of the stairs are a technology-free zone. All the toys were selected by Laci and me to ensure you play and learn by doing. No iPads or other technology that does the work for you or have you interact as only an observer or gamer. You get plenty of that at your own home. I know you love those wooden trains, all of the different building sets, and the puzzles, puppets, and dozens of other things that will fill our Grandpa Sunday activities.

You know I am an old guy but probably have no idea what my life was like. You obviously feel really comfortable running all over the house. No rooms are off-limits. Although, I do appreciate that you are respectful of the artwork that I have asked you to "look, but don't touch." Also, I know you like to go into my office on the first floor, and Laci's on the second, where we continue to work during the week. I am sure you have no idea what we do for work, or for that matter, what we have done. To both of you, I am just grandpa which does not get better than that.

My mind wanders. You are so young and have your whole long life ahead of you, maybe, hopefully, more than a hundred years. At 72, I realize that I have a lot more years behind me than in front of me. I, too, am hoping to see my 100th birthday and see you in your 30s solidly building a life of your own, but no one knows what tomorrow will bring. So, carpe diem—seize the day.

I am back to focusing on the need at hand, how to get the wheels on that amazingly complex car that you are building and planning to test by rolling it down the stairs from the loft to the dining room below. I see the engineer in you. You just see the fun in destroying something and then building it again to see if it can survive another test down the stairs from the loft. Funny, no matter how solid we build it, you figure out a way to destroy it. Actually, that sounds like some really good engineering. Design, build, test, learn, redesign, rebuild, retest, learn more, and on and on. Nice work, kiddos. Grandpa is proud of you.

Oh, I have told you, although you probably don't understand a word that I said, that I was an engineer, and a scientist (actually a physicist), and a naval officer, and a business leader, and a world traveler, and a lifelong learner, and one of the most curious people that you will probably ever know. I have showed you all the foreign money, coins, and currency I collected over the past 40 years, my Lieutenant Commander shoulder boards and collar devices, and some other memorabilia of my career that I have stashed in my office. You were completely uninterested and unimpressed. I totally understand for now but hope that will not always be the case.

I also have had an incredible life filled with amazing experiences, great relationships, and an opportunity to develop and live a set of values and principles that have guided me for the past 70 years and will guide my path for the rest of my time with you. I would love to share that with you, but at your very young age, you have no context or experience to understand anything I would be saying.

Oops, you are off to the next thing. You are headed downstairs to the pantry for a snack and then back to the kitchen counter to see how much the crystal trees have grown. Amazingly, the crystals are actually forming leaves on the cardboard trees we cut out and colored. Wonderfully, you actually tell me that you are excited to see what was going on. I have a little opportunity to talk about the science behind crystal growth. You listen for a moment, and then you are gone again. You go back upstairs to build a pretty complex train track, and you start to play with the wooden trains. You make some choo choo sounds. No technology here—just some good solid playing, creativity, and learning. I love it.

The next few hours are filled with hide-and-seek with Laci and grandpa, an impromptu puppet show always involving a puppet fight at the end, puzzles, upstairs, downstairs, until the whole loft and a good portion of the kitchen and adjacent living room are covered in parts of a variety of building kits, science experiments, the wooden train set, hand puppets, puzzles, fossils, and polished stones.

I just got a text that your mom and dad are on their way to pick you up. Wow, that was another incredibly fun day. I ask what you would like to take home—the crystal trees for sure and a small plastic sandwich bag for each of you with a few fossils and rocks that you especially like. When your parents get here, you are not ready to leave, but with a little coaxing, you put on your shoes and head for their car. That was another successful Grandpa Sunday, and hopefully, we created some memories you take away all with a little more understanding about how much I love you, who I am as a person, and what it means to have a fun day exploring, learning, and being a curious person. Maybe you even learned a bit about what it is like to be an engineer and a scientist. Bye-bye, Sean and Kyle. Thanks for the great day. Whew, Grandpa needs a nap.

> "You can never go wrong if your career decisions always combine personal and professional growth. Career progression is never linear. Success isn't always about achieving a goal."
>
> —*Robert Danna, 2022*

THINKING ABOUT MY over 70 years on this earth has been quite cathartic. I learned that life is so complex; it is unfathomable as a child. Each person is unbelievably complicated, a result of "nature" and "nurture" that performs a beautiful dance every minute of every day. Personality, attitude, curiosity, hard work, learning, teaching, chance and luck make up the stew. The result is our journey through life. Just do your best. Develop and live your values. Be a good person. I hope you might say that I have succeeded at that. As an old man, that is in fact my legacy.

Like peeling an onion, I have exposed you to only a few of the outer layers of myself. I have hundreds of stories and experiences that are still stored away in my very cluttered brain. I have a lot more of that "useless information supposed to fire my imagination." Thank you again, Rolling Stones, for that terrific line.

So, what is important now? Get a great education. Learn to always question what you are told. Develop a high sense of integrity. Find a north star to guide your decisions. Be a good person. Really figure out what "living aloha" means. Be a sponge. Take it all in. You will reference it sometime in your future. You got to love that "useless information" even if it seems boring and irrelevant now. Once you believe you have done this, be ready to repeat and refine it for the rest of your lives despite challenges, obstacles, and changes that will be coming down the path during your life journey.

Finally, what is the meaning of life? That is an interesting question. I believe it is to learn, to grow, to teach, to lead, to challenge respectfully, and to share. Although I have been able to become financially secure (not rich), that was never my goal. In fact, many of my decisions have resulted in me making less money and accumulating fewer "assets." Two things come to mind. I read about the life of Albert Einstein when I was a teenager and young adult and reflected on the fact that this great scientist lived a very modest life for all of his incredible accomplishments. He literally changed the world of physics and contributed to the science that underlies all the technology we take for granted today. I actually wanted to be him. Wow! That would be amazing. I internalized a lot about what the meaning of life is from how he lived his life.

One other reference that I would you like you to consider is a song, *In Held Twas in I*, written and performed in the late 1960s by Procol Harum. A couple of verses sum it all up for me:

> At a time like this, which exists maybe only for me
> But is nonetheless real, if I can communicate
> And in the telling and the bearing of my soul
> Anything is gained, even though the words
> Which I use are pretentious and make you cringe
> With embarrassment, let me remind you of the pilgrim
> Who asked for an audience with the Dalai Lama

He was told he must first spend five years in contemplation
After the five years
He was ushered into the Dalai Lama's presence, who said
Well, my son, what do you wish to know?
So the pilgrim said
I wish to know the meaning of life, father

So the Dalai Lama smiled and said
Well my son, life is like a beanstalk, isn't it?

The Dalai Lama, a source of great knowledge and wisdom, has no F-ing idea—none. Neither do great religious leaders, pundits, philosophers, and prophets have any idea either—none. Who does? The answer is this: the scientists and engineers—those who deal with logic, facts, and evidence. Ask them, and then, be skeptical about their answers until you can satisfy yourself that what they are saying can be verified and trusted. As you know, this song is one of six songs that are in a very short play list that illustrate who I am and what I believe in. Please listen to it. Closely listen to it. Let it wash over you. Reflect on it. Play it again. It tells about me, who I am, and my story.

Additionally, in high school social studies, I learned about the Nootka Native American tribe and a ceremony that the northwestern Native Americans practiced—the Potlatch. In Potlatch ceremonies, possessions are shared and given away to show "wealth" and generosity. I have always led with kindness, enjoy giving more than receiving, paying rather than being paid for, and sharing what I own (including time with me on vacation at timeshares that I have purchased). My credit card is always the first on the table when we go out with friends and family. When my mom died, you'll recall my brother and I literally organized a Potlatch for her. We gave away all her household items, including hundreds of her collectables, to all her friends and family.

So, I would hope that you and others who might read this memoir would say that Bob lived modestly but was always generous with his time, knowledge, experiences, money, property, and anything else that made me Bob. There are times that this becomes a bit frustrating. When is your generosity being taken for granted, never acknowledged or "repaid" in fact, in principle, or in kind? As far as I've experienced, that occurs often. In fact, it occurs almost always. There is an abundance of takers and very few givers. Even saying "thank you" appears to be a problem for most, let alone actually doing something nice in return for the giver's generosity.

That is where I rely on Living Aloha. That becomes the icing on the cake; never expect "repayment" in any way. That makes who I am easier for me. Giving is everything with no need to ever have it returned in kind. Yes, that is the meaning of my life.

Aloha, Sean and Kyle, and Mahalo for bringing an incredible amount of joy and hope into my life. I hope you live a life filled with curiosity, incredible experiences, and the joy of living every day to its maximum.

I am, and always will be, your loving Grandpa.

Lyrics to Songs that Reflect Who I Am

Listen carefully to these six songs to know everything about me.

Imagine (John Lennon—1971)
Imagine there's no heaven
It's easy if you try
No hell below us
Above us, only sky

Imagine all the people
Livin' for today
Ah

Imagine there's no countries
It isn't hard to do
Nothing to kill or die for
And no religion, too

Imagine all the people
Livin' life in peace
You

You may say I'm a dreamer
But I'm not the only one
I hope someday you'll join us
And the world will be as one

Imagine no possessions
I wonder if you can
No need for greed or hunger
A brotherhood of man

Imagine all the people
Sharing all the world
You

You may say I'm a dreamer
But I'm not the only one
I hope someday you'll join us
And the world will live as one

God (John Lennon—1970)

God is a concept

By which we measure
Our pain
I'll say it again
God is a concept
By which we measure
Our pain

I don't believe in magic
I don't believe in I-Ching
I don't believe in Bible
I don't believe in Tarot
I don't believe in Hitler
I don't believe in Jesus
I don't believe in Kennedy
I don't believe in Buddha
I don't believe in Mantra
I don't believe in Gita
I don't believe in Yoga
I don't believe in Kings
I don't believe in Elvis
I don't believe in Zimmerman
I don't believe in Beatles

I just believe in me
Yoko and me
That's reality
Dream is over
What can I say?

The dream is over
Yesterday

I was the dreamweaver
But now I'm reborn
I was the walrus
But now I'm John
And so dear friends
You just have to carry on
The dream is over

Sniper (Harry Chapin—1972)

It is an early Monday morning.
The sun is becoming bright on the land.
No one is watching as he comes a walking.
Two bulky suitcases hang from his hands.

He heads towards the tower that stands in the campus.
He goes through the door, he starts up the stairs.
The sound of his footsteps, the sound of his breathing,
The sound of the silence when no one was there.

I didn't really know him.
He was kind of strange.
Always sort of sat there.
He never seemed to change.

He reached the catwalk. He put done his burden.
The four-sided clock began to chime.
Seven AM, the day is beginning.
So much to do and so little time.

He looks at the city where no one had known him.
He looks at the sky where no one looks down.
He looks at his life and what it has shown him.
He looks for his shadow it cannot be found.

He was such a moody child, very hard to touch.
Even as a baby he never smiled too much. No, no. No, no.

You bug me, she said.
You're ugly, she said.
Please hug me, I said.
But she just sat there
With the same flat stare
That she saves for me alone
When I'm home.

When I'm home.
Take me home.

He laid out the rifles, he loaded the shotgun,
He stacked up the cartridges along the wall.
He knew he would need them for his conversation.
If it went as he planned, then he might use them all.

He said Listen you people I've got a question
You won't pay attention, but I'll ask anyhow.
I found a way that will get me an answer.
Been waiting to ask you 'till now.
Right now!

Am I?
I am a lover who's never been kissed.
Am I?
I am a fighter who's not made a fist.
Am I?
If I'm alive then there's so much I've missed.
How do I know I exist?
Are you listening to me?
Are you listening to me?
Am I?

The first words he spoke took the town by surprise.
One got Mrs. Gibbons above her right eye.
It blew her through the window wedged her against the door.
Reality poured from her face, staining the floor.

He was kind of creepy,
Sort of a dunce.
I met him at the corner bar.
I only dated the poor boy once,
That's all. Just once, that was all.

Bill Whedon was questioned as stepped from his car.
Tom Scott ran across the street, but he never got that far.
The police were there in minutes, they set up barricades.
He spoke right on over them in a half-mile circle.
In a dumb struck city his pointed questions were sprayed.

He knocked over Danny Tyson as he ran towards the noise.
Just about then the answers started coming. Sweet, sweet joy.
Thudding in the clock face, whining off the walls,
Reaching up to where he sat there, answering calls.

Thirty-seven people got his message so far.
Yes, he was reaching them right where they are.

They set up an assault team. They asked for volunteers.
They had to go and get him, that much was clear.
And the word spread about him on the radios and TV's.
In appropriately sober tone they asked, "Who can it be?"

He was a very dull boy, very taciturn.
Not much of a joiner, he did not want to learn.
No, no. No, no.

They're coming to get me, they don't want to let me
Stay in the bright light too long.
It's getting on noon now, it's goin' to be soon now.
But oh, what a wonderful sound!

Mama, won't you nurse me?
Rain me down the sweet milk of your kindness.
Mama, it's getting worse for me.
Won't you please make me warm and mindless?

Mama, yes you have cursed me.
I never will forgive you for your blindness.
I hate you!

The wires are all humming for me.
And I can hear them coming for me.
Soon they'll be here, but there's nothing to fear.
Not anymore though they've blasted the door.

As the 'copter dropped the gas he shouted, "Who cares?" .
They could hear him laughing as they started up the stairs.
As they stormed out on the catwalk, blinking at the sun,
With their final fusillade his answer had come.

Am I?
There is no way that you can hide me.
Am I?
Though you have put your fire inside me.
Am I ?
You've given me my answer can't you see?
I was!
I am!
And now I will be
I will be

The Great American Eagle Tragedy (Earth Opera—1972)

And call out the border guard
The kingdom is crumbling
The king is in the counting house
Laughing and stumbling
His armies are extending
Way beyond the shore
As he sends our lovely boys to die
In a foreign jungle war

The queen is in the garden
Moaning and weeping
She spied the execution of Spades
While he lay sleeping
The kingdom judge and jester
Leaped together from the tower
Lie still as fallen statues
In the cultivated bower, bower

And call out the border guard
The kingdom is crumbling
The king is in the counting house
Laughing and stumbling
His armies are extending
Way beyond the shore
As he sends our lovely boys to die
In a foreign jungle war

The orchestra assembles
And tries in vain to tune
While outside in the stable yard
The hounds are howling at the moon
A blind man in the far off jungle
His bamble hurt in flames
Sits and whispers to his flute
All the unremembered names

And call out the border guard
The kingdom is crumbling
The king is in the counting house
Laughing and stumbling
His armies are extending
Way beyond the shore
As he sends our lovely boys to die
In a foreign jungle war

The scarlet cloaked and white horsed huntsman
Rides upon the meadow green

His silver arrow scars the sky
And I can hear the eagle scream
The peasants watch in dumb struck wonder
The gay procession passed them by
The victory silence is consuming me
And we've at last the eagle's cry

And call out the border guard
The kingdom is crumbling
The king is in the counting house
Laughing and stumbling
His armies are extending
Way beyond the shore
As he sends our lovely boys to die
As we send our lovely boys to die
As you send our lovely boys to die
In a foreign jungle war

Why people, I can't stand it anymore!
I, I, I, I, I can't stand it anymore!
I can't stand it!

I God!
Oh God! Oh God! Oh God! Oh God!
Where is that place?

Bye bye bye bye bye bye
Die die die die die die
Bye bye bye bye bye bye
Die die die die die die
Oh no! Oh no! Oh no!

Stop the war!
Stop the war!
Oh please! Stop!

In Held 'Twas In I (Procol Harum—1968)

In the darkness of the night
Only occasionally relieved by glimpses of Nirvana
As seen through other people's windows
Wallowing in a morass of self-despair
Made only more painful by the knowledge
That all I am is of my own making

When everything around me, even the kitchen ceiling
Has collapsed and crumbled without warning
And I am left, standing alive and well
Looking up and wondering why and wherefore

At a time like this, which exists maybe only for me
But is nonetheless real, if I can communicate
And in the telling and the bearing of my soul
Anything is gained, even though the words
Which I use are pretentious and make you cringe
With embarrassment, let me remind you of the pilgrim
Who asked for an audience with the Dalai Lama

He was told he must first spend five years in contemplation
After the five years
He was ushered into the Dalai Lama's presence, who said
Well, my son, what do you wish to know?
So the pilgrim said
I wish to know the meaning of life, father

So the Dalai Lama smiled and said
Well my son, life is like a beanstalk, isn't it?

Held close by that which some despise
Which some call fake, and others, lies
And somewhat small for one so tall
A doubting Thomas, who would be?

It's written plain for all to see
For one who I am with no more
It's hard at times, it's awful raw

They say that Jesus healed the sick and helped the poor
And those unsure believed his eyes
A strange disguise
Still write it down, it might be read
Nothing's better left unsaid
Only sometimes, still no doubt
It's hard to see, it all works out

Everything Louder Than Everything Else (Meat Loaf—1993)

Wasted youth!
Wasted youth!

I know that I will never be politically correct
And I don't give a damn about my lack of etiquette
As far as I'm concerned the world could still be flat
And if the thrill is gone then it's time to take it back
If the thrill is gone then it's time to take it back

Who am I? Why am I here?
Forget the questions, someone get me another beer
What's the meaning of life? What's the meaning of it all?
You gotta learn to dance before you learn to crawl
You gotta learn to dance before you learn to crawl

So sign up, all you raw recruits
Throw away those designer suits
You got your weapons cocked, your targets in your sights
There's a party raging somewhere in the world
You gotta serve your country, gotta service your girl
You're all enlisted in the armies of the night

And I ain't in it for the power
And I ain't in it for my health
I ain't in it for the glory of anything at all
And I sure ain't in it for the wealth
But I'm in it 'til it's over and I just can't stop
If you want to get it done
You gotta do it yourself
And I like my music like I like my life

Everything louder than everything else
Everything louder than everything else
Everything louder than everything else
(Everything louder, everything louder, everything)

Everything louder than everything else
Everything louder than everything else
Everything louder than everything else
(Everything louder, everything louder, everything)

Wasted youth!
Wasted youth!
Wasted youth!
Wasted youth!

They got a file on me and it's a mile long
And they say that they got all of the proof
That I'm just another case of arrested development
I'm just another wasted youth
They say that I'm in need of some radical discipline
They say I gotta face the truth
That I'm just another case of arrested development
I'm just another wasted youth

They say I'm wild and I'm reckless
I should be acting my age
I'm an impressionable child in a tumultuous world
And they say I'm at a difficult stage
But it seems to me to the contrary
Of all the crap they're gonna put on the page

That a wasted youth is better by far (wasted youth!)
Than a wise and productive old age (wasted youth!)
A wasted youth is better by far (wasted youth!)
Than a wise and productive old age (wasted youth!)
A wasted youth is better by far (wasted youth!)
Than a wise and productive old age (wasted youth!)
A wasted youth is better by far (wasted youth!)
Than a wise and productive old age (wasted youth!)
A wasted youth is better by far (wasted youth!)

Than a wise and productive old age (wasted youth!)
A wasted youth is better by far (wasted youth!)
Than a wise and productive old age (wasted youth!)

Louder, louder, louder, louder
Louder, louder, louder, louder, louder!

If you want my views of history, then there's something you should know
The three men I admire most are Curly, Larry, and Moe
Don't worry about the future, sooner or later it's the past
If they say the thrill is gone then it's time to take it back
If the thrill is gone then it's time to take it back

So, sign up, all you raw recruits
Throw away all those two-bit suits
You got your weapons cocked, your targets in your sights
There's a party raging somewhere in the world
You gotta serve your country, gotta service your girl
You're all inducted in the army of the night

And I ain't in it for the power
And I ain't in it for my health
I ain't in it for the glory of anything at all
And I sure ain't in it for the wealth
But I'm in it 'til it's over and I just can't stop
If you want to get it done
You got to fight for yourself
And I like my music like I like my life

Everything louder than everything else
Everything louder than everything else
Everything louder than everything else

Everything louder than everything else
Everything louder than everything else

Everything louder than everything else
(Everything louder, everything louder, everything)

Everything louder than everything else
Everything louder than everything else
Everything louder than everything else
(Everything louder, everything louder, everything)

Everything louder than everything else
Everything louder than everything else
Everything louder than everything else
(Everything louder, everything louder, everything)

Everything louder than everything else
Everything louder than everything else
Everything louder than everything else
(Everything louder, everything louder, everything)

Representative Technical Publications and Presentations (1983–1998)

1. R. Danna, K.J. Rebeck, *"Failure Prevention Program Development: An Application of Pressure Vessel and System Recertification and Inspection Planning,"* **Failure Prevention and Reliability—1983**, American Society of Mechanical Engineers, pp. 109–117 (1983); also presented at the 1983 ASME Design and Production Engineering Technical Conferences, Dearborn, MI.

2. R. Danna, *"Overview of Configuration Management Program Development and Implementation for Ground Based Pressure Vessels and Systems,"* presented at the NASA Pressure Systems Seminar, White Sands Test Facility, Las Cruces, NM, September 1983.

3. R. Danna, C.S. Trent, *"Implementation of a Configuration Management Program for Nuclear Plant Simulators,"* Transactions of the American

Nuclear Society, **45**, pp. 558–559 (1983); also presented at the 1983 Winter Meeting of the American Nuclear Society, San Francisco, California.

4. C.S. Trent, R. Danna, *"Development of a Configuration Management Program for Nuclear Plant Simulators,"* **All About Simulators, 1984**, Society for Computer Simulation, **14**, pp. 18–24 (1984).

5. K.J. Rebeck, R. Danna, G.S. Miller, R.T. Hollingsworth, *"Recertification Analysis and Inspection Planning for Environmental Test Facilities,"* Proceedings of the Institute of Environmental Sciences, pp. 328–335 (1984), also published in the Journal of Environmental Sciences, **27**, pp. 33–39 (1984).

6. E.G. Landauer, R. Danna, *"The Need for Technical Staff Training,"* Transactions of the American Nuclear Society, **46**, pp. 44–46 (1984).

7. D.E. Sharp, R. Danna, J.E. Stoneking, T.G. Carley, *"Failure Prevention Program Implementation: A Case Study of High Pressure Gas Storage Vessels,"* American Society of Mechanical Engineers, 84-PVP-66, pp. 1–6 (1984).

8. J.P. Davis, R. Danna, *"De Minimus Concentrations of Radionuclides in Various Waste Media,"* Transactions of the American Nuclear Society, **47**, p. 101 (1984).

9. D.W. Chan, R. Danna, J.P. Davis, et al., "Election *and Evaluation of Potential Very Low Level Wastes (VLLW) From Nuclear Power Plants,"* **Waste Management '85**, Proceedings of the Symposium on Waste Management, Volume 2, pp. 395–399 (1985)

10. D.W. Chan, J.P. Davis, R. Danna, et al., **Evaluation of the Potential for De-Regulated Disposal of Very Low-Level Wastes from Nuclear Power Plants**, National Environmental Studies Project, Atomic Industrial Forum, Inc., AIF/NESP-035 (1986).

11. R. Danna, D.E. Sharp, *"Survey of Documentation on Blast Waves Resulting from Failure of Gas Filled Pressure Vessels,"* presented at the NASA Pressure Systems Seminar, Johnson Space Center, Houston, TX, September 1987.

12. S.P. Shores, D.E. Sharp, R. Danna, F.E. Lundy, M.G. Olsen, *"Life Assessment as Applied to Pressurized Gaseous Storage Vessels,"* **Advances in Piping Analysis and Life Assessment of Pressure Vessels and Piping**, PVP-Vol. 129, edited by S.J. Chang, R.C. Gwaltney and T.Q. McCawley, American Society of Mechanical Engineers, pp. 89–92 (1987).

13. R. Danna, D.E. Sharp, B.L. Webb, *"A Guide for Recertification of Ground Based Pressure Vessels and Liquid Holding Tanks,"* Eastern Space and Missile Center Technical Report ESMC-TR-88-01, available through the National Technical Information Service (NTIS), NTIS #AD-A190935, December 1987.

14. M. Coleman, M. Cain, R. Danna, C. Harley and D. Sharp, *"Review of Energy Release Processes from the Failure of Pneumatic Pressure Vessels,"* Eastern Space and Missile Center Technical Report ESMC-TR-88-03, available through the National Technical Information Service (NTIS), NTIS #AD-A207549, August 1988.

15. R. Danna, *"Paperless Inservice Inspection Programs,"* presented at the NASA Pressure Systems Seminar, Ames Research Center, Moffett Field, California, October 1989.

16. R. Danna, *"Recertification of Pressure Vessels and Tanks,"* invited presentation at the Petrochemical Technology Seminar, sponsored by MQS Inspection and APTECH Engineering, Houston, TX, May 1989.

17. R. Danna, D.E. Sharp and B.L. Webb, *"Development of a Methodology for the Assessment of Residual-Life of Pressure Vessels at Government Facilities,"* **Nondestructive Evaluation: NDE Planning and Application**, NDE, Vol. 5, edited by R.D. Streit, pp. 35–44 (1989); also presented at the 1989 ASME Pressure Vessel and Piping Conference, Honolulu, Hawaii; reprinted in the Proceedings of the 1991 JANNAF Interagency Propulsion Committee, Safety and Environmental Subcommittee, Chemical Propulsion Information Agency (CPIA) (1991).

18. R. Danna, C.R. Harley, Z.P. Quandt, A.C. Weinstein, *"The Impact on Pressure Systems of Upgrading Propulsion Test Facilities,"* 26th Joint Propulsion conference, Paper #90-2502, American Institute of Aeronautics and Astronautics (1990).

19. A.C. Weinstein, R. Danna, *"Failure Prevention of Autoclaves and Hydroclaves by Implementation of Periodic Inspection and Safety Assessments,"* Proceedings of the 1990 Joint Army-Navy-NASA-Air Force (JANNAF) Interagency Propulsion Committee, Safety and Environmental Protection Subcommittee, Chemical Propulsion Information Agency (CPIA) (1990).

20. R. Danna, *"Risk Management and Prevention Program Elements and Analysis Workshop: Inspection, Maintenance and Training Considerations,"* invited

presentation at the Community Awareness and Emergency Response (CAER) 3rd Annual California Statewide Conference, Sacramento, CA, May 1991.

21. R. Danna, *"Assuring the Mechanical Integrity of Critical Components in Facilities Subject to Continual Change,"* Process Safety Management Conference, sponsored by General Physics Corporation in Houston, TX (August 1991), Philadelphia (October 1991), and Chicago (October 1991).

22. R. Danna, *"Overview of Process Safety Management: OSHA 29 CFR 1910.119,"* presented at the NASA Pressure Systems Seminar, Stennis Space Center, Bay St. Louis, MS, November 1991.

23. R. Danna, *"Management of Change,"* Process Safety Management Conference, co-sponsored by General Physics Services Corporation and Jones and Neuse, Inc., in Houston, TX (May 1992) Baton Rouge, LA (June 1992), Oakland, CA (June 1992), and Long Beach, CA (July 1992).

24. R. Danna, *"An Integrated Methodology for PSM Program Development and Implementation,"* PSM Report, Volume 1, Number 4, pp. 6–10, Knowledge Base International, Houston, TX, September 1992.

25. M. Mannan and R. Danna, *"The Use of Compliance Audits and Assessments in Establishment of Program Baselines and Plans for 29 CFR 1910.119,"* **Petro-Safe '93 4th Annual Environmental, Safety and health Conference and Exhibition for The Oil, Gas and Petrochemical Industries**, Penn Well Conferences and Exhibitions, Book III, Volume VII, pp. 165–177, January 1993.

26. R. Danna and H.H. West, *"Development and Implementation of a Management of Change Program in Response to Requirements of 29 CFR 1910.119,"* **Petro-Safe '93 4th Annual Environmental, Safety and Health Conference and Exhibition for The Oil, Gas and Petrochemical Industries**, Penn Well Conferences and Exhibitions, Book III, Volume VII, pp. 115–124, January 1993; also presented at the 1993 Petro-Safe Conference in Houston, Texas.

27. R. Danna, *"Implementing Process Safety Management Programs for Hazardous Chemicals and Processes—A One Day Seminar,"* sponsored by GPS Technologies and its SE Asian subsidiaries General Physics Asia and General Physics Malaysia in Singapore and Kuala Lumpur (twice each in June and November 1993).

28. R. Danna, H.H. West, *"Management of Change: Process Safety Management Practice,"* **Proceedings of the 28th Annual Loss Prevention Symposium**, Session 20, Risk Analysis & Process Safety Management, American Institute of Chemical Engineers, Atlanta, GA, April 1994.

29. H.H. West, M.S. Mannan, R. Danna, E.M. Stafford, *"Make Plants Safer with a Proper Management of Change Program,"* **Chemical Engineering Progress**, American Institute of Chemical Engineers, June 1998.

My Reflections on Several Bible Stories

I WOULD LIKE to share why I think the fundamental teachings of the three major religions based on the "God of Abraham" are flawed based on several Bible stories that were repeated over and over again as part of the church's teaching in my childhood. I will try to understand the mind of God from these four sections of the Bible.

GENESIS 2:4–3:24: ADAM AND EVE AND THE GARDEN OF EDEN (EXTRACTED)

Remember that God is all-knowing and all-present, and He is a loving God. He actually knew what Adam and Eve would do and effectively set them up for the Fall. So, what does the Bible teach us?

Verses from the Bible	My reaction and questions
Adam and Eve	
15 The Lord God took the man and put him in the Garden of Eden to work it and take care of it. **16** And the Lord God commanded the man, "You are free to eat from any tree in the garden; **17** but you must not eat from the tree of the knowledge of good and evil, for when you eat from it you will certainly die."	Two items catch my attention. First, it looks like God was interested in man taking care of the planet—a very good thing. In fact, we have not been very good stewards of the environment. Additionally, it looks like ignorance is valued over knowledge. Why is that?I am unsure how good and evil are defined by the Bible.
18 The Lord God said, "It is not good for the man to be alone. I will make a helper suitable for him."	It looks like a women's role, From the "origin" story, it looks like a woman's role is clearly to be just a helper to a man. She does not even have a name at this point.
25 Adam and his wife were both naked, and they felt no shame.	
The Fall	
6 When the woman saw that the fruit of the tree was good for food and pleasing to the eye, and also desirable for gaining wisdom, she took some and ate it. She also gave some to her husband, who was with her, and he ate it. **7** Then the eyes of both of them were opened, and they realized they were naked; so they sewed fig leaves together and made coverings for themselves.	I guess that knowledge of nakedness is the evil that we are talking about? Oh, no! Wait! It is probably the knowledge of sex that we are talking about. Now, I get it.
	The message here is this: It is all the woman's fault. By the way, I think the serpent is a bit player in this story. So, God sets up Adam and Eve to be tested. Eve shows her independence, seeks knowledge, and gets Adam to come along. Then, they get slammed for doing so.

11 And he said, "Who told you that you were naked? Have you eaten from the tree that I commanded you not to eat from?"

12 The man said, "The woman you put here with me—she gave me some fruit from the tree, and I ate it."

13 Then the Lord God said to the woman, "What is this you have done?" The woman said, "The serpent deceived me, and I ate."

14 So the Lord God said to the serpent, "Because you have done this,

  "Cursed are you above all
      livestock and all wild animals!
  You will crawl on your belly and
      you will eat dust all the days of
      your life.

15 And I will put enmity
      between you and the woman,
      and between your offspring[i]
      and hers;
  he will crush[j] your head,
      and you will strike his heel."

16 To the woman he said,

  "I will make your pains in
      childbearing very severe;
      with painful labor you will give
      birth to children.
  Your desire will be for your
      husband, and he will rule
      over you."

Eve is cause of the fall. Knowledge is bad. Ignorance is good. Sex is evil. Mankind is doomed. Great.

This is the best part. Adam is proven to be a spineless worm. Adam immediately throws Eve under the bus and acts like he knew nothing about what he was doing. Eve gets all the blame, and God will now determine the punishment for such a heinous crime. Oh, He might as well ask one question as part of the trial.

The woman has only one excuse. It is lame. It was the snake. It was all preordained. So, it really does not matter. God knew all of this was going to happen—that "all knowing" thing.

Now, it is time for the punishment. The serpent gets punished first. Note that we are not talking about Satan here. We are only talking about the snake—the bit player. God knew all of this beforehand and is just playing out the story.

17 To Adam he said, "Because you listened to your wife and ate fruit from the tree about which I commanded you, 'You must not eat from it,'

"Cursed is the ground because
of you;
through painful toil you will
eat food from it all the days of
your life.
18 It will produce thorns and thistles
for you,
and you will eat the plants of
the field.
19 By the sweat of your brow
you will eat your food
until you return to the ground,
since from it you were taken;
for dust you are
and to dust you will return."

The poor snake definitely drew the short straw here and gets hammered.

Now, here comes the really bad news, Ladies. You get nailed big time. You have to bear the children and suffer, yes, suffer childbirth. It's your burden for seeking knowledge. By the way, you will now have to be subservient to the A-hole who threw you under the bus. WTF. Are you actually good with all of this?

Adam is reminded by God that it is all Eve's fault that he is now going to be cast out of Eden and have to work for a living, not to mention *not* be immortal! Whoa, I can understand why men treat woman the way they do.

It is clearly dictated by the creator of the universe—the creator of the universe? Really? That seems a little petty, but hey, billions of people believe this.

Nice.

GENESIS 5:32–10:1: WICKEDNESS IN THE WORLD AND NOAH AND THE FLOOD

Remember that God is all-knowing and all-present, and He is a loving God. He actually knew what his creation (mankind) would do and effectively set them up for elimination.
So, what does the Bible teach us?

Verses from the Bible	My reaction and questions
Wickedness in the World	
5 The Lord saw how great the wickedness of the human race had become on the earth, and that every inclination of the thoughts of the human heart was only evil all the time. **6** The Lord regretted that he had made human beings on the earth, and his heart was deeply troubled. **7** So the Lord said, "I will wipe from the face of the earth the human race I have created—and with them the animals, the birds and the creatures that move along the ground—for I regret that I have made them." **8** But Noah found favor in the eyes of the Lord.	It must have been something about all of that knowledge and free will, but it looks like God messed up big time with those human beings. God feels that they are all evil, like everyone and everything: the babies in the cradles, the moms and dads just trying to live their lives as well as they can, the kids playing with their sticks and balls in the fields, the grandmas and grandpas, just everyone. By the way, there will also be little collateral damage—like every other living creature on earth.
Noah and the Flood	
11 Now the earth was corrupt in God's sight and was full of violence. **12** God saw how corrupt the earth had become, for all the people on earth had corrupted their ways. **13** So God said to Noah, "I am going to put an end to all people,	So, what is the solution? Kill them all except for this guy named Noah who God seems to like for some reason. He was probably a groveler and ass kisser. God seems to like that. We will also need to rebuild after the carnage and genocide that will take place. So, the "ark plan" was worked up by God, and Noah agreed

for the earth is filled with violence because of them. I am surely going to destroy both them and the earth.

The Lord then said to Noah, "Go into the ark, you and your whole family, because I have found you righteous in this generation. **2** Take with you seven pairs of every kind of clean animal, a male and its mate, and one pair of every kind of unclean animal, a male and its mate, **3** and also seven pairs of every kind of bird, male and female, to keep their various kinds alive throughout the earth. **4** Seven days from now I will send rain on the earth for forty days and forty nights, and I will wipe from the face of the earth every living creature I have made."

17 For forty days the flood kept coming on the earth, and as the waters increased, they lifted the ark high above the earth. **18** The waters rose and increased greatly on the earth, and the ark floated on the surface of the water. **19** They rose greatly on the earth, and all the high mountains under the entire heavens were covered. **20** The waters rose and covered the mountains to a depth of more than fifteen cubits.[g][h] **21** Every living thing that moved on land perished—birds, livestock, wild animals, all the

to project manage it and execute the plan. By the way, Noah seems to be totally okay with killing everybody and everything on earth other than his immediate family. I guess he had no friends, other relatives, or anyone else he cared about. That is sad.

So, we can go down the checklist: Noah, immediate family, the ark, male and mate for the animals then on earth, some food to eat for 40 days and nights. Looks like that will do it. Just button up the ark and then make it rain baby. Last step—okay God, make it happen.

Holy shit, this sounds like destruction and carnage beyond all reason. Everything and everyone was drowned: dogs, cats, bunnies….., wise men and fools. You get it. Everyone and everything was drowned—all of the "wicked," all of the naughty, and all of the nice. This was a complete "redo."

This is my kind of God—insane? That would be my assessment. You draw your own conclusion.

creatures that swarm over the earth, and all mankind. **22** Everything on dry land that had the breath of life in its nostrils died. **23** Every living thing on the face of the earth was wiped out; people and animals and the creatures that move along the ground and the birds were wiped from the earth. Only Noah was left, and those with him in the ark.

Then God said to Noah, "Come out of the ark, you and your wife and your sons and their wives. **17** Bring out every kind of living creature that is with you—the birds, the animals, and all the creatures that move along the ground—so they can multiply on the earth and be fruitful and increase in number on it."

Then Noah built an altar to the Lord and, taking some of all the clean animals and clean birds, he sacrificed burnt offerings on it.
The Lord smelled the pleasing aroma and said in his heart: "Never again will I curse the ground because of humans, even though[i] every inclination of the human heart is evil from childhood. And never again will I destroy all living creatures, as I have done."

Okay, looks like the plan actually worked. The ark held together for 40 days. Noah and his immediate family did fine. The few animals that made it on board also did fine, and as you will recall, everyone and everything else is DEAD!

Now, the groveler and ass kisser need to pay respect to the all-powerful, insane, world murderer. So, the few animals that were selected for this journey and survived the 40 days on board the ark are now sacrificed. WTF? Really—this God of the universe is never sedated. He wants yet more blood, more killing, and now needs to smell the aroma of burnt flesh.

He is a loving God for sure. He knew all of this when he created the universe and Adam and Eve in the first place.

GENESIS 19: SODOM AND GOMORRAH DESTROYED, AND LOT AND HIS DAUGHTERS

Remember that God is all-knowing and all-present, and He is a loving God. We will now learn about the how God feels about homosexuals—be afraid, be very afraid. So, what does the Bible teach us?

Verses from the Bible	My reaction and questions
Sodom and Gomorrah Destroyed 4 Before they had gone to bed, all the men from every part of the city of Sodom—both young and old—surrounded the house. 5 They called to Lot, "Where are the men who came to you tonight? Bring them out to us so that we can have sex with them." 6 Lot went outside to meet them and shut the door behind him 7 and said, "No, my friends. Don't do this wicked thing. 8 Look, I have two daughters who have never slept with a man. Let me bring them out to you, and you can do what you like with them. But don't do anything to these men, for they have come under the protection of my roof." 14 So Lot went out and spoke to his sons-in-law, who were pledged to marry[a] his daughters. He said, "Hurry and get out of this place, because the Lord is about to destroy the city!" But his sons-in-law thought he was joking.	Sodom and Gomorrah had reputations of being free-thinking cities that embraced all types of people including heterosexuals and homosexuals. Lot, a family man, lived in Sodom with his wife and daughters. I expect there were thousands of people and families like Lot and his family, but the Bible makes a big deal out of this incident to make the point that these cities are amoral and evil. My guess is probably not. So, what is Lot's reaction to these homosexuals (or bisexuals) approaching his house? Well, just offer your two daughters to have sex with these men, and do anything you want with them. This is totally sick. Lot's buddy, God, takes notice of Sodom and Gomorrah and decides, as usual, just to kill everyone. This is a pattern that seems to be a reoccurring theme in the scriptures.

15 With the coming of dawn, the angels urged Lot, saying, "Hurry! Take your wife and your two daughters who are here, or you will be swept away when the city is punished."
23 By the time Lot reached Zoar, the sun had risen over the land. **24** Then the Lord rained down burning sulfur on Sodom and Gomorrah—from the Lord out of the heavens. **25** Thus he overthrew those cities and the entire plain, destroying all those living in the cities—and also the vegetation in the land. **26** But Lot's wife looked back, and she became a pillar of salt.

Lot and His Daughters
30 Lot and his two daughters left Zoar and settled in the mountains, for he was afraid to stay in Zoar. He and his two daughters lived in a cave. **31** One day the older daughter said to the younger, "Our father is old, and there is no man around here to give us children—as is the custom all over the earth. **32** Let's get our father to drink wine and then sleep with him and preserve our family line through our father."

6 So both of Lot's daughters became pregnant by their father. **37** The older daughter had a son, and she named him Moab[g]; he is the father of the Moabites of today. **38** The younger

Only Lot, his wife and his daughters would be spared. Again, this is a recurring theme that associates groveling, ass kissing, and spineless men with God's favor.

The cities are totally destroyed again. Every living thing including the dogs, the cats, bunnies in the fields, babies, toddlers, kids, teens, moms, dads, grandmas, and grandpas (yes, everyone and everything) are not spared. Good thing we took care of those homos. That will teach them.

By the way, Lot's wife is another woman who just does not listen to her husband or follow God's rules. He turned her into a Pillar of Salt. So, we have Lot and his daughters—the only ones surviving from the two cities. The cherry on top for this story is the fact that the two daughters then sleep with Lot (their father), get pregnant and create new lines of the tribe. The lesson for the succeeding generation is this: incest is way better than homosexuality. This is sick, sick, sick. The good news is that the Bible is consistent and does not, in fact, provide us any real moral guidance. There are no values or guiding principles here. There are none to be found here.

daughter also had a son, and she named him Ben-Ammi[h]; he is the father of the Ammonites[i] of today.

JOSHUA 6: JOSHUA AND JERICHO

Remember that God is all-knowing and all-present, and He is a loving God. We will now learn even more about war and God's rath on the loser—be afraid, be very afraid. So, what does the Bible teach us?

Verses from the Bible	My reaction and questions
Now the gates of Jericho were securely barred because of the Israelites. No one went out and no one came in. **2** Then the Lord said to Joshua, "See, I have delivered Jericho into your hands, along with its king and its fighting men. **3** March around the city once with all the armed men. Do this for six days. **4** Have seven priests carry trumpets of rams' horns in front of the ark. On the seventh day, march around the city seven times, with the priests blowing the trumpets. **5** When you hear them sound a long blast on the trumpets, have the whole army give a loud shout; then the wall of the city will collapse and the army will go up, everyone straight in." **20** When the trumpets sounded, the army shouted, and at the sound of the trumpet, when the men gave a loud shout, the wall collapsed; so everyone charged straight in, and they took the city. **21** They devoted the city to the Lord and destroyed with the sword every living thing in it—men	Looks like Jericho is in the crosshairs of God this time with Joshua as the willing accomplice. Joshua is trying to conquer the city, and God will help in any way he can. It's good to have God on your side. So, God and Joshua come up with a plan to conquer Jericho. It was the usual approach: march around for a few days; blow the horns; and, kiss up to God. God will then knock down the walls of the city, and Joshua and his troops can rush in and take over the city. It has definitely worked in the past, and Joshua has the secret ingredient that never fails. The secret ingredient is his good buddy, God So, Joshua executes the plan flaw-lessly, and the city is taken. Now, here comes the good part. Do you accept the surrender graciously and work with the vanquished to broker a long-term peace? What? That is not even in the playbook.

and women, young and old, cattle, sheep and donkeys.

24 Then they burned the whole city and everything in it, but they put the silver and gold and the articles of bronze and iron into the treasury of the Lord's house.

26 At that time Joshua pronounced this solemn oath: "Cursed before the Lord is the one who undertakes to rebuild this city, Jericho:

> "At the cost of his firstborn son he
> will lay its foundations;
> at the cost of his youngest he will
> set up its gates."

27 So the Lord was with Joshua, and his fame spread throughout the land.

Let's see what is in the playbook: once you win the battle you kill every living thing and completely raze the city. Oh, yes, that's it.

Kill them all. Kill the "men and women, young and old, cattle, sheep, and donkeys" and whatever else you can find that is alive. Make sure you grab the booty for the Lord. God does love His silver, gold, bronze and iron.

Then, curse the whole city, and make sure you know what infanticide is. Yes, we will kill your children. God and Joshua were buds for life, and they were famous everywhere. I love it!

ABOUT THE AUTHOR

BOB DANNA IS a scientist, an engineer, a secular humanist, and insatiably curious about the world and the universe. He served as a naval officer in Admiral Rickover's nuclear reactors program before becoming a business leader and ultimately retiring from Deloitte Consulting as a managing director. He is a world traveler, both for business and pleasure, and has accumulated millions of airline flight miles. He is also an "experience junkie" who loves anything live: music, comedy, sports, theatre, you name it. Bob currently lives in Las Vegas with his long-term partner, Laci. He was twice married and divorced, has one daughter, and—most importantly—two grandchildren, who were the inspiration for Bob to start writing.